Out of the Shadows

The New Merchants of Grain

By Jonathan Kingsman

Out of the Shadows—The New Merchants of Grain

Copyright © 2019 Jonathan Kingsman
All rights reserved.
ISBN: 9781704267821
Imprint: Independently published

Table of Contents

	Dedication	5
	Introduction	8
	Preface - Swithun Still	11
	The Role Of Traders - Jason Clay	13
1.	Conspiracy and Competition	21
	Agriculture Is Our Backbone - Karel Valken	27
2.	Feast and Famine	34
	History Is Repeating Itself - Jay O'Neil	41
3.	Going with the Grain	48
	There Are No Fools Anymore - Dan Basse	57
4.	Food, Feed and Fuel	62
	Politics And Biofuels - Patricia Manso	70
5.	Managing Risk	76
	Learning To Navigate - Brian Zachman	84
6.	Managing Change	94
	Trading Is Our DNA - Kristen Weldon	105
7.	André	111
	All In The Family - Riccardo and Emanuele Ravano	117
8.	Continental Grain	124
	Playing For Barcelona - Ivo Sarjanovic	128

9. ADM	135
Trading With A Purpose - Greg Morris	139
10. Bunge	147
Feeding the World – Greg Heckman	151
11. Cargill	155
Trading Is An Art - Gert–Jan van den Akker	159
12. COFCO	166
Trading Is A People Business - Ito van Lanschot	171
13. Dreyfus	179
We Know Where We Are Going - Ian McIntosh	184
14. Glencore	191
Emptying A Silo With A Shovel - Chris Mahoney	196
15. Wilmar	204
Master of Business - Khoon Hong Kuok	209
16. A Competitive Future	222
The New Normal - JF Lambert	232
About The Author	241
Glossary Of Terms	242
References	255

Dedication

I grew up on a farm – more of a smallholding, really – in the county of Kent, in southern England. My father moved there after leaving the army at the end of the Second World War and borrowed enough money to buy a small bakery and teashop in Canterbury. The teashop was one of the few buildings left standing in the city after Hitler tried to destroy British morale by bombing Canterbury Cathedral, home of Britain's Anglicanism. His bombs missed the cathedral, but destroyed pretty much everything else in the city.

My father came from a modest background. His own father had once had a thriving business manufacturing ladies' corsets, using whalebones to keep them rigid. His company went out of business when fashion changed, and my grandfather spent the rest of his life trying in vain to find a new angle, something he could manufacture to add value to people's lives.

The experience was a bitter one, and it left a mark on my father, even if it enabled him to understand the importance of adapting to change. 'No one likes change', he used to tell me, 'but the ability to adapt to it is what separates success from failure'.

My father expanded his teashop, buying old army buildings to open a restaurant and an outside catering business. However, food was in short supply. His only solution was to grow his own. He persuaded his bank to lend him enough money to buy a few acres of farmland on the city's outskirts. He started farming it, eventually building our family home there.

At the beginning, the farm was geared exclusively to produce fruit and vegetables for the restaurant and the catering business. He planted fruit trees on some of the land; the rest of the farm was given over to potatoes and other root crops like turnips and parsnips, as well as cabbages, beans, Brussels sprouts – all of which made up the standard British diet at that time. (It was only later that he branched out into strawberries and even later into asparagus.)

Besides growing fruit and vegetables, he also kept chickens to produce eggs for the restaurant and pigs to eat food waste from the bakery and the restaurant. The chickens and the pigs also produced the manure that served as natural fertiliser for growing the vegetables. It really was a circular, sustainable agricultural operation that grew what we would now call 'organic' food – all with zero waste!

The farm also provided me with a happy childhood, where I learned how to drive a tractor at eight and how to plough a field at 10. I regularly helped out on the farm after school and during long school vacations.

As Britain slowly recovered from the war, food production picked up, and food prices fell. It began to make more sense for my father to buy the food he needed for his catering business, rather than to grow it himself. But he still wanted the pigs to consume the food waste from the restaurant and the unsold bread from the bakery. He abandoned vegetables (except for an acre or so for the family) and planted barley as feed for the pigs. He also bought more pigs, started a breeding programme and within a few years had a small industrial farm, raising and breeding pigs.

Despite his hard work, the operation was never a success. One problem was what to do with all the effluent from the pigs. My father never found an effective solution to this problem, but it – because of the smell – made us unpopular with our neighbours in what had slowly become a residential area.

Another problem was the difficulty of keeping the pigs healthy; they lived in such close confinement that they were often ill, needing a constant supply of antibiotics to keep them free of disease. The veterinary bills soaked up the operation's meagre profits.

The biggest problem was scale. The farm was simply too small to compete with other bigger units both in the U.K. and continental Europe. At the time, U.K. pork prices were low; cheaper pork was being imported from Holland's bigger and more efficient pig farms.

My father tried to tackle the pigs' health issue by giving up barley production and using the land to let the animals roam freely in the open air. The pigs were healthier (and arguably happier), and the vet bills dropped. However, the pigs gained weight more slowly. In addition, my father now had to buy in all the barley and the grain that he needed to feed the pigs. The economics of the operation just didn't work.

My father died at the age of 102, and the family gave up farming, selling the land to the local hockey club. It was just part of the U.K.'s general move from farming (and industry) to services.

However, I am sure that, if my father were alive today, he would still be farming and would have taken his small farm full circle, back to producing organic food with zero waste, and selling his produce at the local markets. I am told that he could've no longer fed food waste to the pigs, as it is now apparently against the law. Without the food waste, it is doubtful whether he could've made a living out of it. But knowing him, he certainly would've tried.

There is an old saying that you can take the kid out of the farm, but you cannot take the farm out of the kid. Upon leaving university, I was offered and accepted an agricultural merchandising position with Tradax, as Cargill's overseas trading company was called.

I was delighted, but my father was less pleased. As far as he was concerned, agricultural merchants were the enemy – always trying to beat him down in price when he sold them his surplus barley or pushing up the price in later years when he had to buy it for his pigs. He thought that agricultural merchants added little value; he would've preferred it if I had chosen a more useful occupation, such as accountancy.

I never could convince my father that working as an agricultural merchant did add value, and I'm sad that he isn't around today to read this book. I dedicate it to his memory.

Introduction

Almost everything that you eat or drink today will contain something bought, stored, transported, processed, shipped, distributed or sold by one of the seven giants of the agricultural supply chain.

Out of an average 44,000 items in a U.S. supermarket, 40 percent contain corn, and 50 percent contain palm oil or one of its derivatives. You are almost certain to have consumed one of them today. Your bread, pasta and morning croissant will have been made from wheat. Meanwhile, your beef, chicken and pork – as well as your fish – will almost certainly have been fed soybeans or corn supplied by one of the big seven.

And even if you haven't eaten or drunk anything today, the bus or car that took you to work will probably have been partially fuelled by crop-based bio-fuel handled or manufactured by one of these seven giants.

The media often refers to them as the ABCD group of companies, with *ABCD* standing for ADM, Bunge, Cargill and Dreyfus. The acronym, though, ignores the other three giants of the food supply: Glencore, COFCO International and Wilmar. The real acronym, therefore, should be CABDCWG, a real alphabet soup of letters that refuses to be organised into a catchy acronym.

A few years back, when Noble, Olam and Wilmar were becoming Asian giants, the media called the group *ABCD NOW*, although no one ever quite worked out what to do with the 'G' of Glencore. Noble has since been acquired by COFCO, while Olam has stepped out of the mainstream grain business to concentrate on niche markets. The industry and the media now simply refer to the seven as the ABCD+ group of grain trading companies.

Together, ABCD+ handle just under 50 percent of the international trade in grain and oilseeds. On the processing side, they crush and process 35 percent of the world's production of soybeans, with a total crush capacity of close to half a billion tonnes.

Cargill is the biggest of these seven giants, with annual revenues of around $115 billion, profits of around $3 billion (in 2018) and over 150,000 employees. By some estimates, they handle 25 percent of the grains and soybeans produced by U.S. farmers, and every year, they trade as much as 140 million tonnes of agricultural commodities worldwide. They are the largest private company in the U.S. If they were publicly quoted, they would have a market capitalisation of $50 billion. (1)

Publicly listed ADM is the second biggest of the seven, with annual revenues in excess of $60 billion, a market capitalisation of more than $20 billion and profits that touched nearly $2 billion in 2018. Founded in 1902, and NYSE listed since 1924, today the company has 40,000 employees, processes as much as 60 million tonnes of agricultural commodities each year, and sells into nearly 200 countries.

Bunge and Wilmar are also publicly listed, but Bunge's market capitalisation of $8 billion is dwarfed by Wilmar's $16 billion. Bunge is the oldest of the group, tracing its roots back more than 200 years and changing both its nationality and headquarters many times over its history. Wilmar was only founded in 1991 and has similar annual revenues of around $43 billion. However, Wilmar has a stronger foothold in China and is viewed as having better prospects for growth. By some accounts, Wilmar handles about 40 percent of the world's trade in palm oil.

Louis Dreyfus Company is the second oldest in the group. Founded in 1851 in Bern, Switzerland, it returned to Switzerland a few years back, setting up its headquarters overlooking the runway at Geneva airport. It is still owned by the Louis Dreyfus family and trades in everything from grains to orange juice, coffee, cotton and sugar. (It is sometimes referred to as the 'breakfast' company, but without the bacon and eggs.) Dreyfus has 18,000 employees, a turnover of around $37 billion and an estimated market capitalisation (if it were listed) of $6–8 billion.

Glencore Agriculture and COFCO International are the new kids on the block; both have had to find room on an already crowded street corner. Glencore Ag was partially spun off from its mining and oil-trading parent in 2015 and has 13,000 employees. The company announced that it trades about 80 million tonnes of agricultural commodities each year. If it were a public company, it could be worth $6 billion to $8 billion.

COFCO International is the disruptor of the group. Founded in 2014 as a majority-owned subsidiary of China's COFCO, a state-owned enterprise, it had a difficult birth. However, the company already has revenues that approach those of Louis Dreyfus and a similar (estimated) market capitalisation. In 2018, the company traded more than 100 million tonnes of foodstuffs. COFCO International is quickly gaining traction, threatening the livelihood of the other giants.

But it isn't just COFCO International that's threatening the other companies' traditional business model of buying, storing, processing, financing, shipping and distributing foodstuffs. The world is better informed now than ever, which has reduced the need for intermediaries along the supply chain. Meanwhile, artificial intelligence and algorithmic trading programmes are making it harder for physical grain traders to cash in their knowledge and experience by speculating on futures markets. As such, the world's 'magnificent seven' grain-trading companies are once again seeking to reinvent themselves to stay relevant in the modern world.

This is the story of those seven companies – and of their continual battle to remain at the centre of the world's food supply.

Preface

By Swithun Still, Director of Solaris Commodities S.A. (1) and President of Gafta (2) 2019–2020, writing in a personal capacity.

I first read Dan Morgan's seminal work, *The Merchants of Grain*, in 2001, two years after starting my own career in the grain business. I was living and working in Paris for a Russian grain-trading company. Coincidentally, we were fixing freight from the same broker mentioned in the first chapter of the book, so it gripped me from the start. I particularly enjoyed the mystique and drama of the Great Grain Robbery, which was not a robbery at all, just canny buying by the Exportkhleb, the Soviet grain-trading agency.

Of course, by 2001, Russia was no longer importing grain, but exporting it. The grain trade was also changing in other ways, and even back then, I thought someone should write an update to Dan Morgan's excellent book.

Eighteen years later, I was enjoying lunch with Jonathan Kingsman on a sunny terrace in Morges, Switzerland. Jonathan had just finished his book *Commodity Conversations – A Brief Introduction to Trading Agricultural Commodities*, to which I had contributed, and he had cycled down from Lausanne to hand me a signed copy.

'You should write an update to *Merchants of Grain*', I ventured.

Much has changed since Dan Morgan's book was published. In the 2017–2018 season, Russia became the world's largest exporter of wheat with 41.5 million tonnes, and at the time of writing, Solaris Commodities S.A. (2) has become one of the top-three traders of Russian wheat. As for me, I have probably traded more Russian wheat in the past decade than any other Englishman!

Jonathan looked rather surprised when I suggested that he write this book. I poured him a second glass of Tuscan wine, and in a flush of enthusiasm, he agreed.

Grain traders fulfil an essential function and assume a lot of risk in the process. This book demonstrates the valuable contribution they make in helping to feed the world and counters the many myths that surround our business. I hope this book will convince you that we, as traders, are well aware of our responsibilities to transparency, sustainability and human rights, and that we act accordingly.

People can get by without buying many things in life, but not food. We're dealing with the very fabric of life, with grains that make our bread, our pasta, our couscous, our biscuits. As the world population booms, our agricultural systems will be tested fully. As merchants of grain, we have a duty to help our farmers and customers make sure that, together, we feed the world without destroying it.

As those of you who follow me on Twitter (3) will know, I believe that our industry benefits from transparency. We work in a wonderful, challenging and fascinating industry. I'm a merchant of grain. I'm proud of the work that we conduct in the grain trade, and I'm glad to enthuse and amuse on all things to do with grain.

The big grain deals of the 1970s were done in face-to-face meetings, backed by phone calls and Telex messages. Today, transactions are made over a multitude of different messaging services. Who knows what traders will be using for communication in another 40 years? One thing that I hope will not change is that traders will still adhere to the Gafta motto 'My word is my bond'.

I trust that you will enjoy this book.

The Role of Traders - Jason Clay

Jason Clay heads WWF–US's work on global markets and trends related to food. He launched WWF's global work on agriculture, aquaculture and market transformation for food and soft commodities companies. He spoke to me by phone from his home in Washington, D.C.

Good morning, Jason, and thanks for taking the time to speak with me. Let's start at the beginning. I understand that you grew up on a farm.

I grew up on a subsistence farm that was too small to be economically viable. It was 156 acres (63 hectares), or just under a quarter of a square mile – the size of a homestead in the previous century. We produced about three-quarters of our food from gardening, gathering, hunting and fishing. We bought food we couldn't produce ourselves.

We got electricity the year I was born, but we didn't have indoor plumbing until I was 15. I slept on a screened porch, even in winter; the coldest it got was -21°F (or about -29°C).

There were four girls and three boys in the family – in that order. I was the eldest boy. I remember it as a happy time. I worked a lot, but I wasn't responsible for anything. Then my father was killed in a tractor accident when I was 15. I had to step up with my mother and manage the farm. That was a totally different experience.

After my father's death, neighbours and relatives helped us for the first couple of years, but there's only so much goodwill. I couldn't manage the farm and stay and do well in high school, so we rented out the land. However, that meant we no longer had access to it for the parts of the year that were critical for grazing or producing hay for our cattle. So, we had to sell the cows. We auctioned all the animals, tractors and machinery and other farm tools. Mom continued to live on the farm with my two younger brothers until each had graduated from high school. She then sold the farm and moved to town.

So how did you go from trying to fill your father's shoes running a subsistence farm to a PhD in anthropology?

My father had an insurance policy; it turned out that he was actually worth much more dead than alive. That money solved Mom's immediate financial issues. It's a sad fact, but his death and the responsibilities I had made me an unusual college applicant and allowed me to get a full ride to Harvard.

As for anthropology, once I was at Harvard, I wanted to understand everyone around me. We were mostly from the same country, but I was different. There were lots of landowners there, but no other farmers. I didn't fit.

Anthropology was a good choice for other reasons, too. The department was a small community, an extended family. I knew everyone. There was funding for research. I spent one summer in Northeast Brazil studying land conflicts and another living with Mayan Indians in Southern Mexico.

After graduating, I didn't need work experience. I had plenty of that on the farm, where I learned more about life than I did at any of the educational establishments that I ever attended. However, those institutions gave me the tools (networks, fundraising skills and credentials) that I needed to make change happen. That's what I wanted to do in my life.

When I left Harvard, I got a fellowship to study at the London School of Economics for one year. After London, I returned to the U.S. to do my PhD at Cornell, which at that time was the best agricultural university in the world. My subject was anthropology, but I wanted to study international agriculture.

I wanted a PhD to open doors to interesting work and access funding, but I never wanted to teach. I've taught a few times – at Harvard and Yale – but every time it just reinforced the fact that I wanted to do some good, not just to teach others. I started my career by working on human rights.

After your PhD, you ended up in a refugee camp in Africa.

It was in 1984–85 during the Ethiopian famine. The camp was on the border between Eritrea, Tigré and Sudan. It was during the height of the Cold War when the U.S. and the U.S.S.R. used indigenous groups as proxies in domestic conflicts, for example the Mosquito in Nicaragua, Kurds in Iraq, Oromo in Ethiopia or Dinka in Sudan. These groups took the money, not because they supported the U.S. or the U.S.S.R., but because it allowed them to pursue their dreams of independence or autonomy.

I was in a refugee camp to collect reliable data on the people there and what it would take for them to go back, for example why they left their homes, how many in each family had been raped, how many killed and who killed them. Our information showed clearly that the government caused the famine, but the aid agencies didn't want the information made public.

And then you went to a Grateful Dead concert.

I had helped found the Rainforest Action Network, and the head of that group had a connection to the drummer of the Grateful Dead. He reached out to him and asked if the Dead would do a concert to benefit the rainforest.

We had some meetings with the band. They said that they would be happy to do it, but only if they understood what the hell they were doing and how it would help. We spent a year going once a month to Bobby Weir's house, teaching the Dead about the rainforest.

A year later, they did the concert, adding one night to a series of 12 in Madison Square Garden. We were thinking, 'Man, who's going to come to the thirteenth concert'? But they came. It was full.

There was an afterparty where the head of Greenpeace–U.S. came up to me and said, 'Hey, there's a guy here who wants to know what he can do to save the rainforest'. I went over to him, and I said, 'Who are you'? and he replied, 'I'm Ben, and I make ice cream'.

A few months later, he called me, and we met in Boston in the North End in a little restaurant that had paper placemats. He told me he wanted me to go to Brazil and bring him back samples of cashew and Brazil nuts. He then gave me all the specs that the products needed to meet. I didn't have a clue. I'm an anthropologist, not a trader! But I scribbled everything down on the paper placemats.

I went to Brazil and began sourcing the nuts that he needed from Brazil's Western Amazon. We set up Rainforest Marketing, the first fair-trade eco-labels in the U.S., and we co-created Rainforest Crunch with Ben & Jerry, as well as more than 200 other products for other companies like the Body Shop.

We financed a nut-shelling plant in Brazil. I carried cash into the country, $100,000 a time, to finance the work. We bought the nuts shelled in the factory, and the nut gatherers tripled the amount of money they received for them.

Previously, Brazil nuts were shipped down river to Manaus, and many rotted on the barges. By building the shelling plant near the source of nuts, we reduced waste from 40 percent to five percent and tripled the price to producers. In the end, all the other buyers doubled the price they were paying to compete with us. No programme has ever increased the value to all producers in any global market so much, before or since. We did this with just 10–20 percent of the Brazil nut market.

Our trading company was set up as a not-for-profit. I hired a trader and another 30 people to work in the company. Our raw materials ended up in products selling for about $100 million in the U.S. and Europe. We provided long-term, dollar contracts to our suppliers, and they used them to borrow money at local banks to expand production and improve productivity.

Does Rainforest Marketing still exist?

We had a line of credit with U.S. Aid for $3.5 million and another $1 million with the MacArthur Foundation for working capital. Our board members were concerned that they would be individually liable for those loans if anything went wrong. They didn't feel comfortable with the risk.

For me, it was all about providing local communities and indigenous people with economic alternatives. I grew up on a small farm, lived on less than a dollar a day for 15 years and had zero economic alternatives. I knew what that felt like. If poor people have a viable economic base, they can take control of their destiny.

The board felt differently. We were miles apart on that issue. I lost a 7–6 vote of confidence.

So the company closed down, and you joined WWF.

My wife had been living in Washington, D.C., so I moved there and joined World Wildlife Fund as a senior fellow.

I had realised over the years that it's far easier to raise money for the environment than for indigenous people. WWF operate in more than 100 countries, and they have budgets that are much bigger than anything I had seen before. Agriculture was a whole new area for them, but an area that some of the leaders were beginning to see as mission critical.

My first project with WWF was to compare the impacts of shrimp aquaculture and shrimp trawling. They wanted to know which to support and help improve.

The WWF seems to be an organisation that looks for solutions to problems rather than just 'naming and shaming'. Is that a fair assessment?

I think that's true. For one thing, we hire a lot of locals, so it's personal for them. They need to live with the results.

'Naming and shaming' is also broad brush; you can name and shame a lot of people who aren't actually the problem. If you want to find solutions, you have to build coalitions, working quietly and more behind the scenes. This is WWF's strategy. To solve most global problems, everyone should be part of the solution. At least, that makes change happen faster.

If you want to focus on deforestation, for example you don't need 200 foresters; you may not need any at all. What you need is an early warning system that tells you where deforestation is happening so you can then find out why, who's driving it and what key parties are making it happen. Then you can begin to develop a strategy.

WWF is a science-based organisation. We base our programmes on science and research. For us, it's 'Get informed, and then get involved'.

WWF has been involved in setting up several sustainability certification programmes, such as the Round Table of Responsible Soy and the Round Table of Sustainable Palm Oil. We started with the companies that have a reputational risk – the biggest buyers of the commodities that have the biggest impacts. We asked them what they needed to make their supply chains more sustainable. We explained that not buying commodities wouldn't really help, because somebody else would buy them. Instead, we helped develop standards that buyers can require of their producers to improve supply chains.

The conditions and timelines were specific and results based. We want to see results, not tell people how to achieve them. If we agree on the problems and what success would look like, the producers can find the best way to fix them.

The fundamental question, however, is, 'Why do we have certification bodies?' The answer is 'because governments aren't doing their job to protect the planet for future generations'.

Consequently, we're creating parallel structures run by people who mostly don't know much about producing products, much less about producing them sustainably. Certification is not the best option, but right now, it's the one we have. Can it be better? Sure.

But you once said that the certification agencies are about certifying the top 10 percent, while it's really the bottom 25 percent that's causing most of the damage and needs the most help.

Unfortunately, we're often quite willing to let the perfect get in the way of the good. But once producers start seeing that better practices achieve better results, they begin to ask how they can implement them, too.

But, at the end of the day, the biggest environmental impacts come from the bottom 25 percent. That's where we need governments. The poorest-performing producers either need to improve or get out. Only governments can make that happen.

Do you think certification agencies concentrate too much on sustainability and not enough on economics?

I think that, in the old days, it was true, but if it's not economically sustainable, it's not sustainable, period. What no one wants to talk about is that many poor farmers work plots that are simply too small or too marginal to be viable. I know, because I was one once. But this is also a global issue. Smallholders need to get better or to get out. It's not a good life for them, and it's certainly not a future for their children.

We have a lot of well-meaning people who've never set foot on a farm but have strong opinions about maintaining small farmers, and by extension, whether they realise it or not, poverty. We have certification programmes that, in effect, certify poverty. That can't be justified. If you want to criticise certification, this is perhaps the place to start.

Deforestation is the biggest issue facing palm oil. But you once said that there is a way to quadruple production without cutting a single tree. How?

There are a lot of areas, particularly in Indonesia, which aren't forested, but which are dominated by a species of invasive grass. These areas are hard for small farmers to do anything with, but they're perfect for palm oil plantations. You could double palm oil production in Indonesia just by planting these degraded and abandoned lands.

Governments must stop the conversion of forests to plant oil palm. But having said that, oil palm is the world's most productive source of vegetable oil. If palm is done correctly, it has the least environmental impact of any vegetable oil. There's nothing else that can touch it. Expanding any other vegetable oil crop would have far bigger impacts on the environment than expanding oil palm. Oil palm makes it possible to turn degraded land into an asset.

But existing plantations can do better as well. Many oil palm plantations – and virtually all smallholder plantations – use genetic varieties that produce between half and two-thirds of what better varieties can produce. You could nearly double production simply by replanting poorer-performing plantations with better genetics. You'd also have more resistance to diseases. And you'd have shorter trees, which would make it easier for the producers to harvest.

Are you seeing any changes in the way palm is being produced?

Not nearly enough. Nobody is interested in increasing yields. When prices are high, no one wants to change what they are doing. When they're low, they claim they can't afford to. Governments are short-sighted. They don't see the value of investing in the future. And oil palm producers don't want to change. In addition, the biggest palm oil processors see smallholders as buffers. If the price goes up, they buy more from them, but if the price goes down, they buy less.

I understand why people are reluctant to do something different, but for a company to survive the next fifty or a hundred years, it needs to innovate and invest now, even if it's beyond what they think is currently viable. They need test plots and to be constantly experimenting.

What's the role of traders in this?

Most people don't understand that commodity traders are efficient at what they do. The problem is that we're asking traders to do more than the commodity trading system was designed to do. Commodity trading allowed buyers to purchase a product that is interchangeable with any other tonne of the same product. If you buy N°2 yellow corn, you receive N°2 yellow corn.

From about 1860 to the 1970s, commodities were defined by physical properties: weights, moisture content, foreign matter, broken pieces and other physically verified attributes.

Since the 1970s, people have begun to ask commodity traders to address such issues as labour conditions (e.g. minimum wages and child labour) and environmental impacts (e.g. pesticides, deforestation, soil health etc). Buyers are asking traders to verify specific traits that pose reputational risks to retailers and brands that are more inclusive than weights and measures and physical properties.

What challenges do traders face to make these changes happen?

Trading companies are trying to find ways to put such verification systems in place, but they have two problems. First, they need buyers to commit to more than one-off purchases. Depending on the commodity, they need multi-year commitments.

If a trader puts systems in place to verify how a product is produced, it costs money. They need multi-year contracts to offset those costs. Otherwise, the trader could be stuck with this initial cost. If traders could get a five-year contract from a company to buy more sustainable palm oil, soy or whatever, they could amortise their one-off costs over that five-year period.

A trading company may make 1.5 to 3 percent on a single trade. If the verification cost is 1 percent, then on a 1.5 percent margin, you've already lost more than half of your profit. But if the initial cost can be amortised over five years, it gets down to a point where it's negligible. For that to happen, downstream buyers have to put the money where their mouth is, but most haven't done that. That's the issue that traders are facing.

Additionally, if Cargill steps in and makes the investment and holds their trade price steady, but Bunge comes along and lowers its price even by 1 percent or less, most retailers and brands will buy from Bunge.

So, we have two issues to address. One: how do we turn retailer and brand commitments into actual purchases? Two: how do we get traders to work together without risk of collusion?

From a sustainability point of view, we need companies to work together to solve sustainability issues. This is not about price fixing. It's about internalising environmental externalities into prices.

We must work together. We can't manage the planet one producer, one trader, one retailer, one brand or one government at a time.

You mentioned externalities. Although consumers say they'll pay for externalities, they don't. What could be done there?

If all commodities were produced more sustainably, consumers wouldn't have a choice. Changing the definition of a commodity could help. Number-two yellow corn could also be more sustainable. It isn't clear that the price would go up, especially if producer prices for less sustainable products declined because they cost society more. We need to get the price signals right – today, sustainable products cost more, but unsustainable products cost society far more. But ultimately, the consumer is the polluter. And the principle is that the polluter pays.

When you see what's happening, how we're living at 1.3 or 1.5 planets per year, do you get pessimistic?

Sure, but we only have one planet, and we must address sustainability issues one way or another. My main motivator is my children's future, but also the future of all other living things on the planet. This is literally about life on earth.

We need to bring together the best thinking to explore ways to address these issues. We need to look backwards – what solutions in the past didn't work for reasons that may no longer exist? Would they work today?

We need to focus on new technologies. However, the solution is not about finding a silver bullet. What are the best alternative proteins? What's the lighting system that's going to let us get away from the sun and soil?

For the next fifty years, farming on most of the planet is not going to look a lot different than it does today. We will still focus on incremental increases in productivity per unit of land, water, labour or other inputs. But the model is likely to be similar to what we have today.

Are there any other solutions that we may be missing and which we should be looking at to make supply chains more sustainable?

There are two. First, we should be looking at different ownership and finance models. We should explore worker and producer equity models as ways to help the transition to a more sustainable food system that poses less risk for both producers and buyers.

Second, *Codex Alimentarius* took health and safety standards for globally traded food out of the hands of thousands of certification programmes nearly 60 years ago. Could a *Codex Planetarius*, run by the FAO, ensure a set of six to eight environmental performance standards for globally traded commodities?

Thank you, Jason, for your time!

Chapter One: Conspiracy and Competition

'As a historian, I'm sceptical about conspiracy theories because the world is far too complicated to be managed by a few billionaires drinking scotch behind some closed doors'.
Yuval Noah Harari – Author and Historian

In 1979, Dan Morgan, an award-winning journalist with the *Washington Post*, published *Merchants of Grain: The Power and the Profits of the Five Grain Companies at the Centre of the World's Food Supply*. (1) It was a best seller and remains the definitive history of the international grain business.

The publication of *Merchants of Grain* followed what has become known as the Great Russian Grain Robbery, a period during the 1970s in which the Soviet Union purchased massive amounts of grain. Their purchases, plus the subsequent inflation and the controversy over the export subsidies paid by the U.S. government, focused media attention on the international grain trade and the merchants that conducted it.

While researching his book, Dan Morgan had considerable difficulty in obtaining information from what he described as 'shadowy and unknown' grain-trading companies. Except Cargill, grain merchants provided minimal assistance – or none – in the preparation of his book.

The grain companies had nothing particular against Dan Morgan; it was just the way things were. Dan Morgan quoted a U.S. senator as saying of grain merchants: 'No one knows how they operate, what their profits are, what they pay in taxes and what effect they have on foreign policy – or much of anything else about them'.

In 1976, the French magazine *L'Expansion* called Louis Dreyfus 'a commercial empire of which one knows nothing'. Pierre Louis-Dreyfus, the company's president, invited Dan Morgan to lunch in his private dining room. The fish with cream sauce was apparently superb, as was the wine, but the journalist left without learning anything of interest about the company.

Georges André, president of André & Cie – and the original 'A' of the ABCD group of trading companies – invited Dan Morgan to 'an excellent lunch of brook trout in a village restaurant', but all he got out of it was historical data.

Although Dan Morgan wrote little about ADM – the new 'A' in the ABCD group after André exited the business – the company was no more open. When Dwayne Andreas became CEO in 1974, one of the first things he did was to eliminate a 27-person public relations department. He once famously said, 'Getting information from me is like frisking a seal'. (2)

Dan Morgan was granted a one-hour interview with Michel Fribourg, president of Continental Grain, but later received a letter from the company saying, 'It has been decided that we choose not to participate in further interviews with you'. Continental had been in the grain business since the start of the nineteenth century, but never published a company brochure.

None of the trading houses was more obsessed with secrecy than Bunge. Dan Morgan wrote, 'Bunge was a private company about which nobody knew and nobody could speak. ... To Bunge officials, public relations meant keeping Bunge out of the limelight'.

But then, the company's controlling families had a reason for staying in the shadows. Five years earlier, in September 1974 in Buenos Aires, the Montoneros – an Argentine guerrilla movement – kidnapped Jorge and Juan Born, 40 and 39 years old respectively, the grandsons of the founding partner and heirs apparent of the company. Juan Born was released six months later, in March 1975, and Jorge in June 1975. No details were ever given about the ransom paid for Juan, but the Montoneros claimed that the Bunge family paid $60 million for the release of Jorge—more than $200 million in today's money, and equivalent to one-third of the annual Argentine defence budget.

Unsurprisingly, after the kidnapping, the family withdrew even further behind a veil of secrecy. Dan Morgan '... did not get near the Hirschs or the Borns, the ruling families of the Bunge Company'. The closest he got was an hour-long interview with the president of Bunge's North American division. After the meeting, Bunge's public relations agent told him that he had 'neither the time nor the inclination for further discussions'.

But why were the grain companies so secretive back in the 1970s? Dan Morgan wrote:

> The companies ... stay in the shadows most of the time. Perhaps it was the ancient nightmare of the middleman–merchant that made them all so secretive – the old fear that in moments of scarcity or famine, the people would blame them for all their misfortunes, march upon their granaries, drag them into the town square and confiscate their stock.

Anti-Semitism may have been another reason for avoiding the limelight. In his book *The King of Oil,* (3) Daniel Ammann wrote:

> For centuries Jews in Europe had suffered from discrimination. They were unable to become farmers, as they were forbidden from owning land. As they were excluded from the craft guilds, they were unable to become craftsmen. ... They were however permitted to perform one function that was proscribed for medieval Christians: making loans with interest. Thus, the Jews became moneylenders and traders in the absence of other options.
>
> It is one of the ironies of history that the persecution and expulsion of the Jews is what made such an efficient trading community possible. ... By the onset of the modern era, the Jewish Diaspora was greater than that of any other people. The scattered Jews had a trading tradition that was second to none and sufficient confidence to enable trade over large distances and periods of time.

A fear of being blamed for food shortages, anti-Semitism and a desire to hide wealth were the main reasons for grain merchants' obsession with secrecy. But secrecy was also necessary for commercial reasons. The grain business has always been fiercely competitive. Grain merchants have always had to fight tooth and nail for a share of the small margins that usually prevail in the markets, and they are just as happy, if not happier, to take a penny from a competitor's pocket than to take it out of the market.

Unlike equity markets, the concept of insider trading does not exist in commodity markets. Information concerning production, government policies and even the grain deals themselves can move markets. Traders with access to market-moving information certainly didn't want to share it with a competitor; they wanted to keep it secret as long as they could. The need for secrecy has always been deeply embedded in the world of trading and always will be.

Having said that, compare Dan Morgan's difficulties in obtaining information for his 1979 book with the ease with which Daniel Ammann gained access to traders for his book about Marc Rich, published in 2010. The author wrote, 'These oil and commodity traders ... shared their thoughts and their memories with me, opened doors and documents, and explained the technicalities of trading and financing. They tried to show me the big picture, and they revealed their little secrets'.

But then, perhaps Mr Ammann was just lucky in his timing. Until the series of interviews that formed the backbone of his book, Marc Rich had systematically avoided reporters and was 'considered the most secretive trader of the notoriously furtive commodities trading community. For years, no one had ever seen a photograph of him. The media had to resort to artists' sketches for their reports'.

Glencore, the successor company to Marc Rich, is now a public company, as too are ADM, Bunge and Wilmar. Cargill and Dreyfus are still privately owned, but both act as if they were publicly quoted. They publish detailed company reports and actively interact with the wider community, whether bond investors, clients, banks or journalists. COFCO International, the new giant among the grain trading companies, is primarily Chinese government owned, but has an active public relations department and a Twitter account.

In fact, all the large agricultural commodity companies are present on social media, actively engaging with NGOs on issues related to environmental sustainability or human rights.

Despite their increasing transparency, agricultural merchants are still being regularly dragged into the town square of public opinion. They are still frequently being blamed for varying misfortunes and often accused of conspiratorial behaviour.

The 2014 book *The Secret Club That Runs the World – Inside the Fraternity of Commodities Traders*, (4) written by Kate Kelly, formally a journalist with the *Wall Street Journal*, reeks of conspiracy. The title alone suggests that commodity traders work together to secretly 'run the world'. In the book's advertising blurb, the publishing company writes:

> ... [I]f the individual participants in the great commodities boom of the 2000s went unnoticed, their impact did not. Over several years the size of the market exploded, and so did prices for raw materials – raising serious questions about whether the big traders were intentionally jacking up the cost of gasoline, food, and other essentials bought by ordinary people around the world. What was really driving all those price spikes?

The publishers add that the author 'takes us inside this secretive inner circle that controls so many things we all depend on'.

If you read the book, you will find that there is nothing in it about a secret club of commodity traders that rule the world. The reason is quite simple: there is no secret club.

Everyone likes a conspiracy theory; people like to believe that secret clubs – or groups of powerful, often sinister, people – control our lives, that they really do rule the world. The political scientist Michael Barkun has argued that people believe in conspiracy theories for three reasons. He writes:

First, conspiracy theories claim to explain what institutional analysis cannot. They appear to make sense out of a world that is otherwise confusing. Second, they do so in an appealingly simple way, by dividing the world sharply between the forces of light, and the forces of darkness. They trace all evil back to a single source, the conspirators and their agents. Third, conspiracy theories are often presented as special, secret knowledge unknown or unappreciated by others. For conspiracy theorists, the masses are a brainwashed herd, while the conspiracy theorists in the know can congratulate themselves on penetrating the plotters' deceptions. (5)

Agricultural commodity merchants have little to no control over neither the markets they trade nor the margins they earn. Competition is fierce, and traders can only make as big a margin as the markets allows. Often, that's not much. As Guy Hogge, an ex-trader and now Head of Sustainability at Louis Dreyfus, told me in my earlier book, Commodity Conversations:

> There is sometimes a view that big companies such as ours try to manipulate markets to influence price. In fact, the opposite is true. We won't participate in a market that is so thin that it can be manipulated; a market that can be manipulated can equally be manipulated against us. We like liquid markets that trade a lot of volume, that provide proper hedging mechanisms, and that reflect the true supply-and-demand situation at any particular moment.

The big trading companies are now more likely to be dragged into the town square of public opinion over sustainability issues; 'naming and shaming' companies that they feel have behaved inappropriately. However, as the WWF's Jason Clay pointed out in his conversation, you can often name and shame the wrong people.

All the big trading companies have taken the view that the best way to effectuate change for the better is to engage with, rather than ban, suppliers that fail to meet social and environmental norms. Refusing to deal with these suppliers doesn't solve the problem; it only displaces it. As Louis Dreyfus' Guy Hogge explained:

> I believe that engagement is better than boycott. Engaging with Indonesian palm-oil producers, for example, can lead to positive change. The same applies to engaging with smallholder farmers as to why education for their children is more important than having a little extra help on the farm.

Avoiding questionable supply chains completely may be an easy way to refrain from dealing with an issue, but it is not the best way to inspire and encourage change on the ground. If you want to address issues, you have to be involved in them, alongside other relevant stakeholders.

Agriculture Is Our Backbone - Karel Valken

Karel W. Valken is Global Head Trade & Commodity Finance (TCF) Agri for Rabobank International. I caught up with him by telephone from his base in Utrecht, Netherlands.

Good morning, Karel. Could you tell me a little bit about your family background and how you became one of the world's top experts in trade and commodity finance?
I was born and bred in Holland. My father was a civil engineer responsible for the country's waterways and ports. I studied business at the Hogere Economische School of Amsterdam. After university, I did my military service as a platoon commander with a Dutch cavalry reconnaissance unit, spending a year in Germany.

After that, I had to work. I wanted to do something internationally. As a good Dutchman, I found our country a little bit too small. It was also a time when the commodity futures business started evolving. So I began looking for something in the commodity trade, and I ended up at a bank called Mees & Hope in Amsterdam, which became Mees Pierson and is now ABNAMRO. Within the bank, I found my way into commodities. I worked for 14 years with MeesPierson, spending eight years in New York from 1989 to 1997.

This was a particularly interesting period, because you may recall that, in 1989, the Berlin Wall came down. This led to the collapse of the former Soviet Union, then to the implosion of Prodintorg and the ExportKleb, and a significant change to commodity trade flows.

In 1996, I was offered the position of Finance Director and Board Member for Nidera, where I stayed until 2006. That year, one of the icons of commodity finance, a former colleague of mine, Diane Boogaard, moved to Rabobank to set up a new trade and commodity finance division, and she asked me to join her. It was a fantastic opportunity, and I leapt at it.

How did you enjoy your year in the Dutch cavalry?
I had a great time. I'm still in frequent contact with the other officers from the regiment. I learned two things during my military service. One is the importance of time, which, incidentally, is why I appreciate that you called me exactly when you said you'd call me and that you agreed to limit the call to one hour. (Author's note: it was actually one hour and three minutes!)

The other thing I learned in the military is what I call my 'Foxhole Theory'. A fox will use one hole to go into its lair, but it will always have another way out. It's about the alternatives in life that allow you to optimise your negotiation and your margin.

Do you still ride horses?

During my officer training, I had to do some riding, but I'm absolutely no good at it. We were invited once to exercise with the British equivalent of our regiment. It allowed me to see the enormous difference in terms of tradition and ability between the British cavalry and the Dutch cavalry, which made me very humble. So, no, I don't ride anymore!

Did your children ever want to follow in your footsteps into banking or trade finance?

Not really. I have 33-year-old twins. Many years ago, they asked me what had gone wrong with my career, because I was still in commodities. I told them that nothing had gone wrong, but that as a Dutchman, I love to travel, to explore; the commodities business allows me to do that. Moreover, financing commodities is a very functional business! In addition, I mostly deal with privately owned companies where the principals have a vested interest in the wellbeing of their company. They're passionate about their companies, and I'm passionate about commodities!

My son works for a British company in social media advertising, while my daughter is working in communications for a private clinic. There is no tradition in my family for banking or trading, so in that sense, I'm an exception.

You mentioned that you met up with the British cavalry in Germany. Why do you think there are so many British and Dutch traders in agricultural commodities?

I'm not sure. Both countries have a history of exploring the high seas, but then, so do the Spanish and the Portuguese. If you look at successful joint ventures such as Unilever or Royal Dutch Shell, the Dutch and British have a good history of working together and of being alike. They both have similar interests to explore.

A Dutch friend of mine once said that the British never tell you what they really think, while the Dutch will always tell you what they think, even when you don't want to hear it!

Yes, the Dutch can be very direct!

You mentioned you were with Nidera. What was it like working for a private commodity trading company at that time?

I remember vividly when I moved there in 1996. I found Nidera a very different kind of an organisation to the bank. It was like a breath of fresh air, as if I had opened a window onto a stuffy room to let in a new spirit of entrepreneurship and opportunism.

However, I also quickly realised that, when you work for a bank, you have the luxury of a legal department, an HR department and an IT department. It was different working for a medium-sized family-owned trading company. I had to be a jack-of-all-trades, and I had to be more creative. The other thing is, I needed to be quicker. A trader wants to have an answer yesterday, not today or tomorrow! I also had to learn to be more stress tolerant.

Nidera was professionally run, but the family exerted control over the company through the advisory board. Ito van Lanschot was CEO while I was there. He called himself 'an ex-con', meaning he was ex-Continental Grain. I learned a lot from him, particularly on risk management and on the overall dynamics of commodity trading.

At a bank, you look at credit, but credit is just one of the many different risks that a trading company needs to manage. There is, of course, price and basis risk, but there's also freight, currency and counter-party risk.

In those days, I travelled frequently with traders. One of my most memorable trips was in a Jeep with four Russians in the middle of winter. We drove south along the Volga River visiting suppliers, to give me a better feel of the risk of giving prepayments to sunflower seed exporters. That was what I would call my Wild West days.

Do you think Nidera would still be going if COFCO hadn't bought it?

You could ask a similar question about Toepfer, which was also family owned but now fully absorbed by ADM. Would Toepfer have survived if ADM hadn't bought them? I believe that the answer is 'yes' for both companies, but probably with a minority Asian partner and a different focus.

Nidera were a bit slow moving into the Black Sea region after the fall of the Berlin Wall. They missed an opportunity there, particularly in Ukraine. Glencore and Toepfer moved quickly into the region after the collapse of the U.S.S.R. Nidera was a little slower to invest in port facilities, as well as in inland storage and transport facilities. They were too conservative.

You moved from a trading company back to banking. Why did you make that move?

I like being commercially active: doing deals with clients. At Nidera, my commercial activities were limited to negotiating down rates with banks and structured finance, which after 10 years became pretty boring. When Rabobank approached me, I was really excited by the challenge of restarting a commodity unit within a bank, with a number of old colleagues from Mees Pierson.

Another thing was that, in Nidera, the family held all the shares, effectively controlling the company. Not sharing entrepreneurial ownership can be detrimental to long-term success. I grew a little frustrated with that.

Moving on to COFCO International, do you think that it was a mistake for them to buy two companies, Noble and Nidera, at the same time?

In hindsight, they should have bought Bunge, but it wasn't an option at that time. Bunge wasn't for sale.

Initially, Nidera was only looking to bring in a minority partner. They were talking to a couple of Japanese companies about selling 10 percent of the company. But then, COFCO came along with an offer to buy 51 percent. The owners knew that the business was changing, that traders were becoming supply chain managers and food companies, and that required capital that they didn't necessarily have. They decided to take the offer.

In hindsight, I believe COFCO should've bought only Nidera. Noble had a different culture, and it has been tough for COFCO to align the two cultures, let alone deal with the business issues.

Do you think COFCO's purpose is to make money, or is it feeding the dragon?

Their objective is to become a global merchant. Two years ago, their CEO told the FT Commodity Conference that they wanted to become the 'Second C' in the group. They've largely already achieved that, admittedly based at least partially on their business in China. Even so, the volume they move into China is still a minority of their business.

You need to have optionality in your trading book to be successful in procurement. That means having third-party trades.

Do you think trade houses are better off as private or as public companies?

I believe that trading companies generally are better off as private companies. The business is seasonal and cyclical. It's also prone to disruption by politics and weather. This leads to fluctuating P&Ls (Profits & Losses) that investors have difficulty in understanding. We've seen that clearly with Bunge; investor pressure has been hindering management's ability to develop a long-term strategy.

But then, it depends on whether you're asset heavy or asset light. Asset-light companies can have choppier P&Ls. A company like ADM, for example, has steadier P&Ls and thrives as a listed company.

Are you worried about the future of the trade houses?

The grain merchandising companies' core business is to buy grain from the farmer, store, transport and possibly process it. That business has become so transparent over the last few years that it has become difficult to create a meaningful margin. As a result, the A.B.C.D.+ (ADM, Bunge, Cargill, Dreyfus, Glencore, Wilmar and COFCO International) players are moving into more value-added businesses to enhance margins. These new sectors are more capital intensive, and this has led to some discussion as to whether they are better off family owned or as a public company.

I believe that there is room for smaller traders in certain products and in certain geographies. It's harder for them to compete in the bigger commodities. There are successful companies, for example trading in pulses or yellow peas, moving them into Asia. These markets are different. They aren't futures related, and the counterparty and country risks can be higher than in the big grain markets.

If we look at our global grain business, we have very few small companies; they don't have a meaningful function in the chain. Small companies will continue to add value in countries and markets that are too small or too dangerous for the bigger companies to get involved in.

Could you tell me a little bit about Rabobank and its involvement in agriculture?
Rabobank is cooperative bank that emerged from small agricultural cooperative banks founded by Dutch farmers. We have members but no shareholders.

Agriculture is our backbone. We understand the seasonality and the complexity of farming. As a cooperative, it can be a challenge to raise enough capital, and for that reason, we tend to be conservative. But the advantage of not being listed is that we can take a longer-term view of the business; we can be more patient. We're perhaps more focused than other banks on contributing to the wellbeing of society.

I saw that your mission statement is 'Growing a better world together'.
I recently did a presentation to the bank's executive board where I looked at the mission statements of the ABCD+ group. They all had similar statements; we're aligned.

Growing stands for sustainable, healthy growth, development and progress. *A better world* goes beyond our clients, employees and members and includes our communities and associations. *Together* is important because, as a cooperative bank, we believe in the power of coalitions. Our strength lies in connecting people and knowledge. It's much more than an empty slogan!

This mission is part of our Banking for Food (B4F) strategy. It entails the meaningful role we want to play in food transition and how we can help feed the nine billion people that will be on this planet in 2050, while respecting planetary boundaries.

In terms of sustainable financing, which commodity presents the greatest challenges?
If you look at my area of responsibility, most challenges are in cocoa and coffee, simply because of their level of complexity and the need to improve the livelihood for smallholders. We spend a lot of time on those two commodities, even though they're much smaller in terms of volume than grains and oilseeds.

Our challenge is to stop deforestation and prevent climate change, while feeding the world: how can those two objectives coexist? We have to embed sustainability in the business and our daily thinking. Our 'sustainable toolkit' includes services and financing from Rabo Foundation/Rural Fund, as well as the fund we established with the United Nations called Agri3 to combat deforestation and enhance the livelihood of smallholder farmers.

Do you think a time will come when Rabobank will only finance commodities that are certified as sustainable?

This year, we were the sustainability coordinator of a $2.5 billion revolving credit facility with green features. Customers are getting discounts on the interest rates they pay as long as they meet certain sustainability criteria. I suspect that, going forward, companies that aren't green, or less green, will still get financing, but they'll have to pay a premium.

It's different for palm oil. The consumer pressure is different. We don't finance companies that aren't RSPO members. We may sometimes make an exception if a company isn't RSPO certified as long as it's committed to become RSPO certified and has put the correct milestones in place. We can help them on that journey.

Could you describe a typical TCF finance?

TCF has traditionally meant *transactional financing*, where we'd finance, say, a Ukrainian wheat exporter to purchase wheat from farmers and to export it. We can finance the wheat from the moment it's in an upcountry silo until the importer's letter of credit is opened and cashed.

We make an important distinction for the ABCD+ group – the seven companies covered by your book. The ABCD+s each have individual credit ratings within the bank, which allows for unsecured financing. We provide them with anything up to $1.5 billion in working capital that they can use throughout the globe for different purposes. We don't finance them on a transactional basis. That's why the distinction between ABCD+ companies and non-ABCD+ companies is so important.

How do you see your business evolving in the future?

There are two strategic drivers for our agri-clients: sustainability and innovation. We divide innovation into two categories: food and feed innovation and digital innovation. The first is to meet changing consumer demands. For example, Dreyfus recently invested in a company producing fake blood from beets for vegetarian burgers. We help our clients with this type of innovation through our franchise. We have a platform called FoodBytes, headquartered in California, which looks at the innovation needed to meet changing consumer demands. We help our clients with start-ups and their incubation to take them to the next step.

On the technical/digital innovation side, we've embedded in our teams a number of people who are looking at, say, blockchain or robotics. If you look at Dreyfus again, they recently signed a joint partnership with a big e-commerce platform in China, which they'll use to sell their brand of soybean oil.

Distribution and marketing are changing fast. A few years ago, I met the former chairman of Cargill Asia, who'd just come back from China, where he'd visited Alibaba. He told me that he couldn't decide whether Alibaba was a potential competitor or a potential distribution partner. I found his comment intriguing.

Traditional TCF is changing. The amount of due diligence that we now have to do is such that smaller merchants will have increasing difficulty in obtaining financing. We don't have the mandate to do business with companies with a capital below $25 million, simply because the income we can create from this kind of client is too small – and the risk is too big.

The world's population is growing, and international trade will have to play an increasing role in keeping people fed. International traders will continue to have a role despite disintermediation and the democratisation of information. Their role will be in logistics and risk management, and having a large global footprint will allow them to maintain optionality in the chain.

Is there anything that you'd like to add?

In the current environment, money no longer has any value. Interest rates are negative to zero, and you can now be paid for taking out a mortgage. We're living in a new economic reality. At the same time, there's excess capacity in operational assets, and commodity prices are low. These two ingredients could speed up consolidation within the sector, which would ultimately bring margins back.

Lenin once said, 'Grain is the currency of currencies'. Money may not have value at the moment, but grain does.

Thank you, Karel, for the time to share your experience with us!

Chapter Two: Feast and Famine

'After that, there will be seven years of famine, and all the good years will be forgotten, because the famine will ruin the country'. Genesis 41:30 (Good News Translation)

Although we didn't know it, the world nearly ended in 1979, the year that Dan Morgan published *Merchants of Grain*.

On 9 November 1979, my 23rd birthday, U.S. military computers detected an incoming Soviet nuclear missile strike. (1) The U.S. military went on full alert, with fighter jets and pilots scrambled into the air. Six minutes before the first missiles were due to strike, the U.S. was on the point of reciprocating, launching a full nuclear attack of their own. Just in time, someone realised that they had put the wrong tape into one of the Honeywell computers that ran the missile detection system. The tape had been part of a training exercise from the previous day, a war game that simulated a Soviet attack on the United States. The U.S. counterattack was stopped with minutes to go, and Dan Morgan's book went on to be a bestseller.

On that day, I was sitting at my desk in the sugar department in Cargill's head office in Minnetonka, Minnesota, watching the first snow of winter falling outside. I was blissfully unaware that the world had nearly ended. And I was also blissfully unaware that the snow would stay on the ground until the following Easter; it was my first taste of a Minnesotan winter.

I had been working in Cargill's head office since the previous September, when I had been transferred from London, after a year on their training programme. My job was to keep track of the company's trading position and to execute the hedging of the company's purchases and sales of physical sugar. I was also given a trading account; my boss told me that he expected me to make $50,000 per day, 'to help pay the overheads'.

While I'd been in London, I had got to know a floor broker on the London sugar futures market, and now that I was in the U.S., he had decided he would help me out with my trading (in exchange, obviously, for brokerage business). Each day, he would tell me what he expected the market would do, predicting its highs, its lows and its daily trading range.

I took his advice and started to make good trading profits, enough to attract the attention of my boss. I never told my boss that I was simply following my friend's advice; I just told him each day what I expected the market to do. Most of the time, it did it.

It was only a couple of years later when I was back in London and enjoying a good lunch with my friend that he told me that he had been executing orders for the Cubans, who then were the world's largest sugar exporters. They weren't allowed to trade on the New York futures markets, so they concentrated their energy and trading ammunition in London. They dominated the market, pushing it around almost at will.

Well, at least they pushed it around for a while, until they were blown out of the water by something bigger.

At that time, the sugar market was under the sway of something called the International Sugar Agreement (ISA), negotiated under the auspices of the United Nations and designed to ensure a fair price for consumers and producers. There had been various attempts over the years to fix sugar and other commodity prices on a global rather than a national level, but this one would prove to be the last.

Each sugar-producing country was given a fixed production or export quota. If prices fell below a certain predetermined 'fair' price, each country agreed to hold back a certain percentage of their production as stocks. When prices rose again, those countries were supposed to release their stocks and dampen prices.

In practice, sugarcane millers were reluctant to hold stocks when prices fell; they needed the money to pay their farmers. When prices started to increase, producers felt comfortable selling into the rally, confident that the price would be contained as other producers released their stocks. However, when prices began to increase, the stocks that should have been there weren't there; prices exploded.

In the end, the U.N. abandoned the idea of trying to ensure fair commodity prices, deciding that the various commodity agreements they enacted over years created more price volatility than would have existed without them. Rather like communism, fixing a price that is 'fair' to both consumers and producers is a lovely idea, but it simply doesn't work in practice.

The Cubans had tried and failed to control the sugar market. The United Nations had also tried (for more altruistic reasons) and failed. And over the years, as you'll see later in this book, various traders and speculators also tried. They all failed.

Accordingly, if neither traders nor speculators determine price, who or what does?

To answer that question, we should go back to 1759, when the Scottish philosopher Adam Smith introduced the idea of an 'invisible hand'. He realised that it's the price of something that brings supply and demand into equilibrium. If demand increases or supply falls, prices increase to encourage supply, while reducing demand. If supply increases or demand drops, prices fall, sending a signal to producers to reduce output or to consumers to increase demand.

He developed the idea further in 1776, when he wrote *The Wealth of Nations* (2), in which he argued that an economy works best in a free-market scenario where everyone operates in his or her own interest – and where the government leaves people to buy and sell freely among themselves. He argued that self-interested competition in a free market would benefit society by keeping prices low, while building in an incentive for a wide variety of goods and services.

But if the market forces of supply and demand determine price, what determines supply and demand?

The weather is one of the most decisive factors in determining the supply of agricultural commodities. Market participants spend a huge amount of their time worrying about the weather.

Governments can also influence the prices of agricultural commodities and differentials between the prices of different origins. At the time of writing, the trade dispute between China and the U.S. has increased the price of Brazilian soybeans relative to the price of U.S. beans.

Events can also impact price. For example, the outbreak of African Swine Fever in China has reduced Chinese demand for animal feed and had a significant impact on the world's import demand for soybeans.

However, the most important factor that affects the supply and demand of a commodity is the price of the commodity itself, both in outright terms and relative to alternative, competing crops. This leads to a circular situation where the price of a certain commodity will depend on its supply and demand, while the supply and demand depend, at least partially, on its price. This is a feedback loop with a time lag; the length of that time lag depends on which commodity you are discussing.

The price of alternative crops can also have a significant impact on the price of a specific commodity. Many farmers in the United States, for example, have the choice each year whether to plant soybeans or corn. Corn takes nitrogen out of the soil, while soybeans put it back, so corn requires more fertiliser than soybeans. Farmers will consider that when they make planting decisions, but the biggest factor in their decisions will be the relative prices of the two commodities.

Similarly, the poor planting weather in the U.S. in 2019 resulted in higher corn prices relative to those for wheat. This increased the demand for wheat for animal feed, as wheat was substituted for corn. As the saying goes, 'The best cure for high prices is high prices – and the best cure for low prices is low prices'.

However, this isn't a precise process. It works with time lags, and a shortage now can lead to a future surplus. Agricultural markets aren't perfect: they overreact in both directions and can take time to correct. Prices tend to rise too far in times of penury and fall too far in times of plenty. They also tend to stay higher for longer and lower for longer than one would expect.

But why should prices stay low for long periods? Surely, when prices fall below production costs, farmers stop producing and leave fields fallow, right?

One reason is that farmers usually don't have any choice other than to keep producing, even if prices are low. They'll continue to plant and harvest if the price at which they can sell their crops covers what economists call the *variable cost* of growing and harvesting them. The price a farmer receives for corn may not cover fixed costs (the rent paid for land and the interest paid to the bank for the loan to buy tractors and build grain storage silos), but the farmer is still better off planting and harvesting corn rather than letting the land lie fallow.

Another reason is that surplus years tend to result in the surplus being carried forward in the form of stocks. It can take time, sometimes years, for those stocks to be run down.

Although speculators play an important role in bearing some price risk in the market, they sometimes drive prices higher or lower than they' otherwise be – or at least should be. This is what the Commodity Futures Trading Commission (CFTC) calls *excessive speculation*; they define it as speculation 'harmful to the proper functioning of futures markets'. (3)

Commodity prices fluctuate continuously as the market moves to match supply with demand. Although price nearly always ensures supply equals demand, that price may be unacceptable (or at least uncomfortable) for many in the market. The price may be too high for some consumers to buy that commodity – or as much of that commodity as they would like. Conversely, the price might be too low and drive a farmer to bankruptcy.

The British economist John Maynard Keynes once famously said, 'The market can stay irrational longer than you can stay solvent'. (4) He was talking about the equity market, but he could just as well have been talking about commodities.

Less famous economists argue that, in the long term, prices revert to what they call the *equilibrium price*, the price at which the marginal supply of a commodity equals the marginal demand for that commodity. The equilibrium price is usually said to be the cost of producing an extra (or marginal) unit of that commodity by the most efficient producer; economists call this the *marginal cost of production*. No matter how high or how low commodity prices go in the short term, they should revert in the long term to a price equal to the marginal cost of production.

Keynes also once famously said, 'In the long run, we are all dead'. While we're alive – and, I suppose, even when we're dead – these various lags and overshoots result in market cycles. These cycles can be long and painful, but to the present, no one has found a better way to establish prices than Adam Smith's invisible hand.

By constantly trading in large volumes, futures and physical commodity markets establish transparent prices all along the supply chain, prices that allow participants to make informed decisions and allow the market to operate efficiently and ensure an efficient allocation of resources. The speculators and traders in the markets ensure that price is transparent, which in turn ensures that future supply meets future demand.

Dan Morgan wrote *Merchants of Grain* at the end of the 1970s, a decade during which grain prices were highly volatile and when grain merchants were earning considerable profits. The 1970s were a sharp contrast to the 1950s and 1960s, when prices were low and trading margins were non-existent. During those previous two decades, the U.S. had struggled to cope with surplus grain and had enacted a complicated and expensive system of export subsidies, as well as grain donations to developing countries.

On the other side of the world, the Soviet Union was struggling to feed their citizens. (5) Their own agricultural system was failing, and food was in short supply. Simultaneously, the U.S.S.R.'s leaders realised that, if they were to survive, they'd have to maintain the goodwill of their people. To do that, they'd have to reallocate resources from industrial investment to consumption, especially the consumption and availability of meat.

Before the Russian Revolution, Russia had been the world's largest wheat producer and exporter. However, production declined with collectivisation, and by the 1970s, the country could no longer feed itself.

In July 1972, Prodintorg, the U.S.S.R.'s state buying agency, purchased 10 million tonnes of U.S. grain (mainly wheat and corn). The sales were equivalent to 30 percent of the average annual U.S. wheat production during the previous five years and more than 80 percent of the wheat used for domestic food during that period. The sales involved a series of subsidies – including a U.S. government credit arrangement of $750 million. In total, these were later calculated to cost the taxpayer more than $300 million, the equivalent of $1.75 billion in today's money.

When the exports sales became known, the domestic price of wheat began to rise, and within a few months, the prices of feed and food grain, soybeans and livestock all turned higher. The price of wheat almost tripled during the year ending in August 1973. The prices of corn and soybeans more than doubled. The wholesale price index of all farm products rose 66 percent, and the wholesale price of food increased 29 percent.

This inflation was partly due to ex-President Richard Nixon's decision to take the U.S. off the gold standard. The resulting collapse of the U.S. dollar enabled U.S. farmers to compete on the export market just as the U.S.S.R. arrived for their massive purchases. Between 1970 and 1973, farm income in constant dollars more than doubled. Even so, the federal government maintained many agricultural price supports and subsidies. (6)

The 1970s' boom inevitably led to bust. In 1979, then-Federal Reserve Chairman Paul Volcker declared war on inflation, the success of which slowly increased the debt burden of farmers. The same year, the Soviets invaded Afghanistan, prompting former President Jimmy Carter to impose a grain embargo. Inflation subsided, and the dollar rose relative to other currencies.

The high prices and good merchandising profits of the 1970s inevitably led to an over-expansion in both agricultural production and merchandising infrastructure. The result was an excess of both grain and logistics, something Jay O'Neil describes so well in the conversation below. Grain trading companies struggled to stay afloat during this down cycle, and by the end of the century, two of the bigger ones had exited the business. (A third, Cook Industries, never survived the price volatility of the 1970s and had already closed down by the time Dan Morgan published his book.)

The slump of the 1980s and early 1990s was just one of many that have occurred over the centuries. Just taking recent history, crop prices doubled during World War I as production collapsed in war-torn Europe. In 1916, the U.S. government added fuel to the fire with the Federal Farm Loan Act, which extended long-term financing to farmers. When the war ended, agricultural production recovered in Europe, and world prices halved. Farmers began defaulting on mortgages during the 1920s, and the crisis led to the Great Depression. Once again, the U.S. government exacerbated the problem by imposing protectionist tariffs that stymied exports.

As the 1930s wore on, then-President Franklin Roosevelt introduced farm subsidies that encouraged production boosted by rising prices during World War II. A post-war slump in the 1950s and 1960s gave way to the boom of the 1970s and the bust of the 1980s and early 1990s. (7)

That slump then gave way to a super cycle during 2003 to 2008 with China, rather than the U.S.S.R., as the main buyer of American crops, particularly soybeans. Government intervention again amplified the boom with the 2005 Renewable Fuels Standard that significantly boosted corn demand for ethanol production.

The boom has again turned to bust – a bust also amplified by government policy when President Donald Trump began a trade war with China by imposing significant tariffs on the imports of Chinese goods. The Chinese retaliated by hitting where they thought it would hurt President Trump the most and imposed tariffs on the imports of U.S. agricultural products, particularly soybeans, but also corn and ethanol.

Meanwhile, the U.S. Environmental Protection Agency began exempting refineries from requirements to add ethanol to gasoline and other fuels, reducing corn demand.

In 2018, President Trump tweeted, 'Trade wars are good, and easy to win'. Unfortunately, trade wars are like real wars: they are never good, and they are never easy to win.

Farmers and traders are currently suffering from overproduction and excess capacity that are a direct result of the previous boom, but once again, ill-timed government intervention is exacerbating the problem.

But even though grain markets are cyclical, they are also driven by structural trends. The structural changes that have occurred in the 40 years since Dan Morgan wrote his book have changed the grain markets almost beyond recognition. I will look at those trends in the next chapter, but before I do, let's talk with Jay O'Neil, who actually lived through the boom and busts of the 1970s and 1980s, experiencing them, first-hand.

History Is Repeating Itself - Howard Jay O'Neil

Jay spoke with me by phone from his home in Southern Oregon. He has recently taken semi-retirement from the faculty at Kansas State University, where he managed the commercial operations of the International Grains Program. He now operates his own private consulting business. When I spoke with him, Jay had recently returned from speaking at a buyers' conference in Thailand organised by the USSEC, the U.S. Soybean Export Council. Before that, he was doing similar workshops in Central America for the U.S. Grains Council.

Good morning, Jay. Could you please tell me how you started in the business?
I started in the grain business in January 1973, straight out of college. I joined Continental Grain in Orinda, California. It was right at the beginning of what was later described as the Great Russian Grain Robbery, and I was right in the middle of it. I stayed with Conti until May 1977, when I was hired by Pillsbury to work as a grain merchandiser in their export grain organisation.

I worked in Omaha, Nebraska, for one year, moved briefly to St Louis, Missouri, their regional office for export trading, and then to their Minneapolis headquarters. I stayed with Pillsbury until 1984, when they sold their grain origination business to Cargill. Pillsbury had quite a sizeable operation at the time, with over 90 domestic facilities.

When the Soviets came in for grain in the 1970s, the U.S. just didn't have the transportation logistics to handle the volumes that they wanted to buy. The U.S. agricultural industry was not ready or equipped for that much demand. There simply weren't sufficient rail cars, barges or export facility capacity to handle the volumes.

By the early to mid-eighties, the U.S. had built the export capacity needed to meet what we expected to be long-lasting Soviet grain demand. But Russian demand slowed down. They didn't have enough money to continue buying the volumes they'd been buying.

The industry found itself in a horrendous position with an overcapacity of transport equipment and export facilities. People were driving around the U.S. looking for empty rail side tracks where they could store surplus railcars. We were using old military sites, unused industrial sites, anywhere we could find to store them. We parked empty railcars in the expectation that we would need them one day. But it would be many years and hundreds of millions of dollars in industry losses before the excess rail and barge capacity would diminish and balance cargo demand.

I remember one particular meeting at Pillsbury in Minneapolis where the management group turned to the vice president of our barge division and told him to send out teams to look for trees along the Mississippi and its tributaries that were big enough to tie off barges to let them sit.

Everyone was shouldering excess transportation assets and export assets, and everyone was haemorrhaging red ink. In the mid-'80s, Pillsbury's grain division lost more than $200 million in one year, nearly half a billion dollars in today's money. I imagine many of our competitors were in the same position. We were only a medium-sized grain company; bigger companies must have lost even more. Every company in the grain business was losing money.

Pillsbury's management group conducted a study to answer the question: 'When will surplus railcars and barges rust to the point where they go to scrap, or when will demand pick up enough to use those cars?' The group's answer was sometime around 1999–2000! It was a surprisingly good projection. The excess capacity situation also continued through the 1990s, though of course to a lesser extent than in the 1980s. But, boy, were the 1980s bad! We all suffered. We had all over-expanded.

When Pillsbury sold their grain merchandising operations in 1984, I joined Ferruzzi down in New Orleans, managing their feed grain export business in Myrtle Grove, Louisiana.

We are all dependent on the market in this business. You can't dictate what sort of profit margin you can obtain. You can only extract whatever profit margins the market will allow, and back then, it wasn't allowing any. During my time at Ferruzzi, many of the vessels we were loading had negative margins. The entire industry was in a down cycle and incurred negative profitability – negative margins. We were paying more for the barges and the railcars than we were getting from many of the ships we were exporting.

We closed our facility for two months to stop the losses, but the fixed costs of maintaining the facility were higher than expected. We found it was better to continue throughput and obtain revenue to cover some of our variable costs.

That rule still applies today: it's better to keep facilities running, even at low throughput margins, than to close them. It's better to try to extract some revenue to cover something against variable expenses than to have no revenue and still have to pay full overhead costs. We opened the elevator again, but the situation didn't really improve.

I left Ferruzzi in 1986 and took a job with Bartlett Grain Co. in Kansas City, Missouri, where I managed their cross-country grain trading group and export grain operations for 17 years.

Did the Carter grain embargo in January 1980 make the situation worse?
The U.S. has had two grain embargoes: one under the Nixon administration and the other under Jimmy Carter. They were effectively soybean export embargoes. Both were detrimental to the U.S. grain industry. The Nixon and Carter embargoes motivated the Japanese to go to South America and invest capital in the development of the South American soybean industry.

Wouldn't that have happened anyway?
It would have, but not as quickly or on such a large scale. We created our own competition by imposing the two embargoes.

Is history repeating itself now?
I have no doubt that history is repeating itself with the current trade war with China. We're once again helping to create our own competition. China has been put in a difficult situation in terms of grain, both politically and economically. The Chinese are almost certainly telling themselves they can no longer depend on the U.S. as a reliable supplier, and they'll certainly try to diversify their buying options. China is already investing in South America, Sub-Saharan Africa, Russia and the Black Sea to encourage soybean production outside the U.S.

We're again creating our own competition, and that won't be reversible. We'll see grain production increase around the world, and that will make it more difficult for U.S. grain farmers for the next 10 or 20 years and beyond.

But to what extent can China find alternative bean sources? I know the Black Sea region, particularly Ukraine, has expanded corn production, but is corn a substitute for soy?
No, they're not interchangeable. Animal feed has a percentage of starch, usually from corn, but you also need protein, and that comes from the soya meal.

China has a substantial soybean crushing industry that has to be fed by imports. They must import the vast majority of their oilseed needs every year.

You can grow corn in a lot of places, but it's a bit more difficult to grow soybeans. Then again, you have the seed technology companies that are coming up with better, shorter-season soybean varieties that can do well in colder climates such as Canada and Eastern Russia, areas that have previously not been able to grow soybeans.

No one is predicting that these new areas will ever be major oilseed exporters. They'll sell a few million tonnes here and there, but nowhere near the 85-plus million tonnes that China needs each year. China will have to depend on South America and the U.S., but with a growing percentage of that coming from South America.

After you left Ferruzzi, the company tried to squeeze the soybean futures market in Chicago. They failed, and the company went out of business. Is there is a danger that history repeats itself in that sense as well?
Unfortunately, squeezed margins may have prompted some trading companies to try to replace that lost income by taking bigger risks in the futures markets or on the flat price. This has rarely worked.

I've been in the business for 45 years, and I've seen some great companies, Continental Grain, Cook Industries and André, either go bankrupt or exit the grain business. The ones that went out of business did so because someone speculated, took overly big risks, didn't hedge. André got out of the business after big losses in their Italian soybean desk. Cook Industries went bankrupt because of bad positions on crush spreads in soybeans. Even Conti's sale to Cargill followed losses in the Russian bond market. It was always something foolish.

Let's talk a little about ASF (African Swine Fever). Isn't that a bigger problem for U.S. farmers than trade wars?

It is a major problem. In 2017, China imported 95 million tonnes of soybeans, and we were expecting Chinese demand to exceed 100 million tonnes in 2019. But that was before ASF and the tariffs. We now expect China to import 80 to 84 million tonnes, a substantial drop.

Both the U.S. and South America have been ramping up soybean production to supply a 95- to 100-million-tonne China market, and now, we have only 80 to 84 million. I don't know whether you'd call it a perfect storm, but ASF and the trade wars coming together simultaneously are having a major impact on trade.

So the current situation is similar to the 1980s. We have too many beans and too much infrastructure.

I don't see it as being as bad as the 1980s and early 1990s, when margins were negative across the whole industry. It's true we're going through a downturn in export demand. We have surplus transportation, surplus export capacity and surplus ocean transportation. You only have to read the financial results of the big grain companies to see that profits are challenged. But it's not as dark as it was in the 1980s and early 1990s, when profits were negative. Although profits now are poor, they're not negative.

What do you think about President Trump's idea of giving beans to poor countries as food aid?

It's always a question of scale and volumes. We have a 900-million-bushel carryout on soybeans this year, and most expect that to grow to one billion bushels. That's the largest surplus of soybeans that we've ever had in the U.S.: a 23 to 25 percent stocks-to-use ratio. We also have surpluses in wheat and corn. It will take time to solve this problem; it's a multi-year problem. Giving away a few cargoes here and there of beans won't solve the problem.

What about the introduction of GM (genetically modified) crops? Have they contributed to surpluses?

Very much so! Besides improving yields, farmers tell me that, when they plant GM seeds, they're more confident that they'll do well even if the weather is bad. By giving farmers a certain comfort level, GM crops have encouraged them to plant a larger acreage and to get more production per acre.

In addition, we're now planting beans further north and west than they were planted in the past. Historically, in the U.S., we didn't plant large quantities of corn or beans in North or South Dakota; now, we do. The same applies to Western Kansas or Western Nebraska. In the last 15 years, GM technology has led to a dramatic expansion of production into areas that previously couldn't profitably grow these crops. These areas could only grow wheat or barley because of the lack of rainfall and the soil type.

Now, farmers plant GM corn and beans, and they've been displacing barley and wheat areas. The same applies to Canada, where new short-season seeds have led to an expansion of soybean production; it may even double in a few years, although admittedly from a low level.

GM technology has enabled farmers to grow corn and beans in areas that, historically, they couldn't. GM technology has also contributed to yield improvements in traditional growing areas. So GM technology has had a significant impact – and will continue to have an impact.

Why isn't there any GM wheat?

If you ask seed companies, they'll tell you that corn and beans are much bigger crops by planted acres and are commercially more attractive to them than wheat. In addition, soy meal and corn are largely used for animal feed. Humans mainly consume wheat.

In 2008 to 2009, U.S. farmers did ask the seed companies to develop GM wheat; yields weren't increasing as much as in corn and beans. The U.S. was losing wheat acreage to those two crops. But when they asked Japanese flour millers, who are major buyers of U.S. wheat, they said they wouldn't buy U.S. wheat if it were GM. Consequently, GM wheat was put on the back shelf; it was considered too market disrupting.

Some test-plot research on GM wheat has been done in the U.S., Canada and Australia, but so far, there has been no commercial production. There have been three what you might call 'outbreaks' of GM wheat: one in Canada, one in Oregon and now one in Washington state. An environmental group discovered a few GM wheat plants among non-GM wheat and alongside a dirt road, but admittedly, a significant distance – hundreds of miles – from any GM test sites. No one knows how those plants got there.

The Japanese put a temporary embargo on U.S. wheat when it was discovered in Oregon and later on Canadian wheat when it was discovered there. They introduced a testing protocol, but no GM wheat was ever found in any shipment. The embargoes were short-lived.

Going slightly off subject, you recently retweeted a cartoon on Twitter showing organic farming using more land because of lower yields. Is that your view?

Organic farming has lower yields than non-organic farming, so you obviously need more land to get similar production. More carbon is released in the process. A greater agricultural area also means less forest and less biodiversity. Many people believe that organic food is better for them healthwise than non-organic. I don't personally agree with that, but that is the perception among some people, which has created a small percentage of specialised demand for those commodities and products.

Now, changing the subject completely, would you recommend your children become farmers, merchants or neither?

I have two kids: neither has an interest in either farming or grain merchandising. Farming is not a business. It's a lifestyle. It takes place in rural areas, often in isolated areas, takes long hours of hard work, and that isn't for everyone. Thus, many young people don't want to continue family farming. They want the social life and types of jobs that can be found in metropolitan areas.

From an economic standpoint, farming is cyclical. We're currently in a down cycle with low profitability. Hence, it's difficult to obtain capital to buy land or equipment. The farmers that are doing OK now have been farming for generations; they have low debt. It's not a positive economic proposition to buy a farm now and equip it. You have to like the lifestyle and be in it for the long run.

As for grain merchandising, yes, I'd recommend a young person go into it. In the long-term, I expect it to be a financially worthwhile and intellectually interesting career. But many grain companies are currently going through restructuring and laying off staff. We're at that stage in the cycle, but we've been through many cycles before. I trust we'll come through it, as in the past.

Having said that, the rise of the U.S. ethanol industry increased competition for grain in the countryside and made things more difficult for grain merchants. They're no longer the only buyers.

Another thing that has changed is that farmers are now storing crops in their own on-farm storage facilities. Today, 55 percent of grain storage capacity in the U.S. is on farm; only 45 percent is commercial. It used to be easy for merchants to buy cheap grain at harvest time, store it and sell it later. Domestic, as well as export, markets are more competitive now, and handling margins have narrowed.

An additional problem today is that political interference is difficult to predict. It's impossible to guess how long the trade wars will last. Some trade houses expected the trade war with China to be short-lived; they were wrong-footed when it persisted.

But taking everything together, I have had – and continue to have – a fascinating career in the grain merchandising business. It has been challenging, but it has also been rewarding, both intellectually and financially. So, yes, I'd absolutely recommend young people join the sector.

Thank you, Jay, for your time and your input.

Chapter Three – Going with the Grain

'Study grain long enough, and the world shrinks'.
                                                    Dan Morgan

I was transferred in 1979 from Tradax, Cargill's European subsidiary in London, to Cargill's head office outside Minneapolis, Minnesota. That year turned out to be a watershed year, not just for me, but for the world. It was the year in which the world's political and economic tectonic plates shifted.

I had left the U.K., where the punk rock group The Clash were dominating the charts with their hit song 'London Calling'. In the U.S., I found that disco still ruled, with Gloria Gaynor's 'I Will Survive' topping the charts.

In 1979, Sony released the Walkman music cassette player, while Philips introduced the compact disc. The first cable sports channel, ESPN, was launched. And McDonalds introduced the Happy Meal.

Jimmy Carter was President of the United States, and Leonid Brezhnev was Chairman of the Communist Party of the Soviet Union. In May that year, Margaret Thatcher was elected the U.K.'s first female prime minister. Earlier that year, in February, the Iranian Revolution led to the abdication of the Shah of Iran, replaced by the Ayatollah Khomeini. In November, his supporters stormed the U.S. Embassy in Tehran, taking 90 hostages, 53 of who were American.

However, two other things happened in 1979 that, without anyone really paying attention, changed our world forever. The first was the beginning of the opening of China. The second was the beginning of the end of the Soviet Union.

In 1979, the People's Republic of China established full diplomatic relations with the U.S. for the first time since China's communist revolution. It was the first step in bringing China into the global community and opening the country to world trade, something confirmed on 11 December 2001, when China joined the WTO (World Trade Organisation).

Two centuries ago, Napoleon had warned, 'Let China sleep; when she wakes, she will shake the world'. (1) Today, China has awakened, and the world is shaking.

The world has never seen anything like the rapid, tectonic shift in the global balance of power created by the rise of China. In 1979, China accounted for only 2 percent of global output compared to the U.S.'s 22 percent. Today, China's share has climbed to 18 percent, while the U.S.'s has slipped to 16 percent.

Former Australian Prime Minister Kevin Rudd, (2) an astute China watcher, described the country's explosion as 'the English Industrial Revolution and the global information revolution combusting simultaneously and compressed into not 300 years, but 30'.

To give you a couple examples of what that meant on the ground, in the three years between 2011 and 2013, China both produced and used more cement than the U.S. did in the entire twentieth century. In 2011, a Chinese firm built a 30-story skyscraper in just 15 days. Three years later, another construction firm built a 57-story skyscraper in 19 days. Indeed, China built the equivalent of Europe's entire housing stock in just 15 years.

China's urbanisation and rising consumer incomes had a dramatic effect on their diet and food demand. As people get richer, they eat more meat and fish. This significantly increases cereal and oilseed demand for animal feed – and by quite a multiplier. To raise cattle in a feedlot, you need seven kilos of grain to produce one kilo of beef. (3) If you raise pigs, you need four kilos of grain for one kilo of meat. For poultry, the figure is just over two kilos, and for herbivorous species of farmed fish (such as carp, tilapia and catfish), it is slightly less than two kilos.

When people move to cities, they no longer grow fruit and vegetables in their gardens or small farms; instead, they tend to buy more processed food. This accentuates the move away from vegetables to grains. Similarly, urbanisation tends to result in increased food wastage; the food must be moved longer distances, and more food is spoilt in the process.

Meanwhile, Asian people increased their demand for bread and pasta. This increased their demand for wheat for direct consumption.

Contrary to what you might imagine, China's farmers have managed to more than keep pace with the doubling of their domestic demand for wheat, increasing production from 62 million tonnes in 1979 to 132 million tonnes in 2019. (4) They've done even better with corn, increasing production from 60 million to 254 million tonnes over the 40-year period. However, they've failed to keep pace with the rising demand for soybeans for animal feed: soybean imports have increased more than 10,000 percent from the 800,000 tonnes that the country imported in 1979. In 2019, the country imported more than half of the world's total trade in soya.

However, it's not just China. Countries in the Asia–Pacific region are importing an increasing amount of grains and oilseeds to match their growing domestic demand. East Asian countries imported 72.5 million tonnes of grain from around the world in 2019, an increase of more than 50 percent over the last 10 years. Japan and South Korea stand out in corn imports, respectively, the second- and third-largest buyer worldwide, and China has surpassed Saudi Arabia as the largest buyer of barley.

Southeast Asian grain imports, although a third smaller than the amount destined for East Asia, grew even faster, by 129 percent over the past ten years, and are forecast to maintain strong growth in upcoming years – especially considering that wheat consumption in Southeast Asia is far below the global per-capita average of 78 kilos per year and even around three times lower than in China and India. Indonesia, for example is already the second-largest buyer of wheat in the world but has an annual per-capita consumption of only 29 kilos.

Combined, the import volume of East Asia and Southeast Asia accounts for nearly one-third of all grain in global markets.

This huge increase in the demand for protein for animal feed has driven a massive expansion of global soybean production. This has been achieved through an expansion of acreage and yields, especially in the U.S., Brazil and Argentina. In 2019, the world's farmers produced 355 million tonnes of soybeans, almost four times the 93 million tonnes that they produced in 1979. This has been achieved partly through better yields and partly by increased acreage. The average (global) yield for soybeans has increased from 1.82 tonnes per hectare in 1979 to 2.81 tonnes in 2019, while the global acreage has increased 150 percent from 51 million hectares to 125 million.

Trade has also increased sharply, and we've seen significant shifts over the decades, with Brazil now by far the dominant exporter.

In 1979, while China was establishing diplomatic relations with the U.S., Pope John Paul II was visiting his native Poland, the first Pope to ever visit a communist country. This visit, later known as 'the nine days that changed the world', (5) ultimately led to the rise of the Solidarity movement against Communist Party rule. In December 1979, the Soviet Union invaded Afghanistan, a war that they could neither win nor afford. It was the beginning of the end for the U.S.S.R.; the communist bloc officially ceased to exist on 26 December 1991.

Before the First World War, the Russian Revolution and the imposition of communism, Russia had been a major exporter of wheat. By the 1960s, mismanagement had turned the Soviet Union into a major importer of grains. In 1979, the U.S.S.R. imported 12 million tonnes of wheat and 14.5 million tonnes of corn. The Soviet bloc continued to import throughout the 1980s in a desperate attempt to maintain food supplies. In 1984 to 1985, the U.S.S.R. imported a massive 28 million tonnes of wheat and 20 million tonnes of corn.

Domestic grain production fell sharply in the chaos that followed the collapse of the U.S.S.R. in December 1991. The wheat harvest the previous summer had been a record at just over 100 million tonnes, but by 1999, production had fallen to 56 million tonnes. Poor weather played a part, as did a lack of inputs and financing, as well as increased competition from imports. It took time for the collectivised and state farms to be privatised, for funds to be raised and for equipment to be bought. When the Soviet Union collapsed, the bloc had about 25,000 collective and state farms. (6) These have now been broken up into some 285,000 private farms, which generally operate on between 10 and 100 hectares. However, there are some 40 agri-businesses in Russia with over 100,000 hectares.

Both agricultural yields and production have increased massively in the FSU (Former Soviet Union) over the past 20 years. That's partly because of better farming practices, better machinery and increased technology, but also the wider use of fertilisers.

Wheat yields in the entire former U.S.S.R. increased from 1.58 tonnes per hectare at the time of the Soviet Union's collapse in 1991 to 2.54 tonnes in 2018. The corresponding figures for Russia alone are 1.72 tonnes per hectare, increasing to 3.11 tonnes per hectare in the 2017 harvest.

About three percent of Russia's arable land is in an area called the Kuban, the Krasnodar Stavropol region, with a highly productive, humus-rich 'black earth' (*chernozem*) soil. Wheat yields in the Kuban are often over seven tonnes per hectare. Some areas in South Russia have seen yields double in the past 20 years, from four to five to almost 10 tonnes per hectare.

The sanctions imposed following Russia's annexation of Crimea in 2014 have further helped the country to expand domestic agricultural production. The Russian government has made a big push to produce food at home rather than import it. It is now public policy to encourage investments in agriculture, not just in grain, but also in fruit and vegetables, even cheeses.

The Russians are also increasing domestic meat production. Hence, Russia exports little feed wheat. Instead, they use their feed wheat at home to make feed compounds. The same applies to Russia's corn harvest; most goes into the domestic meat and starch industries.

In total, Russia now has about 49 million hectares set aside for grain production, of which 29 million hectares are wheat, split more or less evenly between 15 million of winter wheat and 14 million of spring wheat. However, because the yields of winter wheat are about double those for spring wheat, the actual production ratio is 50 million tonnes of winter wheat versus 25 million tonnes of the spring variety.

Due to less favourable weather, Russia was expected to harvest around 70 to 74 million tonnes of wheat in 2019, a significant drop from the previous year's massive harvest of 85 million tonnes. Domestic wheat consumption is about 44 to 45 million tonnes per year, which leaves exports at around 35 million.

Russian grain production greatly depends on the weather. Most Russian farmland is not irrigated; yields depend on winter snow cover and good spring rains. However, technology such as GPS tracking, increased fertiliser uses and better crop rotations will all boost yields over the long term. This is particularly the case for fertiliser. Much Russian corn and wheat is naturally organic – they don't use mineral fertiliser, particularly in Siberia. It's also non-GMO and, as such, finds willing buyers, particularly in Turkey and South Korea.

Today, Russia is once again the world's largest wheat exporter. In 2019, Russia alone is expected to export more than 36 million tonnes of wheat and three million tonnes of corn. Meanwhile, Ukraine is expected to export over 16 million tonnes of wheat and 28 million tonnes of corn. That is an impressive turnaround that Dan Morgan could've never predicted.

The return of Russia and Ukraine to the world's export markets presents a problem for wheat farmers in Australia, North America and the E.U. where production and transportation costs are higher.

Although year-on-year yields depend on the weather, there is still a potential for increased production concerning both planted area and yields in Central Russia, Urals and the areas bordering Kazakhstan. There is also talk about expanding production in Siberia, where it's too cold to plant winter wheat but where there's potential to grow spring wheat. The growing season there is short, but some remain optimistic that production can be expanded further. (7)

China and Russia have changed beyond recognition, but perhaps the most striking change in the past 40 years has been the almost doubling of the world's population. In 1979, there were 4.36 billion of us on this planet; today, there are 7.7 billion. Roughly 650 million of that increase has been in India, and 500 million has been in China. However, there are also now 100 million more people in the U.S. and about 50 million more in the E.U.

The world's population was about one billion in 1798 when the English clergyman Reverend Robert Malthus wrote his famous 'Essay on the Principle of Population', in which he predicted that the world's population would eventually be checked by famine. Malthus argued that the world's food supply grew arithmetically while the world's population grew geometrically. He wrote, 'The power of population is indefinitely greater than the power in the earth to produce subsistence for man'.

Malthus believed that God had made it that way to teach humankind 'virtuous' behaviour. He believed that humanity could lead a subsistence life, and he predicted a future of 'misery and vice'. Luckily for all of us, he was wrong.

But who would have predicted that, despite a massive increase in population, more people today suffer from overeating than from undereating? Indeed, obesity is now one of the biggest causes of death in the developed world. The sad fact is that, each year, the U.S. population spends more money on diets than the amount needed to feed all the hungry people in the world. (8)

The increase in world grain production over the past 40 years has been nothing short of extraordinary. In 1979, the world's farmers produced a total of 418 million tonnes of wheat. In 2019, they produced 733 million tonnes, an increase of 75 percent. This increase in production in the past 40 years has been achieved through an 85 percent increase in agricultural yield. Over the same period, total wheat acreage has *fallen* 5 percent, from 228 million hectares to 216 million.

In 2019, the world's farmers produced 490 million tonnes of rice, an increase of 87 percent on 1979. During the past 40 years, average rice yields have increased 67 percent, while acreage has increased only eight percent.

In 2019, farmers produced 1.1 billion tonnes of corn, two and a half times their production in 1979. Again, this has been achieved partly through better yields and partly by increased acreage. The average (global) yield for corn has nearly doubled, while the global acreage has increased 50 percent.

What has driven the impressive increases in agricultural yields that have kept the world fed?

Better farm practices have played a part, as has the wider availability of – and technological progress in – fertilisers, herbicides and pesticides. So, too, have economies of scale, as smallholders exited the sector and farm size increased. This has, in turn, led to increased mechanisation and allowed more investment into new technologies.

However, much of the increase in yields – perhaps 50 percent – can be credited to better plant-breeding techniques.

The introduction of Genetically Modified (GM) crops has increased the disparity of agricultural yields across the globe. In 1979, the yield of U.S. corn was about 6.3 tonnes per hectare, and this has since increased to 11.23 tonnes, largely because of the introduction of GM varieties. In Europe, however, GM corn is shunned, and yields have stagnated at around 7.3 tonnes per hectare. This is a significant difference.

Over 90 percent of the corn grown in the United States and Canada today is GM. Grown commercially since 1997, GM corn now accounts for about one-third of the corn grown in the world, most of which has been genetically modified to tolerate glyphosate or to provide protection against natural pests. Glyphosate, sold as Roundup, is a relatively inexpensive herbicide that kills all plants except those with genetic tolerance, which pretty much means all of them.

Monsanto released Roundup Ready Soybeans in 1996, and within 10 years, 80 percent of all soybeans grown in the U.S. were Roundup Ready. (9) Roundup Ready corn received FDA approval in 1997, and it was commercially released in 1998. It used much the same technology as in soybeans, but also had built-in insect protection in the form of a Bt protein, a naturally occurring bacterium that lives in the soil and is toxic to insects.

Scientists also modified corn genes to make the crop more drought tolerant. Drought-tolerant GM corn was approved by the USDA in 2011 and commercialised in 2013.

Over the past 20 years, GM technology has revolutionised farming and transformed the seed and agricultural input business. Previously, much of a farm's cost of production was in purchasing chemicals, fertiliser, herbicides and pesticides; chemical companies made their money selling these inputs. Now, the cost is in the development of the seeds. The result has been a merging of chemical and seed businesses, with large chemical companies buying seed businesses.

Although GM technology has revolutionised the industry, some observers dispute its impact on yields. By one estimate, (10) about 50 percent of yield increases since the 1920s has resulted from breeding, including genetic modification, while the other half has come from improved farming practices. If that's correct, better farming techniques have been just as important as genetics in feeding our growing population.

However, that may be less surprising when you consider that the primary objective of GM crops was not to increase yield. The increases in yield that accompanied GM corn have come in yield protection and stability, not actual increases in yield potential.

The USDA first began to publish corn yield estimates in 1866. Yields of open-pollinated corn varieties in the U.S. remained fairly stagnant, averaging about 1.6 tonnes per hectare for 70 years until about 1936. There was no significant change in productivity during that entire 70-year period, even though farmers' seed-saving practices represented a form of plant breeding. (11)

Agricultural yields began to accelerate with the adoption of hybrid corn in the late 1930s, but the most significant improvement in the annual rate of yield gain began in the mid-1950s in response to continued improvement in crop genetics, increasing adoption of nitrogen fertiliser and chemical pesticides, as well as agricultural mechanisation. Since 1955, corn grain yields in the U.S. have increased at a fairly constant 1.9 bushels per acre per year, sustained primarily by continued improvements in genetics and crop production technologies.

Not only are modern farmers producing more food from less land, but they are also producing more food with fewer people. Way back in the Middle Ages, between 55 and 75 percent of Europe's population was employed in agriculture. That figure has now dropped to between 5 and 10 percent. (12) The figure for the U.S. is now less than 2 percent, a strikingly low number when you consider that the U.S. is a major food-exporting country. But in the U.S., it is not just the percentage number that has fallen; the outright number has also decreased. There are now fewer people in the U.S. employed in agriculture than there were 40 years ago!

Figures for developing countries are higher. About 75 percent of Madagascans and about half of India's population work in agriculture; the figure for China is about 28 percent. As countries grow richer, they need fewer people to produce food.

What is even more surprising is that not only have our farmers increased production to provide enough food for everyone, but they have also provided fuel for our cars. This is another thing that Dan Morgan could've never predicted back in 1979: the global expansion of the biofuels industry. Today, about 40 percent of U.S. corn is used for ethanol production, while around 50 percent of E.U. rapeseed oil is used for producing biodiesel. And despite those huge percentages, biofuels account globally for only about 5.7 percent of land transport fuel use.

When the U.S. ethanol industry started to take off in the mid-2000s, there was a big debate in the press whether corn should be used as fuel: the 'food versus fuel' debate. However, looking back, U.S. ethanol production hasn't seriously impacted either the price or the availability of corn for food or feed. The same can be said for rapeseed in Europe.

Corn contains both protein and carbohydrates; you can use the protein for animal feed and use the carbohydrates to drive your car. When you make ethanol from corn, you get a by-product called *distillers' dried grains with solubles* (DDGS), which can be used as a feed ingredient for livestock.

A similar situation exists in Europe with rapeseed: you use the oil for biodiesel and the high-protein rapeseed meal as feed for animals.

People also forget that, in Europe after the Second World War, 70 percent of a farm's acreage went to feeding (fuelling) its work force, including feed for horses. Today, a rapeseed farmer will see only half of his or her production going for fuel.

Perhaps even more surprising is that, despite increased demand for fuel, arable land acreage in the E.U. and U.S. has been falling since 2008, while forestry and urbanisation have increased.

Farmers must produce enough for food, feed and fuel, but they also must produce starch for both sweeteners and industrial use. This was something else that Dan Morgan couldn't predict back in 1979.

High-fructose corn syrup (HFCS) has taken a significant part of the market for sweeteners in both China and the U.S., largely because it's cheaper than sugar. Isoglucose, as HFCS is called in Europe, has had less impact in the E.U., largely because quotas restricted production. However, these quotas were lifted in 2018.

As Dan Morgan well knew – and as I hope this book will emphasise – the world cannot feed itself without international trade. In 1979, the annual world trade in corn totalled 65 million tonnes and in wheat 68 million tonnes; these figures have nearly tripled in the intervening 40 years to 160 million and 175 million. The international trade in rice, meanwhile, has quadrupled, from 11.6 million to nearly 50 million tonnes.

The biggest increase, however, has been in soybeans. In 1979, 28 million tonnes traded internationally; 40 years later, that figure has skyrocketed to around 150 million!

But our farmers – have they benefitted from this massive expansion in agricultural production and trade?

Agricultural yields are now higher than they were forty years ago, and this will have reduced a farmer's cost per tonne. However, yields have partly increased because of more farm inputs such as pesticides and fertiliser – and these can be expensive. As for labour costs, we have already seen that there are now fewer people employed on farms than there used to be. Similarly, horses have almost completely disappeared. Both humans and horses have been replaced by diesel heavy farm machinery.

The pesticide, fertiliser and diesel costs now mean that there is a reasonable correlation between farm production costs and the price of energy, particularly crude oil. Correspondingly, how have costs behaved compared to prices? Let's look at the numbers on an inflation-adjusted basis.

In 1979, crude oil prices were under $20 per barrel; today, they are over $60 per barrel – a threefold increase.

In 1979, soybeans were trading at around $7.5 a bushel compared to $8.80 in 2019; wheat was around $3.50 a bushel versus $4.60 forty years later. Corn was $2.64 in 1979, compared to $3.75 in 2019.

To put those numbers in perspective, an ounce of gold in 1979 would have set you back $260 compared to $1,325 at the time of writing. And if you had been smart enough to have sold your farm back in 1979 and invested the proceeds in the stock market, you could have spent your life sitting on the beach, watching the S&P 500 Index rise from 100 in 1979 to 2,800 in 2019.

There is an old story about a farmer who wins the lottery. When asked what he will do with the money, he replies, 'I guess I will keep farming until it is all gone'!

There Are No Fools Any More - Dan Basse

Having grown up on a farm in Wisconsin, Dan Basse raised hogs to put himself through Wisconsin State University. He had originally planned to be a veterinarian, but after a few years running the hog operation, he began to realise that some years he made money and could enjoy the university life; some years, he didn't make any money and had to curtail his social life. He told me that was doing the same things in terms of costs, but it was all about marketing.

He began to get interested in markets to try and understand what drives prices. He took some economic courses, fell in love with the subject and switched his major from veterinarian studies to economics. He founded AgResource in 1987 at the age of 30 and is now among the leading analysts in the grain sector.

Good morning, Dan. What do you think first made your reputation as an analyst?
There are two occasions that come to mind. The first was the Carter grain embargo, when we quickly understood that the U.S. government would be buying a lot of the surplus grain stocks.

The second was the biofuel buildouts and the way that the mandates in the U.S., E.U. and elsewhere would lead to a sharp increase in grain and oilseed demand. You could smell, taste and put your fingers on it in terms of projecting future demand. It was therefore relatively easy to see the bull markets that enveloped the markets from 2007 to 2014.

It then became equally as easy to see that agricultural markets would begin to struggle as the biofuel industry matured. We lost that demand driver, but at the same time, productivity and yields continued to improve.

The current situation is less clear. Trade wars aren't as clear as biofuel mandates. The future in terms of politics is far more difficult to predict.

Could the Chinese ethanol programme be the next demand driver?
We think it will drive some demand, but it isn't clear how quickly the programme can be implemented. It should lead to 37 to 45 million tonnes of additional annual corn demand. That will ultimately deplete Chinese stocks by 2021 and lead to increased imports after that date. But unfortunately, when you look at corn yields, technologically, the industry is advancing faster than we thought they would. Yields are increasing faster than demand. But that Chinese ethanol demand will, of course, be helpful to the world corn market.

In the 1960s and 1970s, we were all worried about having enough food to feed the world. And that repeated itself in the early 2000s with the growth of biofuels and the food versus fuel debate.

If you do some long-term modelling of population growth and farm yields, we could start to run out of agricultural farmlands around 2050. Until then, I don't see really what, apart from a weather problem, could alter the situation. I can't see where the next demand driver will come from. Until we find one, any rallies in price are supply based, weather etc. I can't see demand catching up with supply until we get to 2025 or beyond.

What about biodiesel: could it come to the rescue of the U.S. soybean producers?

We've seen record demand recently for biodiesel. It's mandated, so the demand trend will persist. At some point, it may become mature in the same way that ethanol demand matured. We believe that world energy demand will peak somewhere between 2029 and 2031. As we start to use more electric vehicles, the biofuel demand will slow, but for the moment, it keeps gliding upwards.

The U.S. has anti-dumping cases against a number of biodiesel producers, so we've been trying to keep supply out of the domestic market.

Have GM crops aggravated these surpluses? Looking back, could you argue that the world didn't or doesn't need GM crops to feed itself?

I think we need GM crops to feed the world, particularly as population continues to grow. The problem that has occurred is that farmers always overreach when they see profitability; they've brought in more land than we needed. It's not just GM that has enhanced yields – it's also farm technology, GPS, drones etc., as well as better fertiliser, pesticides and herbicides.

Looking back to the 1800s, it has always been demand shifts, whether war, biofuels or the growth of Asia, that have jumpstarted our grain demand. Our current trade wars are disruptive in terms of flows of grain rather than overall grain demand. So, it's a question of shifting the chairs around the table, rather than putting more food on the table.

Do you think that ASF – African Swine Disease – is a bigger problem globally than trade wars?

There's a range of estimates for the number of hogs in China, somewhere between 470 and 600 million. Most of us believe in a number of around 550 million. There's no census, but more than half the world's hog herd is in China. That's what makes ASF so important in terms of the grain industry.

The point is that China was our only consistent annual demand increase, somewhere between five and seven million tonnes of soybeans each year. Now, with ASF, that demand growth has gone. Poultry and aquaculture production is increasing, so that will stabilise bean imports going forward. But again, the key is that Chinese demand isn't increasing. Parts of West Africa are helping us in wheat, but the volumes aren't significant. Corn may be better placed with the increase in the Chinese demand for ethanol, but that won't be significant.

But couldn't the Chinese replace bean imports with pork imports? Could we feed our surplus beans to pigs and then export the meat to China?

That's the hope for the future. We estimate that the U.S. could eventually export 40,000 hogs per day to China, but for the moment, we're nowhere close to that. The Chinese producers are liquidating their domestic hogs, and this is depressing domestic prices. So the import margins don't work. But at some stage, that will end, and imports should again become profitable, first from the E.U. and then from the U.S. That could happen as early as late summer here. You could also see China importing more poultry, beef and even fish.

Staying on the subject of meat, do you concur with the view that Russian grain exports will peak as the country builds their domestic meat production?

I don't think that Russian grain exports have peaked. The Russians have been trying to build their livestock and poultry herds for some time now, and they've also struggled with ASF. The disease moved across Africa, through Europe, then Russia and now into China. So, the Russians have some of the same issues. I believe it will be a while before the Russians export a significant amount of meat. They'll do some trade into Kazakhstan or Northwestern China, but their herd expansion needs to be more robust, particularly in hogs.

The Europeans have learned to live with ASF; the Russians are trying to learn to live with it. The Chinese will try to do the same. Pharmaceutical companies have spent millions of dollars trying to find a cure or a vaccine for the disease, but so far have come up with nothing. It's an old disease, first discovered in the early 1900s in South Africa. It's virulent. I call it the Ebola of the swine industry because the organs bleed from the inside. We're at least five years from a vaccine or antidote.

What about lab-based meat or the growing popularity of vegan and vegetarian diets? Is that a concern for grain and oilseed farmers?

Lab-based meat is rather like cellulosic ethanol. We can do it relatively well in the test tube, but it's difficult to scale up to commercial production. I believe that we're still 10 to 20 years from the moment when we can really scale this to a point where it has an impact on global agriculture. As for plant-based meat, veggie burgers and the like use pea protein.

What about the anti-gluten movement – is it affecting wheat demand?
It hasn't had a sizeable impact. In the rich Western nations, there is some drop in bread and carbohydrate demand, but we're seeing more demand coming in from Africa. On a global basis, wheat demand is still increasing at an annual rate of about 1.7 percent.

And what about the trend towards organic production?
U.S. farmers are looking for alternative markets, including organic grains. But we don't see demand for organic production having any significant impact on global grain flows.

We're more worried by current developments regarding glyphosate. There are now 1,300 cases pending against Monsanto and their parent company, Bayer. You have to wonder if the EPA (U.S. Environmental Protection Agency) won't one day ban the product or whether Bayer will remove it from the market because of liabilities. Remember, food companies are now testing for it in their products.

If they did remove it from the market, it would result in a significant change in global agricultural production. We don't have a cheap substitute. So if you were to ask me what could change our world, the answer has to be glyphosate.

If it were banned or withdrawn from the market today, what effect would it have on global grain production?
There isn't a good substitute except for manual or mechanical cultivation to remove weeds. Cultivators were widely used to remove weeds around crops until the introduction of glyphosate in the late 1980s and early 1990s. If it were banned or removed from the market, we'd probably go back to more crop rotations to keep weeds and insects at bay.

It would be a huge deal. We could lose 15 to 20 percent in yields. And of course, if we go back to tilling, we'd have more carbon in the atmosphere, and we'd have to have more passes over the fields. And we'd have to bring in more land to produce the same amount of food.

What other challenges are facing the sector?
We believe that climate change is having more and more of an impact every year. As both poles warm, the jet stream has more angulations, leading to weather patterns getting stuck. If you look at 2018, much of Eastern Europe and Western Russia had hot, dry weather, while Reykjavik in Iceland only saw three days of sunshine during the whole summer.

Weather patterns tend to get stuck. The temperature gradients between the poles are lacking, and this leads to lots of rain or lots of dryness. We're seeing this currently in the central U.S., with cold and wet weather impacting plantings.

Climate change is real; you can see it in the data. It's already affecting grain production and will continue to do so. However, the sun is dramatically cooling, and this could have an impact later if the planet cools.

What about grain merchants: are there any signs that they might see better margins in the near future?
I'm afraid that grain merchants may have to put up with low margins for a few more years. We don't see any change in that. It's the globalisation of supply with producers in both hemispheres. The buyers have become more short-term in nature. The consolidation among the merchants will continue.

Farmers also have more information than they used to, and farm storage has grown. Grain merchants can no longer pick them off at harvest time. Sophistication has increased all along the supply chain. There are no fools anymore; everyone is well-versed in where their margins should be.

Large farmers are increasingly selling directly to the end user, and this is something that blockchain may facilitate. However, it's unlikely that a farmer will sell to China, so there's still a role for the international trader.

Thank you, Dan, for your time and insights!

Chapter Four: Food, Fuel and Feed

'Drink the best, and burn the rest'. Anonymous

In 1979, when Dan Morgan published *Merchants of Grain*, he didn't mention biodiesel or ethanol once. That was perhaps an oversight.

During the 1970s, the world had endured two massive spikes in the price of oil. In inflation-adjusted terms, crude oil prices rose during the decade from $23 to $54 a barrel; in 1979, they doubled again, before peaking (again in inflation-adjusted terms) at $123 a barrel in 1980. (1) Oil-importing countries were beginning to look at alternative fuels, and Brazil's military government found a domestically produced solution with sugarcane. To be fair to Dan Morgan, ethanol from corn only began to really take off in the U.S. in the 2000s.

Between 37 and 40 percent of the U.S. corn crop is now used each year to produce ethanol. Between 30 and 35 percent of U.S. soy oil is used for biodiesel production. The corresponding figure for E.U. rapeseed oil is 50 percent.

Although that may sound like a shocking diversion from food to fuel, improvements in crop yields, through better seeds and better farm technology, have enabled farmers on both continents to produce enough corn, soybeans and rapeseed to fuel people, animals and cars without significantly increasing area. Agricultural area in the E.U. has actually fallen during the past forty years.

Farmers have succeeded in meeting this extra demand from fuel without putting pressure on food prices or contributing to inflation. In the U.S., retail food price inflation rates are subdued – lower than the 'headline' inflation rate for the overall economy. The mean annual average food price with inflation has averaged just 2.2 percent since the RFS (Renewable Fuel Standard) was enacted in the U.S. in 2005; this is a significant deceleration from prior decades.

Globally, the world food price index maintained by the FAO finished 2018 at its second-lowest level since 2009. This is a different situation than existed in 2007, when food prices were rising sharply. The situation was acute in Mexico, where the price of flat cornbread, the main source of calories for many of the country's poor, increased by over 400 percent. (2) That year, thousands of people marched through Mexico City to protest the rising price of tortillas. Some blamed the problem on increased demand for corn for ethanol production in the United States. However, the white corn that Mexicans use for tortillas is different from the yellow corn that Mexico imported for animal feed and that the U.S. used to make ethanol.

The 'tortilla riots' were the first in a series of disturbances that year to hit emerging countries from Haiti to Bangladesh, as the cost of agricultural commodities, including wheat and rice, reached all-time highs. (3) But it wasn't just grains that were affected: in India, for example an onion shortage led to localised riots. In 2007, the United Nations Special Rapporteur on the Right to Food called for a five-year ban for the conversion of land for the production of biofuels, claiming that they were a 'crime against humanity'. (4) In 2008, the president of the World Bank added fuel to the fire when he said, 'While many worry about filling their gas tanks, many others around the world are struggling to fill their stomachs. And it's getting more and more difficult every day'. (5)

Two years later, the World Bank backtracked on the role biofuels had played in rising food prices; they admitted that they might have overestimated their impact. They wrote, 'The effect of biofuels on food prices has not been as large as originally thought, but the use of commodities by financial investors (the so-called *financialization of commodities*) may have been partly responsible for the 2007–08 spike'. (6) (They were wrong on that, too. See Chapter Five to find out why.)

Although the ethanol industry in the U.S. didn't really begin to develop until the mid-2000s, it can trace its history (7) back 40 years to the passing of the Energy Tax Act in 1978, intended to reduce the nation's vulnerability to oil shortages. In 1980, the U.S. government – to ensure that domestically produced ethanol would be the only cost-effective source of ethanol in the nation – placed a tariff of 54 cents per gallon on imported ethanol. That same year, it became possible for prospective domestic ethanol producers to apply for government-guaranteed loans for up to 90 percent of plant construction costs.

Between 1979 and 1990, U.S. ethanol production increased from 20 million gallons (over 75 million litres) to 750 million gallons (around 2.84 billion litres). In 1990, small-scale producers were awarded an additional tax credit of 10 cents per gallon. By 2004, U.S. ethanol production had reached 3.6 billion gallons.

The Energy Policy Act of 2005 attached a booster rocket to the sector by mandating annual conventional biofuel consumption at 7.5 billion gallons by 2012. In 2007, that target was increased to 15 billion gallons by 2015. In addition, many cities were introducing their own biofuel requirements. In 2007, Portland, Oregon, became the first U.S. city to require all gasoline sold within city limits to contain at least 10 percent ethanol.

The sector received a further boost when it was discovered that methyl tertiary–butyl ether (MTBE) was contaminating groundwater. MTBE had earlier replaced lead in gasoline as an oxygenate additive to reduce carbon monoxide emissions, but by 2006, it had been banned in almost 20 states. This opened a new fuel market for ethanol, its primary substitute.

Ethanol was a win–win for politicians, farmers, environmentalists, producers and consumers. It reduced the U.S.'s dependence on imported crude oil at a time of war and turmoil in the Middle East. Environmentalists were happy to be rid of MTBE and delighted that a renewable fuel was replacing it. Politicians were happy because ethanol increased farm incomes and supported rural economies; it was an obvious vote winner.

Not everyone was happy. A 2010 study by the Congressional Budget Office (CBO) found that, in fiscal year 2009, biofuel tax credits reduced federal revenues by around U.S.$6 billion, of which corn ethanol accounted for U.S.$5.16 billion. In 2010, the CBO estimated that it cost the taxpayer $1.78 to replace one gallon of gasoline with corn ethanol. Similarly, without considering potential indirect land use effects, it said that the costs to taxpayers of reducing greenhouse gas emissions through tax credits were about $750 per tonne of CO_2-equivalent for ethanol. Partly because of this report, the U.S. Congress allowed the import tariff to expire.

Even without the tariff, some analysts argued that ethanol added about 75 cents to $1 per bushel to the price of corn. Those estimates hint that $4 per bushel corn might be priced at only $3 without the demand for ethanol fuel. (8)

As the arguments raged, the U.S. car industry was building a fleet that could run on blends of up to 10 percent ethanol. In addition, by 2013, about 11 million E85 Flex-Fuel cars and light trucks were in operation. (*E85* refers to ethanol–gasoline blends containing from 51 to 83 percent ethanol.) However, the actual use of higher ethanol blends was limited; most fuel stations did not have the tanks or the pumps to offer the new blend. In November 2013, the EPA said that these physical infrastructure difficulties were preventing the blending of ethanol above 10 percent. This limit became known as the *blend wall*.

Aside from the subsidy issue, most of the controversies surrounding U.S. ethanol fuel production and use are related to corn ethanol's energy balance, along with its social and environmental impacts, especially compared to sugarcane ethanol. Producing ethanol from sugar is simpler than converting corn into ethanol. Converting sugar requires only a yeast fermentation process. Converting corn requires additional heating and the application of enzymes. By some estimates, (9) corn ethanol costs 30 percent more than ethanol from sugarcane juice, as the corn starch first must be converted to sugar before distillation into alcohol.

In 2017, the USDA issued a report, *A Life-Cycle Analysis of the Greenhouse Gas Emissions of Corn-Based Ethanol*, (10) that found that GHG (greenhouse gas) emissions associated with corn-based ethanol in the United States were about 43 percent lower than gasoline when measured on an energy-equivalent basis. The report concluded that, by 2022, given current trends, the GHG profile of corn-based ethanol was expected to be almost 50 percent lower than gasoline.

Previous estimates had included allowances for 'indirect land use change' – land converted from grasslands and forests to crop production because of increased demand for corn used in ethanol production. But the USDA argued that farmers worldwide have been using their available land more efficiently, rather than expanding the amount of land used for farming. Instead of converting new land to production, farmers in Brazil, India and China have increased double cropping, expanded irrigation and reduced unharvested planted area, fallow land and temporary pasture. (11)

However, in May 2019, GAO. the U.S. Government Accountability Office (12), reported that ethanol mandates have had a 'limited effect, if any, on greenhouse gas emissions'.

These divergent government reports show that the battle over ethanol's climate benefits is just as contentious as ever. The question really revolves around the extent to which ethanol mandates drive land-use change – and that is a tough question to answer.

However, there is one area where everyone agrees that corn ethanol has an advantage: it returns about one-third of the feedstock to the market in the form of Distillers' Dried Grain with Solubles (DDGS).

Currently, more than 90 percent of U.S. fuel ethanol is produced using the dry mill process, with the remaining coming from wet mills. The main difference between the two processes is the initial treatment of the grain.

In dry milling, the entire grain kernel is first ground into meal, then mixed with water to form a mash. Enzymes are added to the mash to convert starch to sugar. The mash is cooked, cooled and transferred to fermenters. Yeast is added, and the conversion of sugar to alcohol begins. After fermentation, the resulting 'beer' is separated from the remaining stillage. The ethanol is distilled and dehydrated, then blended with about 2 percent denaturant (such as gasoline) to render it undrinkable. It is then ready for shipment.

Meanwhile, the stillage is sent through a centrifuge that separates the solids from the solubles. These co-products eventually become DDGS, as well as corn distillers' oil.

In wet milling, the grain is first separated into its basic components through soaking. After steeping, the slurry is processed through grinders to separate the corn germ. The remaining fibre, gluten and starch components are further segregated. The gluten component (protein) is filtered and dried to produce animal feed. The remaining starch can then be fermented into ethanol, using a procedure like the dry mill process.

Corn ethanol industries are developing in other countries. In China, all gasoline sold on forecourts must contain 10 percent ethanol (E10) by 2020, a plan that should require an additional 4 billion gallons of ethanol. China's installed ethanol production capacity is currently estimated at around 1 billion gallons, leaving a 3 billion deficit that might first be met by ethanol imports, and then, once capacity has been built, by corn imports. (See Patricia Manso's comments below.)

By comparison with the U.S., the E.U. ethanol programme is relatively small. (14) This is mainly because of the importance of diesel in the European fuel mix, accounting for about 70 percent of all transport fuel sold in Europe. Diesel's dominance over gasoline can largely be explained by its favourable tax treatment. Biodiesel accounts for about 80 percent of the E.U. biofuels market, while ethanol makes up 20 percent.

All petrol currently sold in the E.U. is E5, containing up to 5 percent ethanol. However, the vast majority of commercially available petrol vehicles built since 2000 can run on E10, a fuel currently available in Belgium, Finland, France and Germany. E10 now accounts for 32 percent of petrol sales in France and 63 percent in Finland. Meanwhile, E85 is widely available in Sweden, France, Germany and more sporadically in Hungary, Austria, the Netherlands and Spain. E85 requires dedicated flex-fuel vehicles (FFVs), which can run on ethanol, petrol or any mixture of the two, without the need for separate fuel tanks.

Brazil was the first country to introduce FFVs, and today, they account for more than 90 percent of new car sales in that country. The country has a small but growing corn ethanol sector centred on the grain belt in Mato Grosso and Parana, where the local climate supports two crops. Farmers first plant soybeans, and once the bean harvest is over, they plant a *safrinha* (second planting) corn crop. Mato Grosso and Parana are where the high logistic costs of getting corn to port are prohibitive; hence, corn ethanol plants in the region have a steady supply of cheap feedstock.

The USDA estimates that Brazil's corn ethanol production in 2019 will reach 1.4 billion litres, an increase of 609 million litres compared with 2018. Brazil's Corn Ethanol National Union (UNEM) forecasts that the country will produce 2.6 billion litres of corn ethanol in 2020 and 8 billion litres by 2028.

This figure is still dwarfed by Brazil's sugar cane ethanol output, which yielded nearly 35 billion litres in the 2019 crop year. Some local producers predict that corn ethanol could eventually consume 30 million tonnes of Brazil's corn production. At the time of writing, the country is harvesting a record corn crop of 101 million tonnes, with 34 million tonnes to be exported. (15)

DDGS plays a large part in the economics of the sector. Mato Grosso is Brazil's leading cattle producer, with 14 percent of the country's total of 220 million head. The livestock industry in the state is seeking to boost feedlots, reducing feeding on pastures, and DDGS is seen as a valuable feed ingredient.

It may seem odd that the country that has built such a large sugarcane ethanol industry is now expanding into corn ethanol, but sugarcane ethanol mills have also been adding corn processing capacity, finding that they can use corn to keep the mill operating until the next cane harvest starts.

Brazil first began using ethanol in vehicles as early as the 1920s, and the trend gained urgency during the oil shocks of the 1970s. However, sugarcane ethanol's popularity took a hit when the country almost ran out of hydrous ethanol in the late 1990s, when sugar prices rose and mills switched to the more profitable product, leaving drivers of hydrous ethanol-driven cars stranded. Brazil's ethanol sector, therefore, received a major boost in 2003 with the introduction of FFV technology that allowed cars to run on gasoline, hydrous or anhydrous ethanol – or any mix of the three.

Anhydrous ethanol (ethanol with little water content) can be blended with gasoline at levels ranging from 5 to 27 percent. Hydrous ethanol (with a higher water content) can be used by itself only in specially designed engines. FFVs can use any combination of gasoline, hydrous ethanol or anhydrous ethanol. Ethanol mixed with gasoline is a high-octane fuel that helps prevent engine knocking and generates more power in higher-compression engines. All gasoline sold in Brazil includes a blend of 18 to 27 percent ethanol.

But why should grain trading companies care about Brazil's sugarcane ethanol programme? Because they invested heavily in it.

Louis Dreyfus and Bunge both invested heavily in the sector in the 2000s, encouraged by rising oil prices and the optionality that the business gave between sugar and ethanol, and between ethanol and gasoline.

Bunge first put their toe in the water of the Brazilian sugarcane industry in 2007, when together with Itochu, a Japanese trading company, they bought the Santa Juliana mill in Minas Gerais. They liked what they found, and in 2010, they took a major strategic decision to sell their Brazilian fertiliser operations to Vale S.A. and use the proceeds to acquire five sugar mills from the Moema Group. The following year, Bunge opened, again with Itochu, their first greenfield cane crushing plant in Pedro Afonso.

Bunge was hit from the outset by a shortage of cane due to poor weather. The company's combined mills had a cane crushing capacity of 21 million tonnes, but in their first full year of operations only crushed 13 million tonnes. They did slightly better in 2012 with 17 million tonnes of cane, but in October 2013 – only three years after purchasing the mills – Bunge's CEO suggested that the company was launching 'a thoughtful comprehensive review' of its Brazilian milling operations. He estimated the replacement value of its milling assets at more than $3 billion but admitted that it had been challenging for Bunge to transfer its strengths in other agribusiness areas to sugar. The company quietly put the mills up for sale. Several potential buyers kicked the tires, but there were no takers.

It was Louis Dreyfus, though, that made the biggest investment into the sector. The company later spun off the business into Biosev, a company quoted on the São Paulo stock exchange, but with Louis Dreyfus as the controlling stakeholder. Biosev operates 11 sugarcane mills in Brazil (compared to Bunge's eight) and has a crushing capacity of 36.4 million tonnes of cane per year. This makes the company the second-largest cane crusher in the world, employing about 17,000 people, managing 340,000 hectares of cane land and working with 1,200 sugarcane farmers.

Biosev now has an annual production capacity of approximately 2.8 million tonnes of sugar and 1.8 million cubic metres of ethanol. However, the company has insufficient cane to feed its mills, and it operates below capacity. Louis Dreyfus, as a controlling shareholder, has helped finance the company through pre-payment loans linked to sugar-export contracts.

In 2018, the Louis–Dreyfus family foundation that owns Louis Dreyfus Company doubled down and injected a further $1.05 billion into Biosev to unlock an agreement with a group of banks to refinance the accumulated debt. About $800 million of the capital increase was used to reduce liabilities, with the rest strengthening Biosev's cash position. Biosev also reached an agreement with 11 lenders to extend the maturity of banks loans totalling 3.66 billion reais ($1.1 billion). (16)

But why did these Brazil sugarcane investments turn out so badly? It was really a perfect storm of adverse moves on the exchange rate, rising local costs, a series of poor harvests and bad weather. Most importantly, the Brazilian government effectively capped the price of ethanol by fixing the cost of domestic gasoline. As one grain–trader–turned–sugar mill–owner told me, 'I had always thought that wheat was the most political of commodities, but it isn't a patch on sugarcane!'

Another issue is that the grain companies did not realise that processing sugarcane is not the same as crushing soybeans. Beans just turn up at your factory gate; sugarcane must be coaxed. Mill owners must be actively involved in the cane supply – and that usually includes growing the stuff.

As a rule, traders don't make good farmers. Traders tend to concentrate on the short term; farmers, on the long term. Traders like to quickly get out of a losing position; farmers do not sell their farm just because of one bad crop.

The grain trading companies have learned some hard lessons in Brazil's sugarcane sector over past years, and they're putting what they have learnt into practice. This is helping them to turn around the business. In addition, Brazil's government is now letting domestic gasoline prices fluctuate in line with world prices, thus helping the competitiveness of Brazilian hydrous ethanol. Meanwhile, the government's ambitious RenovaBio programme sets out guidelines for future support.

In July 2019, Bunge merged their Brazilian sugarcane assets with those of the British energy company BP to form a joint venture named BP Bunge Bioenergia. The joint venture will manage 11 sugarcane mills in Brazil with the capacity to crush 32 million tonnes of cane per year. Bunge received cash proceeds of $775 million as part of the agreement and took an impairment charge 'in the range of $1.5 billion to $1.7 billion' related to the 'cumulative currency translation effects' of its business in Brazil. (17)

At the time of writing, Louis Dreyfus is soldiering along with their mills.

Biofuels and Politics - Dr. Patricia Luís-Manso

Patricia is Head of Biofuels Analytics at S&P Global Platts, the leading independent provider of information, benchmark prices and analytics for the energy and commodities markets. Previously, Patricia was Head of Sugar and Ethanol Research at Louis Dreyfus Commodities, where she managed a global team focused on developing critical market analysis to design trading strategies.

Good morning, Patricia. Back in 2005, a U.N. official called biofuels 'a crime against humanity'. How are biofuels viewed now?

The debate is less antagonistic than it was a few years back. It's no longer black or white – neither all bad nor all good. The debate has evolved, and the main discussion now is on the sustainability of the feedstock and the supply chain. The issue of ILUC, Indirect Land Use Change, has somewhat been clarified. There has also been more, and better, government regulation. This is particularly the case in the E.U., where RED 2, the new E.U. Renewable Energy Directive, will start to be implemented in 2020.

In addition, there's now more urgency surrounding climate change. There's more awareness that governments and individuals need to do something and do it quick. Biofuels are an available technology. They reduce carbon emissions, and the infrastructure already exists. They're part of the solution.

There's also more of a focus on advanced, second-generation biofuel, most particularly renewable diesel or HVO, hydro-treated vegetable oil.

Could you tell me a little about that?

Renewable diesel can be made from waste and residues through the process of hydrogenation, resulting in a chemical composition identical to fossil diesel. You make traditional, first-generation biodiesel by esterifying vegetable oils or fats to remove the glycerine. This is OK, but the quality of traditional biodiesel varies according to the raw materials used; some will gel at low temperatures.

Because of our cold winters, biodiesel blends are limited in some months of the year, depending on their cold filter plugging point (CFPP) and cloud point properties. Renewable diesel doesn't have these constraints.

So the debate is over: biofuels have won?

Not entirely. There's still an issue on the way the feedstocks, the crops, are produced. Pesticide use is controversial, particularly in Europe with rapeseed. The loss of biodiversity is another issue: biofuel feed stocks are monocrops. But these issues aren't specific to biofuels; they're general issues around agriculture.

Today, the debate is around deforestation: should we be cutting down our forests to grow crops to drive our cars? The E.U.'s RED 2 makes progress on this. It classifies feedstock as either high or low risk in ILUC terms. RED 2 classifies palm oil as high risk; this means that it must be phased out as a biofuel feedstock by 2030 and excluded from the E.U. biofuels supply chain. However, that doesn't mean that palm oil can't be used in other products like processed foods or shampoo. In addition, there are exceptions to the biofuel ban. Palm oil produced by smallholders is exempt from the ban, but as you might imagine, there's some debate as to who a smallholder is.

There's another, perhaps more important issue. Biofuels are currently compared to fossil fuel in terms of GHG (greenhouse gas) emissions. That's fine, but if we're moving to a complete decarbonisation of the economy, then biofuels will have to be compared to carbon-free technologies, such as electricity generated from hydro or wind power. When you make that comparison, they're obviously not so good. For the moment, many of these technologies are either not yet available or not yet economically viable. But I stress the word *yet*.

The electrification of vehicles is another big issue. Some environmentalists argue that we shouldn't encourage biofuels, but instead concentrate our energies toward accelerating the move to EVs, electric vehicles. They have a point, but you still have to fuel the existing vehicle fleet. Besides, you also have to consider the entire supply chain for EVs, their batteries and the way that the electricity is produced. How sustainable is it?

So, yes, there's still plenty to debate. But the debate has become less antagonistic as more stakeholders, particularly the NGOs, become more positively involved.

The E.U. Parliament approved RED 2 last year. What are its main features?
First, as I said earlier, RED 2 classified biofuels as high and low ILUC risk and is phasing out palm oil as a biofuel feedstock.

Second, the earlier RED 1 set a target of 10 percent renewable fuel use in transportation in 2020. This is increased under RED 2 to 14 percent by 2030, but traditional crop-based biofuels are limited to only 7 percent. The other 7 percent has to come from advanced biofuels or EVs.

So, everything is sorted?
We've still got an argument with Indonesia and Malaysia over the palm oil ban. We also have discussions ahead over the smallholder exemptions. There's also a question as to whether palm oil residues are also banned. Some of these residues are an important feedstock in renewable diesel.

In terms of regulation, the ILUC issue has been resolved, but there are still some issues concerning implementation. Remember that all palm oil used for biodiesel already has to be certified as sustainable by one of the major sustainability certification bodies, such as the RTSP, the Round Table on Sustainable Palm Oil.

What is the main ethanol feedstock in the E.U.?
Around 65 percent of E.U. ethanol is produced from grains; the majority from corn, but some wheat is used, depending on the relative prices of the two. Depending on the crop, sugar beet can account for as much as 20 to 25 percent; other grains, such as barley and cellulosic, account for the rest.

The E.U. imports some ethanol from the Americas, Guatemala and Peru, but the majority of Europe's ethanol demand is met by domestic production. The E.U. used to have anti-dumping duties on U.S. ethanol imports, but these have now been lifted. All ethanol sold in the E.U. has to be certified as sustainable. Certification costs time and money, and few U.S. producers are certified.

There is another evolution in terms of regulation that I need to mention. Mandates have traditionally been based on energy content or volume. There's now a trend, started in Germany, for mandates to be based on GHG savings.

How do the various types of ethanol stack up in terms of GHG savings?
Cellulosic biofuels will have the highest savings, followed by sugarcane ethanol, which has a typical GHG savings of around 70 percent. Sugar beet has a savings of around 60 percent. Depending on the age and type of technology used, the typical savings for wheat or corn is between 35 and 65 percent, although EPure, the E.U. ethanol producers' lobby, argues that the typical GHG savings from European-based grain is 70 percent. The savings for corn is lower.

What about the greenhouse gas benefits of biodiesel? Are they as good as ethanol?
Renewable diesel is comparable to ethanol, but traditional biodiesels are lower, with GHG savings of between 35 and 60 percent.

Are E.U. biofuel producers making money at the moment?
According to our crushing margins model, European ethanol producers are making money, but biodiesel producers are struggling due to low-priced imports of PME, palm oil methyl ester, from Indonesia and Malaysia. SME (soy methyl ester) imports are also coming in from Argentina.

Unlike ethanol, about half of the E.U.'s biodiesel demand is met through imports, of which palm is about 25 percent and soy, 10 percent. These imports are mixed into a blend called FAME (fatty acid methyl ester). In winter, you have to use more RME (rapeseed methyl ester); in summer, you can use more PME (palm methyl ester) and SME (soy methyl ester).

What percentage of E.U. diesel comes from UCO (Used Cooking Oil)?

UCOME (Used Cooking Oil Methyl Ester) and other waste make up about 10 percent of the E.U. biodiesel market. Some of the UCO is imported, particularly from China. If the E.U. stops importing palm oil or PME, then the gap will have to be made up by rape and soy.

However, renewable diesel production is growing, with new capacity coming on-stream in France and Italy this year. A lot will depend on whether the E.U. will still allow palm oil residues to be imported and used as a feedstock for renewable diesel.

What about other ethanol and biofuel programmes around the world?

In 2017, China announced an important biofuels mandate of 10 percent by 2020. This announcement came at the peak of their corn stocks. Since then, they've been investing in capacity while slowly increasing their blend.

We know that, if China really wanted to do it, they would. But first, I think they'll look at meeting domestic ethanol demand through their own domestic production capacity, which is currently far from what's needed to meet the 10 percent mandate. We're tracking every new plant coming online; the pace of construction is currently too slow to reach their goal.

We also have to look at this in the context of the current trade war with the U.S. If China did decide to meet their mandate through imports, the U.S. would be the cheapest supplier. But would they want to depend on the U.S. for their programme?

We don't think so. If China really wanted to reach a 10 percent blend, the majority would have to be imported. So, given all these issues, we forecast a 3 percent blend this year, rising to 5.5 percent in 2025 and then 10 percent by 2030.

China will slowly increase ethanol consumption as they build production capacity, depending, of course, on the availability of corn. All in all, we don't expect the Chinese ethanol programme will have much effect on grain markets in the short to medium term.

Could wider use of E15 in the U.S. have an impact on global grain markets?

The Environmental Protection Agency in the U.S. has lifted restrictions on the summertime use of E15. The blenders are not happy with this, and nor are the oil companies. Some environmental groups are also opposed. But it's 'permission to use', not a mandate. Just letting people use E15 will not mean that they'll use it. It's just another blend that you can use; it's a choice for the consumer. Not every state in the U.S. allows E15. And it's not everywhere that the gas stations will invest in another pump. So, there's no question that the U.S. will move from E10 to E15 right away or that ethanol demand will increase by 50 percent.

Our forecast for the U.S. ethanol consumption forecast in 2019 is pretty close to the 10 percent overall. A couple of years ago, we were talking about a blend wall of 10 percent, but with E15 and E85, it's no longer a wall. It's an average.

Are there any other ethanol programmes coming along?
India has been increasing their ethanol consumption because of their recent big sugarcane crops. However, if sugarcane production falls, then this trend could cool or reverse.

A number of other countries have biofuel mandates: Australia, Canada, Brazil, Argentina and Colombia. Mandates are being discussed in some African countries: Sudan, Malawi and Mozambique. In Asia, China has a mandate, as does the Philippines. Japan also has an ethanol programme based on Brazilian ethanol exported to the U.S., converted into ETBE and then re-exported to Japan. But Japan had recently changed its programme, and corn ethanol can now be imported.

We expect more countries to implement biofuel programmes to meet their commitments under the Paris Climate Change Agreement. Long term, we expect biofuel demand to grow slightly faster than fossil fuel demand.

What do you think of Brazil's prospects?
Brazil has a new programme RenovaBio, which should be introduced in 2020. If it is, it should stimulate extra demand for ethanol. We're therefore optimistic on the demand side, but we're concerned that supply may be constrained by a lack of production capacity. This year, the mills are already close to max ethanol on cane.

Corn ethanol production is growing in Brazil, but it's still small, only 3 to 4 percent of the country's total production of ethanol. Traditional sugar mills are also investing in corn ethanol capacity. Brazil exports about 5 percent of their domestic ethanol production. Some ends up in Japan as ETBE, but California is the main pure ethanol importer under their advanced biofuel programme. Brazil also exports industrial-grade alcohol to South Korea, but it's not significant.

Where could future growth come from?
When we look at growth rates in our long-term forecast, it's clearly Asia that's growing, but a lot will depend on India and China. They're the big players.

What are the biggest challenges facing the industry?
Look at the big markets, and you'll see that ethanol remains a largely domestic affair. The majority of the product is domestically produced; international trade is small. There are traditional routes like Brazil to California or to Japan, but it's still a small share of total production. As a result, most of the sector's challenges will be domestic; that means politics.

And looking to the future in a 10- to 15-year time frame, biofuels will be in competition with electric cars. However, the biggest challenge for the industry is to be environmentally sustainable in an economically viable way. Technology is improving, and the new plants are not only bigger but also more efficient. However, the feedstock has to be produced sustainably.

And the opportunities?
Personally, I believe that the future lies with advanced biofuels, such as renewable diesel and other high-GHG-savings biofuels. The future is less clear for cellulosic ethanol; it has yet to prove itself on an industrial scale.

There are also opportunities for biofuels in aviation and shipping. New fuel emissions standards will be introduced for shipping from 2020, reducing sulphur emissions from 3 to 0.5 percent. For the moment, no one is talking about that in terms of biodiesel, but it's something we're keeping an eye on.

So, you're optimistic about the future?
I'm more optimistic about biofuels than I was five to 10 years ago. A lot of advances have been made in technology, and these have been helping production economics. Regulation is taking the edge off some of the environmental issues. Advanced biofuels, such as renewable diesel, are gaining traction.

Looking further forward, electricity will most probably take a growing role in the future for transportation in terms of reduced emissions and climate change. However, it will take time for the existing vehicle fleet and infrastructure to be replaced. Biofuels are already here, and they're better for the environment than fossil fuels. We should welcome and embrace them!

Thank you, Patricia, for your time and comments.

Chapter Five: Managing Risk

'Commodity trading can be best defined as selling something that you don't have to someone who doesn't want it'. Anonymous

Humankind first planted crops about 11,000 years ago, and agricultural commodity traders have almost certainly been around since then. In their daily lives, agricultural traders/merchants, and the companies they work for, transport, store and process the food that we eat. Without them, both our diets and our lives would be considerably poorer.

Libanius wrote in the fourth century:

> God did not bestow all products on all parts of the earth, but distributed his gifts over the different regions, to the end that men might cultivate a social relationship because one would have need of the help of another. And so he called commerce in to being, that all men might be able to have common enjoyment of the fruits of earth, no matter where produced. (1)

Libanius knew that not all crops grow equally well across the world; some countries have a comparative advantage over other countries in particular crops. Traders transport food from areas where it grows well (and cheaply) to areas where it grows less well or not at all. They transport it from areas where it is not needed to areas where it is needed. They transport food from surplus areas to deficit areas.

Some of the wheat grown in Canada will be consumed in Canada, but the country's excess wheat production (around 25 million tonnes) will be exported, mainly to the United States and Central and South America. Some of the soybeans produced in Brazil will be consumed in Brazil, but the excess production (around 80 million tonnes) will be exported, much of which to China.

If a commodity is worth more money in a deficit area than it is in a surplus area – and if that difference is more than the cost of shipping it there (plus a little profit margin to make it worthwhile) – a trader will make it happen.

But to make it happen, the trader will take many risks. Ocean freight rates may increase before the trader can lock in the cost of the transport. So, too, could the cost of insuring the commodity during transport. And as the commodity will also have to be moved from the farm to the port, the trader may find that the local truck drivers (or the dockworkers who have to load the commodity onto the ship at the port of origin and then unload it at the port of destination) have gone on strike for higher wages.

The trader's biggest risk, however, is that the price of the commodity in the deficit area falls before the commodity arrives there. To reduce the risk of that happening, the trader may try to sell the product in the deficit (destination) country as he or she buys it in the surplus (origin) country. Unfortunately, that is not always possible, and he or she could end up selling the commodity for less than anticipated.

Competition is fierce in the trading community; a trader will almost certainly not be the only person to have noticed the difference in the price of a commodity between the origin and the destination countries. If a trader moves quickly and the ship carrying the commodity is the first to arrive at the destination, that person will get a better price for the merchandise than if his or her ship is fifth in the queue to discharge at the port. Speed of transport can often be of the essence. In olden days, this usually meant that the trader with the fastest sailing boat won.

If the price does fall in the destination market before the commodity arrives there, the buyer of the commodity may default on the contract. This risk, like all others, must be managed. That is why trading companies will always limit the amount of risk that they have with any particular contract counterparty. No matter how big a company that counterparty is, all trading houses will self-impose a risk limit on the amount of business that they transact with that company.

A trading house will also self-impose a risk limit on the amount of business that they will do with any one country. Governments change, and even when they do not, they change their minds. To protect local farmers, governments in importing countries may react to falling local grain prices by imposing a ban on grain imports.

The risks in international trade are so significant, one might imagine that the profit margins in trading are enormous. That is certainly the impression that one gets from reading the newspapers or by following social media. However, competition between traders is so intense that profit margins are wafer thin – and have grown thinner over the years. (I will discuss why that has happened in the next chapter.)

Commodity traders do not just move commodities from surplus to deficit areas. They also store and process those commodities. Traders store commodities at times when they are not needed until a time when they are needed. Traders also process those commodities from a form in which they are not wanted to a form in which they are wanted.

An example of the first would be when a trader buys grain from a farmer at harvest time, stores it in a warehouse (called a *silo*) and then sells it gradually throughout the following year to a flour miller. An example of a processor would be the flour miller who buys the wheat from the trader and then grinds it into flour before selling it to a consumer. Most humans do not eat wheat directly; it has to be transformed into something else (flour) first.

Another example of this processing function is when a trader buys soybeans from a farmer and crushes them in his factory, separating the soy meal from the soy oil. The former is used mainly for animal feed while the latter finds its way into all sorts of processed food products, cooking oil or biodiesel.

Commodity trading is usually defined as: 'storing and/or transporting and/or processing a commodity from when, where or in what form it is not needed to when, where or in what form it is needed'. (2)

If commodity traders did not exist, breakfast wouldn't make it to the breakfast table: wheat wouldn't end up as toast, sugar as jam or palm oil as chocolate spread. Indeed, there wouldn't even be the tablecloth on the table; the raw cotton would be still sitting in some warehouse somewhere waiting for a trader to transform it into cotton thread.

When one thinks about this a little, it becomes clear that what a trader is most interested in isn't the outright price of a particular commodity, but the difference in the price of that commodity in its different geographies, times and forms.

A Russian wheat farmer obviously cares about the outright price of wheat; the higher the price, the more money he makes to feed his family and pay his costs. However, it makes little difference to a trader whether wheat costs $300 per tonne or $200 per tonne. What matters to the trader is the price at which he or she can buy wheat from the Russian farmer, transport it and then sell it to the Egyptian importer. It is the price differential that matters, not the outright price.

Similarly, a flour miller is not too worried about the outright price of wheat; what matters to him or her is the differential between the price of wheat and the price of flour. If flour is too cheap compared to wheat, the miller can't cover the cost of running a mill. The same applies to a soybean crusher: what matters to that person is the price differential between the unprocessed soybeans and the processed soy oil and soy meal. Of course, the same also applies to a trader who buys corn from a farmer and stores it, slowly selling it to buyers who will then turn it into animal feed, fructose syrup or ethanol.

Contrary to what one might imagine, traders and trade houses like to limit their exposure to the outright (or flat) price of a commodity. They usually hedge their flat price risk, preferring to make their money on differentials.

However, as we'll see in the next chapter on André & Cie, a trader may get into trouble even if he or she is perfectly hedged. As a futures contract relates to a transaction that is due to take place in the future, the purpose of the futures exchange is to act as intermediary and mitigate the risk of default by either party in the intervening period. To achieve this, the futures exchange requires both parties to the transaction to put up an initial amount of cash, called the *original margin*, to guarantee against default. The more volatile a market, the higher the original margins are likely to be.

It's often the case that the price of a commodity varies significantly between the moment that the contracts are entered into and the moment they're either delivered or liquidated (sold or bought back). To mitigate against default due to these price variations, a futures exchange will each day, after the market close, calculate variation margins corresponding to the amount that the price has moved during the day. All positions are marked to market at the end of each day.

If the market goes up during the day, the shorts will be asked to deposit funds with the exchange equivalent to the amount that they would've lost if they had bought back their positions at the close of the market session. Against that, the exchange will credit those funds among the accounts of those who are long. If the market has gone down during the day, the longs will be asked to deposit funds with the exchange equivalent to the amount they would've lost if they had sold out their positions at the closing price of the day's trading session. Those funds are then credited to the shorts' accounts.

This system of margins may be a protection against default, but it can also be a source of stress for hedgers. Imagine a grain merchant who buys a cargo of wheat and then sells futures against it, in theory protecting him or her from future price moves. However, if the price of wheat were to increase before the cargo is shipped, the trader will be obligated to put up variation margins against the short position on the futures. A company that originates a significant quantity of grain may have to post hundreds of millions of dollars in variation margins if prices rise before the grain is shipped. This can sometimes put a severe strain on cash flow.

Every participant in the food supply chain is a trader, more interested in price differentials rather than outright prices. The farmer is the big exception. His livelihood depends on the outright price of his crop. Final consumers are obviously concerned about the outright price of a food product, but even there, they may be more concerned about the differentials between competing products. *Should I buy chicken or beef for dinner – or peaches or apricots?*

A farmer will usually sell all or part of his crop before it's harvested; a food processor will usually buy some his inputs before he or she needs them. They both do so to reduce their price risk – the risk that the price will move adversely in the intervening period.

Although a farmer will, if he or she is wise, try to sell at least some production in advance, that transaction isn't without risk. There may be a drought, and he or she may not produce as much as expected. If that happens, that farmer would still have to honour the sales contract; he or she would have to buy the shortfall, either by washing it out (buying it back) with the person he or she sold it to or by buying what's needed from a neighbour.

It is, therefore, risky for a farmer to sell wheat not yet planted, but it may be less risky than not selling it. After all, he or she expects to have the wheat when it's harvested; he or she also expects the wheat price to be lower at harvest time. Besides, the farmer's local bank branch will be more likely to lend him or her money to buy the seeds, fertiliser and diesel needed if he or she has locked in prices for at least part of the production. The bank will often want to see sales contracts before disbursing loans.

Everyone involved in that supply chain is taking and managing price risk. The farmer takes a risk by planting wheat in the first place, but then offsets that risk by selling some of it in advance. The trader takes a risk when he or she buys wheat from the farmer, but offsets that risk by hedging in the futures market. The miller also takes a risk when buying wheat, but can offset that risk by hedging in the futures market or by buying the wheat as close as possible to the time when he or she sells the flour.

The baker and the biscuit manufacturer also have a risk that wheat prices rise, increasing their input costs. If the price of wheat rises, they may not be able to pass on all of the increase to their buyers. They might, thus, also mitigate that risk by hedging in the futures market.

When someone, a farmer or a trader, sells something that he or she does not already own, it is called *selling short*. If one has sold a commodity not owned and has an obligation to supply it sometime in the future, one is described as being *short* of that commodity. If one owns a commodity that one hasn't yet sold, that person is described as being *long* of it.

It's often difficult to grasp the concept of selling something short – selling something that one doesn't have in the hope that one can buy it back later at a cheaper price. After all, if one doesn't own something, how can it be sold?

The answer is that one can't sell something that one doesn't already own if it has to be delivered immediately. However, if one must deliver it sometime in the future, one can sell it without owning it first. A person has time to buy at a later date whatever it is that was sold and deliver it to the buyer when the time comes. The farmer does just that: he or she sells part of his or her crops before they've been harvested.

It's not just a farmer who can sell something not already owned. Let's take the example of a trader who has a client in West Africa looking to buy a cargo of white rice for delivery in three months' time. The trader may take the view that the price of rice will fall between now and when the rice must be delivered. In such a situation, he or she could sell the rice without buying it first; he or she could sell short now in the hope of buying in the rice at a cheaper price before it must be delivered.

Investors or speculators can also sell short, even if they aren't involved in the physical commodity market. If investors believe that the price of a commodity will fall in the future – and if they have a futures trading account – they could sell futures now and buy them back later. If they're wrong – and prices rise instead of fall – they'll make a loss on the deal. If they are right and prices do fall, they'll make a profit.

In the equity markets, being short is normally considered riskier than being long. If an equity investor buys a particular share, he or she can hold onto it forever, keep it for his or her grandchildren. However, to sell a particular share not already owned, the investor must borrow it from someone else. The short seller knows that, at a prearranged time, he or she will be asked to deliver that share to the buyer. The short seller will have no choice but to buy the share at whatever price is prevailing at the time. This time constraint could cause the short seller to be squeezed.

Conversely, an investor who is long of a share cannot be forced to sell it and can never be squeezed. The risk of being long or short of equities is, therefore, asymmetric: there's more risk in being short than in being long. This doesn't apply to commodities.

If a short seller of a particular commodity runs out of time, he or she risks being squeezed: at some stage, he or she will have no choice but to buy the commodity, whatever the prevailing price. However, if a trader is long of a commodity, he or she also risks being squeezed and having to ship and sell the commodity at whatever the prevailing price is.

As we've seen earlier, a trader transforms a commodity in one of three ways: space, time or form. The trader likes to limit risk exposure on the outright price of a commodity and prefers to concentrate his or her energies on the different prices of his commodity, depending on where, when and in what form it's delivered. A trader will buy a commodity from a producer and then move and transform it along the supply chain from producer to consumer.

A trader is a contract principal on the deal. At one stage or another in the process, he or she will actually own the commodity involved in the transaction. As such, he or she runs a *price risk* (if not properly hedged) or a *basis risk* (if hedged and the price of the commodity owned moves adversely relative to the hedge). A company that trades in physical commodities is usually called a *trade house*.

A *physical broker* deals in a physical commodity. He doesn't take a price risk but puts together a buyer and a seller for a commission. The only risk a broker has is losing his or her commission if one or both parties to the contract fail to perform. As such, the loss is limited to the broker's commission, but then so, too, is profit.

A *futures broker* is someone who executes an order on a futures exchange on behalf of a client. Most futures brokers are clearing members of the exchange on which they're executing orders, but they don't have to be.

A broker isn't the same as an agent. A broker works equally for both the buyer and the seller and favours neither. An agent works for one party only. For example, a soybean producers' cooperative in Brazil may have a sales agent in China who represents the cooperative's interests in China and works to find buyers for their beans. Alternatively, a soybean-crushing plant in China may have a buying agent in Brazil who works on behalf of the Chinese plant to source the best beans at the best price.

A market participant who isn't a physical trader or merchandiser is usually called a *commodity speculator*. The U.S. Commodity Futures Trading Commission, or CFTC, refers to such a participant as a *non-commercial*, which is perhaps a better descriptive term. A non-commercial is an entity – it could be an individual, a hedge fund, a pension fund or a bank – that isn't involved in the physical transformation of the underlying commodity. It isn't directly involved in the commercialisation and transformation of the commodity on its journey from producer to consumer.

However, a non-commercial is indirectly involved in that journey, adding value to the supply chain in the process. A non-commercial assumes (some of) the price risk that commercials (physical traders) don't want. They're an integral part of the supply chain; without them, physical traders would have to either assume more price risk, buy at the same time as they sell or sell at the same time as they buy.

Producers like to lessen their risk by selling in advance, and consumers like to reduce their risk by buying as late as possible, often for immediate delivery. Non-commercials resolve this mismatch in the appetite for risk by buying forward from the producers and selling spot to the consumers. They assume some of the risk in the supply chain that producers and consumers are happy to lay off. They perform a useful function. The process works better with them than without them.

Non-commercials may have different motivations for being involved in the markets. Pension funds may like to hold commodities as part of a diversified-risk portfolio of equities, bonds and property. Hedge funds and banks may believe that they can beat the market and predict future price movements better than others. Some smaller speculators may just like the thrill of the risk.

Non-commercials inadvertently play a role beyond risk assumption. By buying before a supply deficit hits or selling before a surplus hits, speculative activity often results in the price moving before the deficit or surplus event occurs. This can mean that supply and demand balances itself out quickly, and that helps to prevent crises. By anticipating problems, speculative activity can help markets solve them before they occur.

Learning to Navigate – Brian Zachman

Brian is President of Global Risk Management at Bunge. He joined Bunge from Millennium Limited Partners where he traded agricultural commodity derivatives as a portfolio manager.

Prior to that he was a Portfolio Manager with SAC Capital from 2012 to 2014, and has served in various commercial, merchant and trading roles with Cargill, ConAgra and Bunge. He holds a Bachelor of Arts in Economics from the University of Minnesota-Duluth.

I met with Brian in Bunge's office in Geneva.

The views and opinions expressed in this interview are those of Brian Zachman and do not necessarily reflect the official policy or position of Bunge Ltd.

Good morning, Brian. My first question is, how did you start in the business?

I'm from St. Michael, a small town in Minnesota, just northwest of the Twin Cities. My family was in the dairy farming business, but it was never really my hope to have a career in the family business. My choice of university, the University of Minnesota–Duluth, even came with an added bonus: it was too far from the farm for my dad to call at 3 p.m. and ask for a hand milking the cows at 5 p.m.!

I was interested in markets and studied Economics and Math in college before applying to Cargill, but for a position in their financial markets department. Cargill likely saw the farming background and instead offered me a merchant trainee job in their Oilseed Processing Division in West Fargo, North Dakota. It was the only multi-seed facility Cargill operated at that time in North America, crushing sunflowers, flax and canola and shipping both crude and refined vegetable oil.

It was a stroke of luck to start a career in this particular facility, as it provided a well-rounded exposure to both domestic and international import/export markets; truck, barge and rail logistics; value-added refining; international currencies; commodity hedging in futures and options; flat price and basis risk management; and plant operations.

A year into my tenure as a trainee, the existing commercial manager in West Fargo accepted a transfer, so I was promoted to a commercial role, responsible for establishing the plant's crush schedule and for maximising the facility's gross margin. The West Fargo commercial staff was quite small, only five merchants, but all of my colleagues were experienced professionals and were extremely generous with their time; they all were very patient with me and taught me a lot about markets and about business more broadly.

What happened to the family farm? Is it still going?

My parents sold the milking cows and the young stock in the early 1990s, when Mom and Dad reached retirement age and when no obvious succession plan emerged for the farm – all of my five siblings also chose professions other than farming. Dad still lives on the farm, although suburban development and the resulting increase in land values mean less and less of the land is directed to agricultural uses. It's a tale as old as time, a pattern likely to continue throughout rural America.

So you escaped the farm and are in West Fargo, working as a commercial manager for a crushing plant. Then what happens?

Cargill transferred me to their head office in Minneapolis as a soybean oil merchant in their Domestic Soybean Processing group, responsible for managing the crude soybean oil flows and associated price risk from their 14 domestic soybean crush plants. It was a chance to learn about and manage risk in a much larger industry, the soybean processing industry. This job also brought a lot more exposure to futures markets and how they work, particularly the economics of making and taking delivery, which are such an important driver of price discovery. It was my first real opportunity to trade proprietary risk in the futures markets, and I loved it.

Also in Minneapolis, I worked with a team that managed not only domestic soybean processing but also price risk for Cargill customers as well as the international price risk exposure for Cargill; that brought an appreciation of the global nature of the agricultural markets. Reflecting on it now, I was 24 years old, sitting in one of the largest agribusiness companies in the world, in one of their core businesses, and learning from some of the best people in the business. It was a remarkable opportunity.

But then you left Cargill?

It was a really tough decision. There was some discussion of sending me to the Philippines to work in their copra crushing and coconut oil business, a move that didn't materialise for whatever reason. Cargill was at the start of some large organisational changes, and I was open to other opportunities.

Ultimately, I left Cargill to join the ConAgra Trade Group in Omaha, Nebraska, led by Greg Heckman who, incidentally, is now CEO of Bunge. ConAgra was putting together a team to consolidate and manage global commodity price risk for their retail and foodservice brands and their grain, livestock and processing businesses. Part of that process was trading in international markets as procurement for overseas brands and to better inform risk decisions elsewhere.

At the time, ConAgra was also looking to build a soybean crushing facility and ultimately decided to focus mainly on their branded businesses. I found the downstream part of the business very interesting, as it was a chance to learn something new, but I missed the commodity and more market-oriented elements of the chain.

During my two years at ConAgra, I got to know Bunge as both an international and a domestic supplier of vegetable oils and meals. Bunge was undergoing a transformation that sounded exciting. They were moving from a conglomerate of businesses to having a greater focus on their grain-trading and oilseed processing core. Bunge was moving away from a model as an FOB supplier toward one with international distribution, and they wanted to build a commodity research and price risk apparatus to serve the new business model. It seemed like a great fit, so I joined Bunge in a trading and price risk management role. That was in 1999, the same year Bunge moved their headquarters from São Paulo to White Plains, New York.

Professionally, the move to Bunge was just right for me. I was going back to oilseed processing, a business I really enjoyed and one where my knowledge and experience could be useful. I also liked the idea of building something from the ground up and being part of something that was growing. It really couldn't have been a better move at that time.

Is this the time that you had the most fun in your career?

Hopefully, the most fun is yet to come, but to this point in my career, yes, that period was probably the most fun. When I think about the professional learning curve, the evolution of the company and the people in it, and the evolution of the commodity markets during the early 2000s, it was a great place to be. The ag markets and the broader financial markets experienced nearly every extreme during that time.

The period 1999 to 2001 was a dreadful time for the agricultural markets in terms of oversupply and inventory overhang. The Brazilian currency devaluation led to rapid production expansion, and the industry broadly had too much elevation and processing capacity. Price ranges were extremely narrow, and the trading houses were suffering. Remember, that was the period when André got out of the business, and Continental Grain sold their trading operations and asset base to Cargill. Trading houses were shrinking and making a lot of good people redundant just when Bunge was looking to expand once again into international markets.

As a result, we were able to attract capable and experienced people just as the agricultural markets were turning. We took on people from other companies, from different backgrounds. The combination formed something unique. There was a Cargill way of doing things and an André or a Continental way, and the result was a merger of those different approaches. It was an outward-looking and well-networked group; it was exciting to be a part of it.

Bunge shares became publicly traded in 2001, and there were obvious requirements for a better and more robust risk management process. Among our responsibilities was to build an analytical process that could serve the entire company in helping identify market opportunities, then to help position the physical and futures markets, and to coordinate the company's positioning in markets.

The ag markets, from 2005 until probably 2015, experienced a period of relative scarcity in grain and oilseeds inventories and significant volatility in many parts of the value chain. It brought higher prices for producers; it brought more opportunities for all value chain participants, including physical merchants and managed funds. With the benefit of hindsight, that period was likely the exception, not the norm. Probably many will look back on that particular decade with fondness and hope for a repeat.

What caused that cycle?

Several bullish inputs seemed to intersect in the same decade. Global GDP growth led to huge increases in meat and feed demand in some of the largest populations. During this time, demand from the biofuel sector also grew from insignificant to extremely meaningful volumes of vegetable oils, corn and sugar cane, driven in part by government mandates and pulled by higher energy prices. The energy price spike also flowed through to the cost of production in crops, shifting the cost of production higher. Interest in commodity indices and the idea of commodities as an asset class also brought a lot of buy-side participation in commodity futures markets; the increased financial flow was non-traditional, not initially understood and brought about increased volatility. Finally, the weather's impact on crop production is always a factor for pricing, but those marginal impacts have a larger price impact when balance sheets are tight. Meanwhile, higher prices drove a large need for investment in all the associated production, crop input, transport, throughput and processing infrastructure. In the middle of it all came the global financial crisis of 2008–09, and prices of ag commodities were roughly halved before staging a significant recovery. It was an extremely volatile but opportunity-rich environment.

And then you left Bunge to join a hedge fund.

Yes, another tough decision! In 2012, I'd been with Bunge for 13 years. My wife and I had a long-term plan to move to California by 2019 to be nearer her family. I was pushing for a move to Minnesota, but she wasn't interested in cold winters! I had no long-term professional plans in California, maybe write about experiences in markets, maybe do some teaching, but I had definite long-term plans to continue trading in the commodity markets with my own capital.

Some questions always exist whether traders can be successful outside of a big apparatus, if they do not have real-time visibility of value chain economics. I was very happy at Bunge. Most of my best friends were also my colleagues, but I wanted the challenge of managing capital on the outside to see if I could do it successfully.

And what was it like being with a hedge fund?
I really enjoyed the experience. The 'reason for being' is very clear in a fund. It's about delivering results, and that clarity has a way of creating the right kind of focus. Also, maybe contrary to popular perceptions, my experience is that hedge funds are very disciplined organisations. There's a real recognition that outcomes are uncertain and that one doesn't know anything with certainty, so a big part of the business revolves around managing risk.

My primary frustration in the managed money space was being limited to the Exchange-traded instruments and not being able to take positions in the underlying physical commodities (the basis) or in any other part of the value chain. The analytical process is the same in both settings – oftentimes at the fund, we had very solid opinions about value migration in parts of the chain, but with no way to express our opinion in those markets.

Having an actual presence in the physical markets is far more interesting, because one has a multitude of transportation, elevation and processing assets in a value chain – those components within the chain are constantly shifting in value on the basis of supply and demand. The intellectual challenge of solving that puzzle is more worthwhile, or at least the conclusions can be more readily deployed when one is involved in the physical parts of the commodity value chain, not just the financial ones.

What about the size of the positions that you took at the hedge fund; were they similar to those that you took at Bunge?
The public perception is that hedge funds take big swings in the market, and no doubt, some of them do. I actually managed much smaller positions in the fund space than I did in Bunge. Because of its physical merchandising business and global scale, Bunge often has no choice but to take big positions in the futures markets – maybe a simpler way to express that is to say that Bunge does not determine when their upstream farmer customers choose to commercialise grain or when their downstream food/feed consumers choose to buy it. They're largely in the middle of those value chains managing risk, many of which are put to them. Contrast that to a hedge fund, where risk is a lot more selective and where the obligation to assume risk does not exist. If a fund doesn't like the risk, they simply don't assume it.

An analogy I've heard likens managing positions in Bunge to that of driving a bus versus managing positions at a fund to that of driving a sports car. Smaller positions at a fund have an ability to weave in and out of traffic more quickly (while still obeying speed limits!).

Bunge moves large volumes of physical commodities and is obviously less manoeuvrable than a hedge fund. At the same time, we have a responsibility to a lot more stakeholders in the value chains where we operate: our suppliers, our customers, our employees, our communities. So 'driving a bus' involves a lot more permanence and responsibility. The bus must be out there in all conditions; the sports car has an option to remain parked in the garage!

So you get to 2019, you've learned how to successfully manage capital, and you honour your promise to your wife to move to the West Coast, where you'll write a book, become a teacher and trade your own capital.

Well, not exactly! I'd known Soren Schroder, the CEO of Bunge at the time, for a long time; in the fall of 2018, we began discussing the possibility of my returning to Bunge. The more we spoke, the more excited I became about the opportunity. I was very familiar with the businesses of Bunge and the markets in which they operate. I liked the people in the Company, and I believed that my experience in the fund space could bring a useful perspective.

Bunge had been a huge part of my professional life and meant a lot to me, so I convinced myself very quickly. Then I spoke with my wife. She's a planner, and the California plans had been set for a long time. Her first response was not very enthusiastic, but she ultimately came around. California deferred, on a couple of conditions – please don't ask what the conditions were!

If you'd gone to California, would you have managed other people's money or just your own?

It's a tough question. When you manage someone else's capital, particularly if an investor is paying fixed management fees, you're a steward of that capital; in that situation, my belief is that you have a fiduciary obligation to be on point and involved 24/7. A lot of stress comes from that obligation, and the pace required is demanding. That lifestyle is a grind, has a shorter shelf life, and chews up a lot of one-person asset managers.

Contrast that to a situation where one is managing only their own capital and answers only to themselves. If they don't like the current opportunity set in a particular market, they have the flexibility to bow out and go hiking for a couple of weeks. The standalone asset manager generally doesn't have that freedom. That isn't to say it cannot work. It really comes down to the understanding forged between capital provider and manager – the alignment just comes more easily when those people are one and the same.

But you're managing other people's capital at Bunge.

That's definitely true, but I'm not managing it alone. That makes a big difference. Responsibility and accountability ultimately roll up. They need to, but it's necessarily a team effort and doesn't come down to any single person. There's a certain amount of gratification with doing something on your own. At least for me, it's more rewarding to be a part of something bigger. I get a lot of fulfilment from feeling that I've contributed to the success of that bigger something.

What do you do in your current position?
Bunge is a public company, and one of the clear messages from investors and from the board of directors is that they want less volatility in earnings. We're working on a number of changes in processes and reporting in an effort to move in that direction. We're segregating the risk-taking areas – we call them *buckets* – and giving them all individual drawdown limits. The idea is to increase diversification across the portfolio; we know all areas won't make money at the same time, but we want to reduce the risk of any single area creating an unacceptable loss at the level of the overall portfolio.

At the same time, risk is a part of the fabric in agribusiness; we have no choice but to embrace it and manage it. An important area of focus is in working with colleagues that manage the operating businesses of the Company and framing the existing market environment. If we can create an informed and accurate view of the future or at least properly assess the range of outcomes, we'll take on risks that are not just sound but that are appropriately sized for the current market and margin environment. (He laughs.) It's just that easy, and it's just that difficult!

What do you find the most challenging in the current environment?
Markets are always challenging enough, but now, geopolitical risks have risen to a level that I haven't seen before in my career. People who were around in the 1970s and early 1980s and lived through the grain embargoes might be more accustomed to the current situation, but it's new for me.

When China was admitted to the WTO in 2001, I remember thinking that, from now on, markets were going to be driven by economics and that the world would really benefit from what would be a more efficient allocation of resources. And from the perspective of a trader, when you understand the economics in that world, you have a real advantage; granular research can derive big benefits. Now, geopolitics is such that everything can change at the stroke of a pen or a tweet. This is creating binary risks that are tough to manage.

Otherwise, if you look at what's happening in the broader space, there's a lot of pain in the industry right now. I believe that it's mostly about where we are in the cycle. Surplus markets mean less frequent opportunities, and those opportunities tend to be smaller. So if a lot of your traditional income is coming from trading and positioning in markets, then that element of the business is challenged in the current environment. What will change is time, in the form of the commodity cycle or else a more transitory supply shock.

At the same time, digitalisation is making markets more rapid. Millennium, a fund I used to work for, has a division called WorldQuant managing some portion of their assets. Already, about a year ago, the WorldQuant founder wrote publicly that they have 10 million alphas (archived in their databases and that their short-term goal is 100 million in the next few years!

The traditional trade houses are never going to compete with that. However, we have a significant upside in that our physical business produces a lot of proprietary data, generated by our asset base and our global scale. If we can gather and analyse that data correctly, it will provide insights not easily replicated. Also, parts of our business embed a lot of flexibility and optionality, which represents value.

A common perception is that the big grain trading and processing companies make outsized profits to the detriment of other players, namely farmers and consumers, in the supply chain. That's totally false. You just have to look at the value the stock market puts on these companies. The low multiple that investors assign to our shares reflects the reality that this is an ultra-competitive business. The investment in permanent assets is expensive, the outcome on those investments is not easy to forecast, and the assets themselves act to make supply chains more efficient, which results in higher prices for farmers and lower prices for consumers.

Are you optimistic or pessimistic about the future?

I'm optimistic. We're global players with a global asset base. We're an integral part of the food supply chain and will remain so if we can adapt to what our customers want. It appears the trend is toward better quality, greater reliability and traceability. We physically originate 70 million tonnes of grains and oilseeds each year and have an end-to-end presence in the supply chain; that's an inherently strong structural position, which is not easy to replicate.

From the standpoint of price risk management, our network also provides us with a lot of proprietary information that helps us optimise our value chains. In a way, our asset base is a call option on volatility in the supply chain.

Also, the business of feeding the world will never go away. It is changing, no doubt, and the hand we're dealt is never the same. Our job strategically is to change with it; our job tactically is to do the best we can with the hand we're dealt.

Do you think commodity trading is a zero-sum game?
It's often described that way, but the reality is that most transactions in any market are mutually beneficial. Adam Smith talked about price as 'the invisible hand that efficiently allocates resources'; I marvel at how true that is in the ag markets. Inefficiencies are arbitraged out of markets quickly, and surplus commodities flow to deficit areas like water. It's just super-efficient.

Of course, if you had a market with only two speculators, then one would lose and the other would win. That's zero-sum. But the vast majority of transactions serve a need and really are mutually beneficial.

What advice would you give to a young person starting a career in commodities trading?
Wow, how much time do you have? (He laughs.) After 25-plus years in this business, we could spend an entire day talking about that!

My first piece of advice would be to remain intellectually curious. It seems to me that some of the most successful people in the business always ask the next question, not in the interest of information overload, but in the interest of drawing connections between cause and effect in the markets: What's driving this? Why is this happening? Does it have any knock-on effects? What does it mean?

Second, be humble. If you don't already possess humility, the market will eventually provide it to you – but it's almost always more expensive that way!

Accept that you give something of yourself when you put on a position; it exposes your vulnerability to failure. In reality, markets can reward you, even when your underlying logic was flawed, and a bet can go badly, even when your underlying logic was sound.

Some of the best advice I received went something like 'be less concerned about defending your logic and "being right", because you don't have all the facts; be more concerned about the outcome and managing your capital'. When it's framed that way, you realise a bad bet isn't an indictment on your intelligence. Being wrong on occasion is just a part of the business. Get over it, let it go, and move on. Being wrong only becomes a problem if it's either the chronic state – or if it results in a spectacularly bad outcome because you stubbornly held on too long in the belief you were right!

Third, never say never. You can say that there's a low probability of something happening, but you shouldn't say it will never happen. We've all seen too many things happen that we thought would never happen. The options markets have this pretty well figured out.

Fourth, find what works for you, and develop your own style. At the same time, though, seek the counsel of people that you trust, who can ground you in moments of emotion and the extremes, and who can help you put things in perspective.

Finally, appreciate the place that commodities have in the world. … We're in a relevant business with great purpose!

Thank you, Brian, for your time. I think you should write that book!

Chapter Six: Managing Change

'There is nothing more difficult to take in hand, more perilous to conduct, or more uncertain in its success, than to take the lead in the introduction of a new order of things.'
Niccolo Machiavelli

The Soviet buying in the 1970s created tremendous opportunities for the grain trading companies. But the huge volumes and massive price volatility also created tremendous risks.

Continental Grain learnt this the hard way (1), when their traders underestimated the depth of Soviet buying; the company sold physical corn short, expecting to cover the sales when prices fell later in the year. But corn prices didn't fall. They continued to climb, and the company covered their shorts at the top of the market.

For Michel Fribourg, the owner of Continental Grain, this was a traumatic event, and he declined to offer further tonnage when the Soviets came back for more in October 1975. A few months later, he reorganised the company, firing traders and employing risk and business managers instead. As Dan Morgan wrote, the risk in these big sales was just too big: 'The glory days of the grand slams in the Russian trade were over. … Most of the companies now insisted that the Soviet Union share more of the risks'. (2)

Back in the 1970s, most commodity imports were handled by central government agencies within the importing country. Governments were generally assumed to be more reliable counterparties than the private sector, but this belief was shaken when, in early 1975, wheat prices fell and Turkey's wheat-importing agency cancelled the wheat import contracts it had concluded at higher prices with Continental, Bunge and Cargill. (3)

Simultaneously, these state buying agencies had begun to attract the U.S. government's attention regarding the inducements (bribes) that the grain companies paid to civil servants and politicians to get business done. A new light was being shone on these practices. A new morality began to take hold within the U.S., leading to the Foreign Corrupt Practices Act passed in 1977.

New light was also being shone on the shipping and transportation of the physical grain, leading to an FBI investigation in 1975 into alleged short loading and falsified shipping documents at Mississippi grain loading terminals. Meanwhile, the grain companies were under the spotlight for anti-competitive practices in inland grain transportation.

Despite the price volatility and the disruption in trade flows resulting from Soviet buying, physical trading margins within the agricultural supply chain remained thin. The big trading companies largely made their profits by taking positions on the futures markets that they themselves dominated.

But there again, a new morality was beginning to take hold, with the formation in April 1975 of the Commodities Futures Trading Commission, a new independent government agency to police the exchanges. It was formed 'with fewer "policemen" than the Rockville, Maryland Police Department' (4) and appeared to get off to a slow start, but it was a sign of things to come.

Perhaps more importantly, the big trading companies were already – in the 1970s – beginning to lose their domination of the agricultural futures markets. Large, well-financed speculators were moving in. The most famous were the Hunt brothers, who had made a fortune early in the decade by squeezing the silver market and then tried to do the same with soybeans.

Their buying pushed prices higher and helped speed the demise of the publicly quoted Cook Industries, a former cotton trading company that, by the mid-1970s, had begun to rival traditional grain companies. (5) Cook was forced to sell its U.S. grain elevators, allowing the Japanese trade houses Mitsui and Marubeni to gain a foothold into the U.S. grain business.

Taking all this together, the traditional grain business was already beginning to fundamentally change in the 1970s. The catalyst was the massive price volatility and subsequent general inflation that followed the Soviet grain purchases.

The grain companies had been hoping for such an event all through the doldrums of the 1950s and 1960s, but the consequences were greater government intervention and increased transparency, as well as the entry of well-financed speculators into markets that had previously been quietly local.

Bring those elements into a sector that was already struggling to cope with higher volumes and greater counter-party risks, and one can begin to see that the writing was already on the wall. The seat-of-the-pants era of buccaneering trading was on the way out; professional risk management, cost control and a new morality were on the way in.

The environment in which the big trade houses operate has continued to change since *Merchants of Grain* was published in 1979. The agricultural trade houses have done their best to change in response – and as we will see with André and Continental – some even decided that the best response was to leave the business completely.

But what has changed so dramatically over the past 40 years? What have been the drivers that have transformed the industry?

Information technology has resulted in both the spread and the speed of information increasing dramatically, leading to better and more quickly informed clients, reduced price differentials and lower or negative trading margins.

Meanwhile, there has been an increase in the level of general education all along the supply chain. A wheat importer in Jakarta is almost as likely to have studied at Harvard (or another top university) as the grain trader sitting in Geneva who is selling him or her the wheat.

The ease of communication and the spread of information have led to what's known as *disintermediation*. This phenomenon is not limited to the grain trade; it has occurred in numerous supply chains. When I started in the business, I'd call a travel agent to book a flight or hotel; now I do it directly through the Internet. I no longer need the travel agent to act as an intermediary between the airline and myself. Similarly, a buyer, either the consumer or importer of a commodity, can bypass the trade houses completely by getting in direct touch with the seller.

The mix of better information and better education has also resulted in a shift of market power along the supply chain. In the past couple of centuries, farmers slowly lost pricing power to the merchants who moved the food to market. The merchants then gradually lost their market powers to food processors and retailers. The growth of the Internet and, in particular, of social media has in turn weakened the power of the brands and the supermarkets, empowering consumers at the expense of farmers, merchants, processors and retailers.

Consumers in rich countries want to know where their food comes from. They want to know that it has been produced sustainably. Consequently, many organisations have been set up to certify that their food – or their cotton – hasn't harmed either the environment or the social welfare of those involved in its production.

This led to a shift from tradability to traceability. *Tradability* is taken to mean the ability to trade a commodity in terms of switching origins or destinations in response to changes in relative prices of the commodity and of the shipping rates. *Traceability* is the ability to trace a particular (usually certified) commodity all the way back along the supply chain to the farm or even the field where it was produced.

Blockchain technology is making traceability easier. In 2018, Cargill used blockchain to allow consumers to scan a code on the packaging of their Thanksgiving turkey to locate the farm where the turkey was raised. (6) As the technology becomes more widespread, the costs of traceability will fall. However, being less able to switch origins reduces merchants' flexibility and, hence, their profits.

The solution, of course, would be to have all commodities certified. That way, traders could respond to changing market conditions by switching or swapping one certified product for another. However, because of the costs involved, only a small percentage of most commodities are currently certified, and progress is slow.

Certification and traceability can increase costs if products must be kept separate in warehouses, port terminals and ships. It can sometimes lead to the underutilisation of these assets. However, most certification schemes allow for what's known as *mass balance*. If a trader buys 40,000 tonnes of certified product from a mill, he or she can put that into a warehouse – and mix it – with other non-certified products and then take out 40,000 tonnes of the mixed product and still sell it as certified. It probably won't be the same product, but one can use certification certificates against it.

It's often said that traceability and certification are turning many commodities into ingredients. *Investopedia* (7) defines a *commodity* as:

> A basic good used in commerce that is interchangeable with other commodities of the same type. Commodities are most often used as inputs in the production of other goods or services. The quality of a given commodity may differ slightly, but it is essentially uniform across producers. When they are traded on an exchange, commodities must also meet specified minimum standards, also known as a basis grade.

It continues:

> The basic idea is that there is little differentiation between a commodity coming from one producer and the same commodity from another producer. A barrel of oil is basically the same product, regardless of the producer. By contrast, for electronics merchandise, the quality and features of a given product may be completely different depending on the producer.

An 'ingredient' can also be a commodity, but it is usually considered a specific grade or quality to make a success of a recipe or to be consumed directly. Cocoa is becoming an increasingly specialised ingredient; buyers are becoming even stricter about the quality of their raw ingredient. In coffee, Robusta coffee is a commodity. Arabica coffee is absolutely not a commodity. It's like fine wine.

As we will see later, many traditional trade houses are trying to move away from low-value and low-margin commodities into high-value and high-margin ingredients. The tonnages are smaller but are – in theory, at least – offset by higher margins. Among the big grain trading companies, ADM has made a strong move into this area.

As consumers, we not only want to be sure that our food is produced in an environmentally and socially sustainable way, but we also want to be sure that it is good for us. Unfortunately, we often receive conflicting or contradictory information about what is good for us: what is healthy and what is not.

This can result in difficult to predict – and fast moving – trends that can leave both farmers and merchants wrongfooted. The demonisation of sugar is probably the best recent example. It has led to a sharp reduction in the growth of global sugar demand. But it has also led to a collapse in the demand for fruit, particularly orange juice. Other examples include the recent pushback against Genetically Modified products in the U.S. or the increase in the number of consumers who are gluten intolerant.

Empowered consumers can lead to increased government intervention, whether in areas of health and safety, or trade relations. Consumer trends can quickly change direction, and governments are rarely far behind. This increases merchants' risks and pushes up their compliance burden. At the same time, consumer empowerment has been accompanied by the media's increased hostility to agricultural merchants. This media hostility has reduced merchants' political leverage and made it harder for them to hire talent.

However, in a strange twist of fate, farmers – particularly U.S. farmers – have also become more powerful. (8) Big farm operators are pushing grain companies for better prices or striking their own deals to directly supply manufacturers, cutting out the middleman. Many farmers ploughed the proceeds from the high grain prices from 2007 to 2012 into on-farm storage. This trend continued in the years up to 2018, when a series of big harvests encouraged farmers to further expand their on-farm storage. In the 10 years from 2007 to 2017, U.S. farms' crop-storage capacity expanded by 14 percent to 13.5 billion bushels – enough to hold nearly all of 2017's corn harvest. This gives them significantly more power in the supply chain.

At the same time, the traditional grain companies have faced competition for crops from livestock operations and ethanol plants.

Improved access to market data has empowered farmers to become tougher negotiators. This has been partly fuelled by a demographic shift. As U.S. farmers' average age climbs above 58, more are retiring, creating opportunities for bigger, wealthier and higher-tech farm operations to expand. Farms generating $1 million or more in annual revenue represent just 4 percent of the U.S. total, but now produce two-thirds of the country's agricultural commodities.

In response, Cargill's North American agricultural supply chain has shrunk its network of U.S. grain facilities from 120 to about 85 in the four years up to 2018, divesting some far-flung grain elevators that aren't near a railroad or river. Overall, Cargill still is merchandising the same amount of grain, directing more volume toward its remaining, higher-capacity facilities. All the same, farmers have bought at least some of the elevators that Cargill sold, further compounding the problem.

On a completely different level of importance, global climate change will present an enormous challenge in the future to farmers and merchants alike. It will increasingly make both crops and trade flows less predictable, increasing the risk when investing in infrastructure such as warehouses and port terminals.

Over the past decades, merchants have found it difficult to make money by doing what merchants do: transforming commodities over time, space and form. They have tried (sometimes successfully, sometimes less so) to leverage the knowledge that they glean from their physical merchandising activities into predicting future price movements. (A trader once told me that he 'went to the futures markets to cash in all that he learned from the physical trade'.)

However, the 'financialisation' of commodity markets, coupled with recent advances in artificial intelligence, has arguably reduced the advantage that physical commodity merchants had in the futures markets.

Agricultural commodities have traditionally been viewed as both too speculative and too specialised for an outside investor. One really had to be an expert in cocoa to invest in cocoa – and one had to be an expert in orange juice to invest in orange juice. The price of each commodity depended on a whole range of commodity-specific fundamental information that needed to be analysed on an individual market basis. Orange juice prices could drop because of changing consumption habits; cocoa prices could rise because of conflict in the Ivory Coast. There was little to no correlation between the two commodities.

In addition, each individual commodity market was relatively small compared to the equity markets and too illiquid to absorb large inflows of investor money from, say, a major pension fund. Most importantly, however, commodities were not considered worthy of investor (as opposed to speculative) interest, as they were considered to be *mean reverting*: prices reverted over time to the marginal cost of production for the most efficient producer.

This way of thinking was fundamentally challenged when Gary Gorton (then of Wharton) and Geert Rounwehorst (of Yale) published 'Facts and Fantasies about Commodities Futures'. (9) The abstract of their paper reads as follows:

> We construct an equally weighted index of commodity futures monthly returns over the period between July of 1959 and December of 2004 in order to study simple properties of commodity futures as an asset class. Fully collateralized commodity futures have historically offered the same return and Sharpe ratio as equities. While the risk premium on commodity futures is essentially the same as equities, commodity futures returns are negatively correlated with equity returns and bond returns. The negative correlation between commodity futures and the other asset classes is due, in significant part, to different behaviour over the business cycle. In addition, commodity futures are positively correlated with inflation, unexpected inflation, and changes in expected inflation.

In other words, the authors found that if you took a basket of commodities rather than just one particular commodity, commodity prices were inversely correlated with the prices of bonds and equities, and positively correlated with inflation.

The report was like an electric shock to the investment industry. It had particular significance for the pension funds looking both for a hedge against inflation and against the bad years when bond and equity prices fell. When equity prices fall, the report basically concluded, the losses on a portfolio would be offset by increases in commodity prices. Pension funds reacted quickly to the report; they loved the idea that commodity indices could be used as a hedge both against inflation and against a fall in bond and equity prices.

By coincidence, the study hit the financial press about when the world was getting excited about China and the country's apparently insatiable appetite for commodities. Iron ore and copper were needed to build skyscrapers and roads, while soybeans were needed to fatten the pigs to meet China's growing demand for meat. The pension funds loved the idea of investing in commodities as a way of participating in the China growth story.

Pension funds rushed into commodity index funds that held long positions in baskets of various commodities, and a whole industry quickly grew up around commodity index fund management, most of it within the banks. The banks built large commodity-trading desks that not only managed investment flows but also traded around those flows.

All this began to attract the attention of the media and the general public, especially as it coincided with rising food prices. Well-meaning commentators naturally blamed the increase in food prices – and the ensuing food riots in several countries – on speculators, particularly on the arrival of index-fund investors into the commodity markets.

But were commodity prices rising because investors were holding supply off the market and pushing food prices out of the reach of a hungry population? Or were investors flocking to the commodity markets because prices were rising due to increased demand-and-supply bottlenecks coupled with a run of bad weather and poor harvests?

Public opinion went with the first explanation, arguing that speculators (and index funds in particular) were pushing up food prices. Many called for the futures markets to be closed (some agricultural–commodity markets were indeed closed for a while in India, even though India doesn't have any commodity index funds). Banks were pressured to stop investing in food commodities (and some did).

In 2010, an article in *Harper's* magazine accused Goldman Sachs of profiting while people went hungry or even starved. The article argued that Goldman's large purchases of call options on wheat futures created a demand shock in the wheat market that disturbed the normal relationship between supply and demand and pushed up prices.

However, a report the same year by the Organisation for Economic Co-operation and Development (OECD) found that there was 'no convincing evidence that positions held by index traders ... impact market returns'. The OECD argued that there was no correlation between the index-fund positions in particular commodities and the price rise for those raw materials. The OECD also pointed out that commodities without futures markets – and, hence, without any index fund involvement – also saw price increases during the period.

However, others have argued that commodities without futures markets saw their prices rise because of the rising prices of commodities with futures markets. For example, there is a case to be made that the rising price of wheat caused the price of rice to rise. The UN Conference on Trade and Development (UNCTAD) said index funds 'can significantly influence prices and create speculative bubbles, with extremely detrimental effects on normal trading activities and market efficiency'.

The brouhaha died down as food prices once again fell, but investment funds remain active in the agricultural commodity markets, in both index and beta funds. (10) The CFTC reported in March 2019 that as much as 70 percent of the volume in the grain futures markets was generated by computer or algorithmic funds run by investors outside traditional grain merchandising.

Many of the changes listed above are good on a global level. Empowered consumers, supported by fast-moving and attentive governments, are leading to improvements regarding environmental and social sustainability and health. However, they're making life tougher for grain intermediaries. What are traditional agricultural merchants doing to adapt?

The first response of any business to squeezed margins is to cut costs, but that is not necessarily the solution, particularly if you believe that commodity merchandising is a zero-sum game.

As Jay O'Neil rightly pointed out earlier in this book, the market fixes the price of a commodity. Commodity producers and merchants are price takers: they can only take what the market offers them. This means that if one participant in the supply chain makes more money, someone else along the supply chain has to make less. The same applies to market share. As demand is static or, at best, growing slowly, if one producer sells more, another must sell less.

They only way people in that supply chain can make a bigger margin is to use their market power to squeeze the others in the supply chain so they make less. Commodity merchants now capture a smaller share of the margins in the chain than they did.

If we accept that a commodity supply chain is a zero-sum game, the only way to increase margins without taking money from suppliers and clients is to cut costs. This can be done in several ways.

Cutting labour costs is usually a company's first response to margin pressure. Reducing headcounts can do this, making the remaining employees work harder or more efficiently and reducing salaries. In the case of traders, bonuses are another option.

Companies can reduce costs by outsourcing tasks in the hope that other companies can perform a function more cheaply that they can. We saw an example of this in mid-2018 when Bunge sold their sugar-trading department to Wilmar, letting them merchandise the production from Bunge's Brazilian sugarcane mills.

Innovation, either in processes or technology, can help companies reduce labour costs and gain efficiency. Obvious examples include better communication between offices, data handling in offices and mechanisation (including robots) in manufacturing and handling. There is no reason to think that innovation will suddenly end. Indeed, there is reason to think that the trend will accelerate, enabling further cost reduction along the supply chain.

Farming is the one part of the agricultural supply chain that has benefitted the most from innovation and technology. Hybrid seeds, more efficient farm machinery, improved pesticides and insecticides, and drone and GPS technology have all helped to reduce costs.

Economies of scale are a common source of cost reduction; building a one-million-tonne commodity processing plant or port loading facility will not cost twice as much as building a 500,000-tonne facility. However, the best way to reduce unit costs is to increase throughput to ensure the capacity built is being used to its maximum.

Last, in everyone's interest, companies can cut costs by reducing waste. The U.N. estimates that food waste and crop losses amount to nearly U.S.$ 1 trillion yearly. That's a huge cost, not just to the environment but also to the agricultural supply chain. Even making small inroads into that waste could significantly benefit the profitability of supply chain actors.

However, in a zero-sum supply chain, the only way to increase profits without picking others' pockets is by reducing costs. Unfortunately, what may work for an individual company (or farmer) may not work collectively.

One farmer can take advantage of innovation and technology to grow the same-sized crop from a smaller area, but his or her instinct will be to plant all his or her available land and produce more. To capture economies of scale, a processor will build a mega-plant, and to reduce unit costs, he or she will seek to maximise throughput. Moreover, obviously, any success in reducing wastage will also increase the available food supply.

There is, therefore, a tendency for cost cutting in a commodity supply chain to result in increased supply. And increased supply usually results in lower prices. Acting alone, an individual player in the supply chain might increase his or her margins by cutting costs. However, if everyone does it, the resulting extra production can result in a fall in price that negates the costs saved.

Looking at this another way, economic theory tells us that the price of any particular commodity is, in the long term, determined by the marginal cost of production of that commodity's most efficient producer. The more efficient the producer, the lower the cost.

So, if cost cutting is not the solution, what is?

Some trade houses are trying to move more into ingredients and out of commodities. Some commodities, such as coffee and cocoa, are already losing their commodity status and are differentiated by origin. End consumers are already willing to pay more for gluten-free or lactose-free or organic or non-genetically-modified or locally produced food. And the big brands are willing to pay more (hopefully) for specific food varieties that fit their recipes.

Some grain merchandisers are attempting to expand their activities beyond traditional trading, expanding along the supply chain towards both the producer and the consumer. In this sense, some trade houses are working to become the whole supply chain – from field to fork – rather than just a small part of it. (This strategy also fits well with blockchain and the movement towards traceable supply.)

Other grain merchandisers are taking this further, working to become fully integrated food companies, producing and managing retail brands. Some are moving the other way, investing in land and becoming farmers. And others are taking an opposite approach by sticking to small product niches or geographical areas such as the Black Sea.

As the reader will see in the following chapters, commodity merchants are adapting to the changes occurring around them. They're embracing these changes, not resisting them, and they're doing so in different ways.

It is not clear which particular strategy, if any, will turn out best. But as Charles Darwin once said, 'It is not the strongest of the species that survives, not the most intelligent that survives. It is the one that is the most adaptable to change'.

Trading Is Our DNA – Kristen Eshak Weldon

Kristen Eshak Weldon is the recently appointed Head of Food Innovation and Downstream Strategy at Louis Dreyfus Company, a title that her father thinks might be a contender for the longest business title in the world.

She was born in New York City and raised in Houston, Texas, before attending Georgetown University in Washington, D.C. There, she was one of about four women and about 200 men in her year to obtain a degree in finance and international business. Kristen told me that she had intended to study marketing, but quickly switched to finance because she liked the concreteness of mathematics.

So, you're a mathematician?
I like facts and being able to resolve problems. In liberal arts, you can always ask another question without reaching a conclusion. With a finance degree, your work was done at the end of the day, versus a liberal arts degree where you always had more reading to do.

I graduated at the height of the dotcom boom; so many of my classmates joined start-ups. I joined JP Morgan, where I went into the markets training programme. Everyone else I knew from Georgetown went into investment banking, rather than trading. I was attracted to the lifestyle of trading, being on your toes, making quick decisions, but not necessarily carrying risk overnight.

I started in fixed income and hated it. It was really boring. I spent my time modelling trades, but in the 18 months that I was there, I only did one trade! One of the group's VPs at the time was moving to commodities, and he took me with him. I started as a salesperson in the metals group, one of two analysts. It was fantastic. I loved the fact that it was real and tangible.

I particularly liked commodity balance sheets, understanding supply and demand, bringing it all together. I also like the precision of a model, when it all comes together. I worked with corporate clients, particularly in base metals.

I have two younger brothers; they're twins. By this point, they had come to New York as well. They're both in the music industry, so we'd laugh that we were all touching platinum in some sort of way! I was trading it, and they were trying to make platinum records. They're immensely successful.

So, you are all high achievers in your family.
Yes, I think my parents are very happy, although they did have their doubts about my brothers when they were younger! We all were raised as one unit, almost like triplets. I was only 16 months older than they were, and I was never treated any differently at home in terms of what I could achieve or what my parents wanted me to do.

I remember when I was about nine or ten. I went one Saturday to my Dad's office, where he was CEO of a hospital in Houston. He had a little mini refrigerator in his office, and I was excited about which soft drink I would choose from it. I sat in his assistant's chair, and I told him that I wanted that chair when I grew up. He got really cross. 'You should want my chair', he told me, 'Not my assistant's seat'.

In 2003, JP Morgan asked me to move to London to cover North American and European consumer and producer clients in both base metals and energy. When I was 14, I had come to London to stay with a friend, and I fell in love with it.

I arrived in London the weekend of the London Metal Exchange (LME) Summer Party: July 4, when the U.S. markets are closed. I was a 25-year-old American woman, and I thought, 'Oh, my God, what have I got myself into?' I stuck it out for as long as I could, but it was tough.

I remember my first LME Dinner, a sea of men in dinner jackets! The drinking went on all night, and I got home at 5 a.m., only to turn right around for a breakfast meeting at 7 a.m. I wouldn't have gone to the Playboy Club, but I was happy to go to the parties. I felt they were necessary to network.

I did my best to fit into this male atmosphere. I think a lot of that speaks to my childhood and my degree. Having two brothers so close in age, our house was full of boys. I was also used to the comments – you know how abusive siblings can be to each other! Then at university, I had a lot of male friends. So the banking and trading environments weren't that alien to me. It was just that the LME was the extreme end of that. The verbal comments eventually got to me. Things like that should not be happening in the 2000s.

Having previously talked to Blackstone about a job in New York, I called my contact and said, 'Listen, I've made a mistake. I'd really like to work with you, but I'd like that to be in London'. And he said, 'Yes'. So I left JP Morgan in June 2004 and joined Blackstone in July. It was a completely different atmosphere from the LME desk at JP Morgan. It was a younger industry.

I stayed at Blackstone for thirteen and a half years. I built a commodity hedge fund platform. It was great fun, and I had a hugely supportive boss. He encouraged me to speak up more in meetings and not to be afraid to ask a question or express a point.

I remember that I was disappointed not to have been promoted during the 2008 review season. I asked my boss why that was. He replied, 'Because you never asked'. So the next year, I asked. I was pregnant with my first child, but I made sure I kept my personal life personal so I would just be assessed on the merits of my performance. I was promoted to Managing Director in 2009 and made Partner in 2013. I was young, and I was the first female partner in London!

How did you manage your work–life balance?

When I was pregnant with my second child, my husband left his trading position at JP Morgan. We took the view that my career at that point was looking positive. His career was going in a different direction, with trading mostly going electronic. His real passion in life is design and architecture, and we had just bought a new house – a major renovation project. We agreed that he would invest his time into the house project, and I would continue to work. We moved into the house three years after that.

My husband is around much more for our children than I am right now. I think that it's really difficult if both parents are going full speed. In any case, society is changing. Dads now take much more of a role in family life. Not seeing their kids can be tough for the dads as well. Child raising is an equal task to be shared.

In 2017, the commodity hedge fund business was slowing. Funds were closing, and the environment was becoming more challenging. I thought it would be a good opportunity to step back, clear my head and at the same time spend more time with my family. My boys were growing and as they say, 'Small kids, small problems; big kids, bigger problems'. I felt it was the right time to spend a bit more time at home.

I applied and was accepted for a Sloan master's in leadership and strategy at the London Business School. The course was amazing. It was a great year for me, even if I didn't spend more time at home!

And after that, you joined Louis Dreyfus?

Yes. I'd known Ian McIntosh for some time, and he called me around May 2018. We discussed his ideas for LDC. I shared with him a lot of what I had learned in my master's course, in terms of innovation and disruption, while keeping the culture of a company: basically, how you disrupt from within. In October, after he became CEO, he asked me to join. I jumped at the opportunity.

You've had a fabulous career so far – and a great opportunity in your new position. Can women have it all: a family and a career?

Women (and men) can have it all. In my experience, it has been challenging to have it all at the same time.

So, where do you start? You arrive at LDC, you're given a long business title, and then what?

Joining Dreyfus was a tremendous opportunity for me in terms of innovation and disruption. My initial focus is on the future of food.

The first thing I had to do was to understand what makes LDC successful as a company. I initially spent little time in London and instead tried to go to the places where LDC has a major presence. I visited industrial assets and wanted to understand industrial processes, but more importantly, I wanted to meet the people and understand the culture of the company.

During this initiation period, I realised that people were often working on the same challenges in different regions, but without necessarily sharing their experiences. It's essential that we leverage best practices across regions, so my first task was to try and link the dots.

The second thing I had to do was to define our investment thesis. The future of food topic is so vast, there are so many things we can be doing. Upstream is logical in terms of looking at helping farmers to be more efficient and more effective, but it's a really crowded space and more the domain of the seed and technology companies. The downstream part has more opportunities and is adjacent to what we already do, but we have to decide what's relevant to us and where we can be impactful.

Could you tell me a little about your company's investment in MOTIF, the food ingredients start-up?

I joined LDC when the due diligence was nearly done. This investment is really exciting, cutting edge, and I'd place it on the far-right-hand side of our range of opportunities as it relates to adjacency. MOTIF leverages biotechnology to create innovative ingredients that replicate animal proteins in terms of texture or taste. The company is based in Boston and was the second start-up to launch from Ginkgo Bioworks. Investing in MOTIF was a way for us to help us understand more about the future of food.

The other agricultural commodity traders have already been serial acquirers in the sector, moving into specialty areas. What will you do differently?

Our intention is not to provide all of the food and beverage (F&B) companies with a blanket solution for all their specialty ingredients, but we'll do it in specific areas and regions. And we'll do it differently. We're looking to work in partnership with other companies in the form of joint ventures or by bringing in external co-investment capital on the innovation side. This will allow us to move quickly.

Don't you think LDC is starting the process a little late in the game compared to your competitors?

Maybe, but one thing that gets drummed into your brain at business school is that there's no such thing as a first-mover advantage. That and 'fail fast'. I would've liked to have had some lessons learned from previous acquisitions, but we're certainly not too late. The timing is still right, and we can add value in the areas and regions that are less trafficked.

In the late '90s, Continental Grain decided that the risks in commodity trading weren't worth the rewards, and they sold their commodity trading operations to Cargill. They then became a major investor in the faster-growing parts of the food chain, almost as a venture capital fund. Is that something that LDC might consider doing, selling off their bulk handling operations?

Absolutely not. The trading part of our business is the DNA of our company. That won't go away. When we look at new areas, we have to ask what we bring to the table and how: are they adjacent to what we know and do best? We can bring industrial scale to a business, as well as our risk management skills. Our geographical footprint helps massively. We already operate in countries where a start-up may not be able to go by themselves – countries where we already understand the regulatory landscape, the political issues etc.

What about brands? LDC has a crushing plant in China, and if I understand correctly, your plan is to take beans all the way from Argentina through to branded bottled oil in China. That's a new venture for you: a branded consumer product.

Branded consumer products are not new to LDC per se. Over the years, we've created a number of branded consumer products, including edible oil brands Vibhor in India, Vila Velha in Brazil or Zephyr coffee in the U.S., together with rice and sugar brands. Today, we plan to go downstream in a more structured approach where we leverage our matrix structure and take experts from our platforms that know these products, and then use our regional resources that understand local consumer demands.

And that leads me to my most important question: what does the consumer want? Is it sustainability, health, human rights, a fair income for farmers or what?

You're asking the wrong question. Different consumers want different things. That's what makes this job so interesting and provides so many opportunities.

First, it depends on where you are in the world. If you look at Europe and the U.S., then health is probably the number-one issue, followed by environmental sustainability and human rights. Farmer welfare probably comes last, but that doesn't mean that it isn't important. In China and other Asian countries, consumers are looking closely at quality and safety, for example. In the poorer parts of the world, the first question usually is, 'How can I meet the daily needs of my family?'

Second, regardless of where they are, different people have different priorities. They may be vegetarian, vegan, flexitarian or whatever. There are opportunities in providing different consumers with different solutions.

As a company, our downstream approach has to be crafted differently for each region and for each market segment. At the same time, we have to keep a focus on the macro picture of feeding the world safely and sustainably. We have to be aware of what our global goals are. We have to look at the entire value chain and where it's impactful.

Every day when you leave the office, you should ask yourself, 'Am I doing the right thing? Is what I'm doing beneficial, and do I feel good about it?'

That's what's really important about what I'm doing at LDC, especially on the innovation side. We want to know that we're delivering a food product in a safe and environmentally sustainable way, that we know exactly where it comes from and that the labour that produced it is being paid market wages.

I want to be someone that does positive things, and I want to work with aligned parties that share our values, whether it's the companies that we invest in or fellow investors in these companies.

Thank you, Kristen, for your time.

Chapter Seven: André & Cie

'Number 5/7 Chemin Messidor, please'.
'Oh, you mean André', the taxi driver replied.
'You know it?' I asked.
'Everyone knows André'.

The year was 1995, and I'd come to Switzerland from Paris to visit my clients in Switzerland. André & Cie, at that time probably the second-largest grain trading company in the world after Cargill, had recently opened a sugar-trading desk. At the time of my visit, André & Cie was already active in the Cuban sugar business.

Cuba had lost their high-priced export market for sugar when the U.S.S.R. collapsed in 1991. The country was desperate to find new export markets for its sugar production and was also desperate for foreign exchange to pay for food imports. This was exactly the sort of business that André & Cie excelled in; in fact, the company had a specialised department, FINCO, which put together complicated barter and countertrade operations.

Throughout the 1990s, André & Cie supplied wheat and other foodstuffs to Cuba in exchange for sugar and other foodstuffs. As one ex-employee later told me later, 'André was feeding Cuba. I don't know what would have happened if André hadn't have helped them'.

My taxi pulled up, and I got out. The company's headquarters, built in 1962, occupied a prime secluded spot amidst a residential area in Lausanne. Large trees made it all the more discreet – almost invisible. Near the building's entrance, half-hidden by shrubbery, was a small sign with the *Andre & Cie* name. It reminded me of the first time that I visited Cargill's head offices, hidden in a woodland outside Minneapolis. André's offices were hidden 'in full sight' in the middle of a city, but just as discreet.

The automatic sliding doors opened into a large lobby with huge picture windows giving a spectacular panoramic view of Lake Geneva with the Alps in the distance. There was a massive orange tapestry hanging on the wall behind where the receptionist sat. The company had come a long way since 1877, when the first Georges André, aged 21, set up a wholesale store in Nyon on Switzerland's Lake Geneva to sell flour, dried vegetables and pasta under the name of his father, a wealthy watch assembler. He used his father's money for the venture and called the company H. André & Fils.

André & Cie was always a family business, with the major part of its capital in the hands of the founding family and related families. Successive generations of the André family have always carried out the main managing functions of the group. Elected president in 1940, it was Georges A. André (1906–1997), the fourth generation of the company, who is credited for building the company to be one of the five top agricultural merchants in the world.

In 1941, Georges André also established a separate shipping venture under the name *Suisse–Atlantique*. The venture was a success, and when I visited their office in 1995, the company owned 12 ships and had another 50 on time charter. Suisse–Atlantique was to play a crucial (non-)role in the demise of André et Cie five years later.

Working with his brother Jean, Georges built the company to a size where it was physically shipping around 25 million tonnes of grain per year. Including all the trading around those shipments, the figure would have been closer to 75 million tonnes. Concerning volume, André & Cie was probably number two at the time, though still quite a way behind Cargill at number one. Even so, they were ahead of Bunge and Dreyfus.

Through his contacts in the U.S.S.R., Georges André had quickly realised that the U.S.S.R. would become a major grain importer in the 1970s. André & Cie were long of physical grains going into the Russian purchases and made a colossal amount of money when grain prices exploded.

The family was – and still is – a deeply Christian one, and faith has always played a major part in the way they conduct business. They are members of a religious group that closely follows the teaching of John Nelson Darby (1800–1882).

Darby was an Irish clergyman who left the clergy in 1831 to join an inter-denominational group of believers now known as the *Plymouth Brethren*. In 1848, the Brethren split into two: the *Open Brethren* and the *Exclusive Brethren*. Darby was recognised as the dominant figure among the *Exclusives*, which became known as the *Darbyite Brethren*. It is to this religious Christian group that the André family belongs.

In her book *Village of Secrets*, Caroline Moorhead writes extensively about the Darbyists and how they helped shelter Jewish refugees during the Second World War. She writes, 'The families didn't think of themselves and doing good. They did what they had always done, giving sanctuary to the persecuted'.

She also explains the Darbyists' reputation for secrecy and withdrawal from society: 'Since it was only possible to be a true Christian when living a life of faith, the solution was to have as little as possible to do with the ways of the world, which was seen as entirely evil'.

The faith taught frugality. The family's frugality meant that all profits were reinvested, rather than paid as dividends. This allowed the company to build significant reserves, helping the company during difficult times. However, it may have given the André family a false sense of security, discouraging them from diversifying or restructuring their activities in response to a changing trading environment.

The policy of reinvesting profits may also have encouraged the family to invest too heavily into flour and cotton mills in Argentina, where the company operated under the name *La Plata Cereal*. These investments turned dramatically sour and contributed to the company's later troubles.

The macro-environment during the early 1990s was a difficult one for agricultural commodity merchants. In many cases, margins were even negative. André & Cie was the second-most export-oriented grain company after Continental Grain, and low world grain prices, along with limited price volatility, created a challenging environment for the company's traders.

As the 1990s wore on, André & Cie sought profit opportunities outside their traditional geographies. When Continental Grain sold their trading operations to Cargill, André & Cie took on Conti's trading team in Italy to develop the local destination market. The team speculated heavily in the CBOT soybean options market, losing close to $100 million – money that André & Cie at that stage could ill afford to lose.

An ex-employee of André & Cie told me that taking on the Italian team had been controversial at the time. The company had by tradition only employed people directly from university or the Swiss apprenticeship system. Once one joined, the training was rigorous; it would usually take seven to ten years before one was allowed to conduct a trade.

However, as the pressure on physical trading margins continued, André & Cie tried to boost their talent pool by taking on experienced traders from outside the company. To attract new talent, the company had to pay high salaries, and this resulted in the 'outsiders' being paid more than traders who had been trained internally. This resulted in jealousies between trading desks, and the working environment deteriorated. The André-trained traders viewed the outsiders as mercenaries, only interested in short-term profits to boost their end-of-year bonuses.

Meanwhile, André & Cie also had problems in Spain, where they had taken a 49 percent holding in a trading and transport conglomerate by name of *Trans Africa*. The conglomerate owned SOCIMER, a small bank headquartered in Geneva. Without informing the André family, SOCIMER bought a bank in Argentina called MEDEFIN that had fallen into bankruptcy. The Argentinean bank's losses spiralled out of control, and SOCIMER tried to hide the losses using client deposits.

The Spanish authorities pursued fraud charges against the André family after the bank collapsed, and it took ten years of legal proceedings to find the family completely innocent of any wrongdoing.

By that time, André & Cie was already suffering from crippling losses on their Argentinean operations. In the preceding half-century, Argentina's government had at various times imposed draconian foreign exchange controls that had made it impossible for foreign companies to repatriate profits. André & Cie had invested their profits in large-scale industrial operations, primarily in soybean crushing and cotton milling. By the end of the 1990s, these investments were losing money and were a real burden on the company.

The company suffered not only from problems caused by recession, devaluation and government intervention in Argentina, but also to a lesser extent in Brazil. André's activities were heavily slanted towards South America and the Former Soviet Union; the two areas represented two-thirds of the company's capital and half of its sales.

André & Cie was particularly exposed to currency devaluations. Until 1998, finance managers at the big trading companies commonly borrowed in Swiss francs or U.S. dollars, taking advantage of low interest rates. They then loaned these sums in local currencies at high interest rates to companies in developing countries. The company lost money when governments devalued their local currencies; the higher local interest rates that had once seemed so attractive failed to compensate for the losses incurred through the devaluation.

When I visited their offices in 1996, André & Cie had working capital of around U.S. $2 billion, most of it loaned in some sort of financing.

Adding to their difficulties, when grain prices rose at the end of the 1990s, the company had to pay enormous variation margins against their short hedges on the futures exchanges. André & Cie was primarily an origination company: they bought grains and other commodities from producers and then hedged their price risk by selling equivalent quantities on the futures exchanges. When commodity prices increased, the exchanges called for variation margin money to guarantee those short positions.

By the end of the decade, the situation was dire; in 1999, André & Cie lost 285 million Swiss francs (CHF). The company had little choice but to go through a major restructuring, cutting a large portion of their trading staff. However, it was 'too little, too late'. By the end of 2000, the company had equity of CHF 19 million and was losing CHF 6 million each month.

The Swiss bank UBS had an outstanding loan to André & Cie of $98 million that came to maturity in December 2000. Given the company's working capital of around $2 billion, the amount was relatively small. However, UBS used the maturing loan to try to force the family to merge the two sides of their businesses, trading and shipping. Although the trading company was losing money, freight rates were strong, and the shipping company was profitable. In addition, the ships that the company owned were extremely valuable. UBS wanted those ships as collateral for their loan and made the merger a condition for its renewal.

The family insisted on keeping Suisse–Atlantique separate. They felt that they had already lost enough on the trading side and that the risk/reward ratio of the trading business did not justify their risking even more of their net worth. UBS called in the loan. On 20 January 2001, André & Cie went into bankruptcy proceedings, and the Swiss authorities appointed a liquidator.

The company sold La Plata Cereal, its Argentinean operations, during the liquidation process to Bunge for $70 million. At the time, some analysts estimated the Argentinean business to be worth twice that.

It took more than ten years for the liquidator to fully wind up the company, but the André family made sure that all obligations were met in full, even using family money to pay employees' redundancy payments over and above legal minimums. Once everything was wound down, all creditors were paid in full. There was even money left over for shareholders.

All this begs the question regarding whether André & Cie could have been kept going. I have asked that question to several of the company's ex-employees, and the answer is always the same. 'The company could probably have been restructured and kept going, but the family no longer believed in the business. Their hearts were no longer in it'.

Some argue that the André family is financially better off now because of exiting trading operations, as their freight operations have been profitable over the years. Others disagree. By exiting grain merchandising when they did, the André family missed the agricultural commodity super cycle that began in 2004.

I can't help but feel that it wasn't just a question of whether the family wanted to keep the business going; there was also the question of whether they had the managerial and strategic skills to keep it going. The agricultural trading business is now very different from when André & Cie was in business. Would the company – and particularly the family – have been able to adapt?

Georges André, the third-generation president of the firm, officially retired in 1986 when his son Henri took over as president. However, Georges remained a presence in the company until well after his retirement. Georges couldn't – or wouldn't – let go. Some of the people who worked there then told me Georges didn't have confidence in Henri; he felt that his son didn't have the drive to do what was necessary to keep the company relevant in a changing macro-environment.

Henri felt hamstrung by George's presence and delivered a damning verdict on his father. 'As long as he was in charge', he said, 'we really had to abandon any ideas of restructuring the group. For him, restructuring meant abandoning a part of what he and his father had built up'.

We will never know who was right: father or son. Georges André died in 1997, when it was probably too late for Henri to make the necessary changes to the business. But at least the father wasn't around to see the end of the company that he had worked all his life to build. Nor did he see the 'A' of ABCD replaced by ADM, a company whose European headquarters is based in Rolle, just a little further along the shores of Lake Geneva.

All in the Family - Riccardo and Emanuele Ravano

Riccardo and Emanuele are President and CEO, respectively, of IFCHOR, an international ship broking company based in Lausanne, Switzerland, with a network of 12 offices in the Asia–Pacific, Europe, Middle East and the USA. I asked Riccardo, the founder of the company, how it all began. He answered:

I come from a ship owning family. I started in the shipping business in 1964 at the age of 20, in Genoa, Italy. At that time, the family still owned some tankers, but I had sold them by 1972. Over the first ten years in business, I developed quite a sizable chartering company.

In the 1970s, politics in Italy began to get really bad, even dangerous. Many of my clients began to move abroad, and in 1976, I decided to follow them. I looked originally at Monaco and then at Geneva. I had a friend who told me that there was a one-room office for rent in his building in Lausanne. I took it.

I started on my own at first with a secretary – who by the way is still with the company, 42 years later! Over the years, we expanded from one room to two floors, … but we remained in the same building!

When I moved to Lausanne, I told our lawyer that I wanted to call the company *ISCHOR*, an acronym for *Italo-Swiss Chartering Organisation*, but either he or the Chamber of Commerce misread my handwriting and registered the company as *IFCHOR*. I was initially surprised to discover that the company's name was IFCHOR, but I was too busy to change it – and the name stuck! We still have a branch office in Genoa.

And Manu, when did you join?

Ours is a family business, so I joined when I was born! I officially started working in 2002, just before the freight super cycle, which lasted about five years, between 2003 and 2008. This was when China decided to boost its production of steel to a level that nobody could even have imagined. To make steel, you need iron ore and coal. The freight market went into a bonanza period.

By the time I joined, IFCHOR had already grown, and we employed 30 to 40 people on the fifth floor of this building. The company was especially active in the Panamax sector, which is still today the most liquid market in dry bulk. Grains are a big component of the Panamax market. There are coal trades, along with minor ones such as bauxite or other ores, but grain is the most important. IFCHOR built its name and expertise in the Panamax market.

How big is the company today?

Today, we're about 180 people around the world. I would say we do between 3,000 and 4,000 transactions a year throughout our various offices and segments. We've never calculated the number of tonnes that equates to, but perhaps we should. It could be good marketing!

Is S&P (sales and purchase) brokerage a big part of your business?
We're fairly active in Greece and in Japan, but we don't view it as one of our core businesses. It currently represents between 5 and 10 percent of group revenues. However, we're looking at how to grow that in the years to come.

Riccardo, what are your other sons doing?
I wanted my sons to gain experience in a big company before joining me in the family business. So I said to them, 'Go out, see what others are doing, and then come back with a different view on the business'.

One of my four sons began his career with André. When André went bankrupt, he moved to Bunge. Another son started with Tradigrain, which has now become Quadra, where he's Head of Freight and a partner.

My third son isn't involved in the business. Manu was the only son to join the family business, and he was the one who hadn't seen anything else! The other two sons never came back!

So two sons went to work in shipping for trading companies. Do the big trade houses each have a shipping department?
All of them do. Over the years, they've developed bigger and bigger departments. Forty years ago, they might have had one guy chartering vessels on a voyage basis, but now they all have separate departments with P&Ls that can reach tens of millions of dollars.

The trading companies developed their freight activities around their grain needs. They wanted to better control their supply chains, while making money in a market that's separate from the commodity.

This has allowed them greater flexibility. Forty years ago, they might sell a cargo to China and then look for a ship to transport it. Now, they can be short or long on tonnage and take positions. It's become a trading market.

Do the trade houses own their own ships?
The big trade houses have been in and out of owning ships, but they're mostly out now. They prefer to charter rather than to own, and they're mostly active on a time charter, rather than a voyage basis.

Manu, that's one big change in the past 40 years. Are there others?

The most important change in the past 40 years has been the development of the market in forward freight agreements (FFAs). These now trade every day in thousands of lots, allowing operators to hedge their freight needs. The FFA market has traditionally been an OTC (over-the-counter) market, where counterparties enter into direct agreements with each other. It's still an OTC market, but since the crash of 2008, all FFAs are cleared either in London or Singapore.

Could you tell me a little about what happened in 2008?

Freight rates collapsed. Panamax time charter rates fell from $70,000 per day to $7,000 per day. People hadn't realised how volatile freights could be, and a number of shipping and FFA-trading companies went into bankruptcy.

FFAs are closely linked to the physical shipping business. It's the physical shipping market that determines the FFA prices, not the other way around.

IFCHOR was one of the first companies to broker FFAs in 1999, and we remained active until 2010, when we decided to focus our attention on the physical market. We keep in close contact with the FFA brokers, and we have a broker screen in our office. There are a lot of FFA traders that have no physical presence, and they like to talk to us about the physical market. We get information in exchange, and we probably know the forward curves even better than if we were brokering the market ourselves.

Are hedge funds active in the FFA market?

There aren't many, but the ones that are tend to be very active. Aside from FFAs, hedge funds have an estimated $5 to $6 billion invested in shipping companies. This was at one stage quite negative for the market because it exacerbated the oversupply situation.

Riccardo, are the grain-trading companies very active in FFAs?

In the FFA market, everyone is watching what the big trading companies are doing. If Cargill makes a big grain sale, they might come into the FFA market to hedge their freight exposure. Everyone is looking at Cargill, and if they buy in volume, other participants may say, 'Wow, Cargill is bullish; we'd better buy as well!' But their activity isn't based on an opinion, but on a need.

Does the Baltic Exchange still have a role?

Forty years ago, the Baltic Exchange was the centre of world shipping. It's now owned by SGX, which clears FFAs, but the Baltic doesn't itself clear FFAs. I would say that the Baltic Exchange's main role is in constructing the indices against which the FFAs trade. They have some reporters who talk to the main brokers (like us) to ascertain rates. In this way, the indices are independent and the most important reference for shipping rates worldwide.

A lot of ships are now time-chartered on floating rates at plus or minus the Baltic indices. The indices are credible.

Who owns the ships?
I haven't seen the latest statistics, but I'd say today that the Chinese and the Greeks own around half of the dry bulk ships. The Scandinavians are still a large presence. But honestly, it's difficult to say. You have Greek owners living in Monaco and Belgian owners living in Singapore.

Manu, in grain, how much is shipped in Panamaxes (vessels that carry on average 60,000 tonnes and can transit the Panama canal), and how much in Handymaxes (vessels that can carry less than 60,000 tonnes)?'
I'd say two-thirds in Panamaxes. Local trades from the Black Sea are in Handymaxes, but the big shipments to China are done in Panamaxes or slightly larger ships (so-called Post-Panamaxes). Capes (that can carry as much as 150,000 tonnes) are totally out.

There are two criticisms of the sugar industry –
You mean, *shipping industry*.

Sorry, yes, the shipping industry! After 40 years in sugar, the word has become hardwired into my brain! One of the criticisms of the shipping industry is that the vessels are operated under flags of convenience.
In the past, these criticisms may have been valid, but the situation has changed significantly in the past 40 years. Although shipping is still a relatively unregulated market, it's getting better, cleaner, more structured and more transparent than in the past. Ship owners can't just do what they want; they have to comply with various rules, for example the International Trade Federation rules or their equivalent.

There's also the IMO, the International Maritime Organization, a United Nations agency with responsibility for the safety and security of shipping and the prevention of marine and atmospheric pollution by ships. There's also RightShip, a private company which works with owners and charterers to make sure that ships are well maintained, environmentally sound, and crews are well looked after.

There are other organisations, such as the Sailors Society, which help the life of seafarers and which are supported by owners and charterers.

Owners understand that shipping is their main resource and it's in their interest for their ships to be well maintained and for their crews to be well treated. However, what ship owners do to fiscally optimise their businesses is not something we can judge. People will always fiscally optimise their businesses if they can, whether it's in shipping or in other sectors.

When it comes to GHG emissions, shipping transports 90 percent of the goods in the world. Simultaneously, the sector burns only 7 percent of global oil consumption. Shipping globally contributes only 3 percent of the GHG emissions in the world.

Recently, the IMO took a major step to implement – as of January 2020 – new regulations to ensure a targeted 20 to 30 percent reduction in GHG emissions, to be achieved principally through the use of low-sulphur fuel.

To comply with the regulations, some owners have decided to invest in scrubbers to scrub sulphur from the high-sulphur fuel, reducing the emissions in that way. The sulphur still needs to be evacuated, but I understand that it's environmentally neutral for it to be put into the sea. I'm personally not convinced that scrubbing is a long-term solution.

Do you think that cargo ships will one day once again have sails?

They may, but I think a more likely transition will be to hybrid electric engines, as in the car industry.

Riccardo, what about LNG: is it an alternative?

There's a lot of discussion at the moment around LNG-fuelled ships, but for the moment, the technology is pricey and difficult to justify economically. Some charterers may be willing to pay more to charter LNG-fuelled ships for environmental reasons, but trading margins are currently so thin that it's unlikely that trading companies could do so and remain competitive. There's also a question of LNG supply at the ports. It isn't easy to organise globally. There's a risk of LNG-fuelled ships being stranded.

So, Manu, what's the solution?

I think it will be a contribution of many things. There might be some sails that work. There might be some solar power as well. There might be some electric contribution to the engine. It will be an evolution that will take another 10 to 15 years before we reach a point of having the right mixture of technology.

What's the average lifespan of a ship?

That's another thing that has changed significantly over the past 40 years. When my father started in the business, the average lifespan of a cargo vessel was 25 to 30 years. Today, it's more like 15 years, especially when you look at all the new regulations coming.

I'm currently working a ship that's 15 years old, and I'm having difficulty in chartering it. BHP Billiton has said that they're not comfortable chartering ships that are older than 12 years, although they might in exceptional circumstances. Other charterers will soon follow their example. Cargill, for example doesn't set age limitations on their vessels, but when you approach them with a ship over 15 years old, they'll only charter it if they have no choice.

Remember, though, some ships are well maintained and safe for carrying grain, even at 25 years old. Others are less well maintained and are a problem at 12 years old. We know which ships are well maintained and which ones aren't.

Riccardo, where do ships go to be scrapped?

It depends on the local price of scrap metal, but now, it's mainly to Bangladesh and India. Turkey has traditionally scrapped vessels, but the price of scrap metal in the country has recently fallen to $150 to $200 per tonne. In Bangladesh, scrap metal trades close to $400 per tonne. That's a big difference.

Containers have been one of the biggest revolutions in shipping in the last 40 years. Has that revolution affected the grain industry?

Not really, although I did see a tender yesterday to ship 50,000 tonnes of wheat, and I was surprised to see a container company winning it. I would've thought that bulk would have been cheaper, but with the container industry structurally oversupplied, owners are sometimes desperate for cargo, especially on return trips.

If you produce wheat in the north of Italy and you sell it to a consumer in central China, containers might make sense. When you ship in bulk, you handle the commodity a number of times: you transport it to the port. You load it on the ship. You unload it at destination, and then you transfer it to the final buyer. With containers, you stuff the container at origin, and the commodity stays in the container right through to the end destination.

Although containers may sometimes have advantages, dry bulk will remain the usual and cheaper shipping method for grain.

Manu, how's the current market?

Panamax rates today from Santos, Brazil, to China are around $40 per tonne. That voyage rate peaked in 2008 at around $70 per tonne. It fell to around $15 to $16 per tonne and hung around the low twenties for a few years. It has now risen to $28 to $30 per tonne.

For the Capesize vessels that can carry 150,000 tonnes, the Brazil-to-China rate peaked in 2008 at around $100 per tonne, but it then fell to as low as $8 to $9 per tonne in 2015–16. To cover running costs, owners need $16–18,000 per day, pending the financing of the ship. Now they're earning $28,000 to $29,000 per day. The owners are comfortable at this level, covering both variable costs and depreciation. We've recovered from the crisis years of 2015 and 2016 when rates were very low, forcing owners to renegotiate their debt or massively reinvest in their businesses.

Where's innovation likely to come from in the future in the industry?

Shipping is facing the same challenges as those faced by commodities. Technology has made communication fast and seamless in both chartering and trading. This has led to thinner margins. As a result, traders are seeking economies of scale, and shipping is evolving with bigger and bigger ships. Port infrastructure is also adapting to accommodate these bigger ships. I wouldn't say it's a challenge. It's a reality. We have to adapt to a world that's faster and bigger.

Thank you, Riccardo and Emanuele, for your time and input.

Chapter Eight: Continental Grain

'You have to constantly reinvent yourself if you want to be successful. At CGC, we've been doing that for over 200 years'. Paul Fribourg (1)

Simon Fribourg founded what later became the Continental Grain Company in Arlon, France (now Belgium), in 1813. The company began as local grain merchants, mainly brokers.

Trading companies often thrive when markets and trade flows are disrupted in some way, and the Fribourg family's first big break occurred in 1848, when Belgium was hit by famine following the failure of the local harvest. According to company legend, Simon Fribourg's son Michel travelled to Bessarabia (now Romania) with sacks of gold, where he bought surplus grain to be shipped back home.

During the 1930s, the company made significant investments in inland grain terminals, port depots and storage facilities throughout the U.S., placing them second to Cargill in terms of origination. This gave Continental a huge advantage once the Second World War was over, enabling the company to prosper during the relatively quiet grain trading years of the 1950s and 1960s. When the Soviet Union's wheat harvest failed in 1964, Continental Grain became the first U.S. firm to export grain to the U.S.S.R, selling the bloc one million tonnes of wheat and rice.

After announcing the $80 million sale, Mr. Fribourg said, 'Anybody can get grain to sell to the Soviet Union. Our business is basically built on ideas and imagination'. The deal, he said, showed that international trade could open channels that diplomacy alone could not – and that trade could also spur economic development in nations. (2)

The profits from the sale allowed the family to begin a programme of diversification that, by 1972, was beginning to attract media attention. The magazine *Business Week* dedicated a cover story to the company, writing, 'There are at least 100 companies under the Fribourg corporate umbrella, and new ventures in many new markets are being added regularly'.

However, Michel Fribourg still had the trader DNA – and he 'felt the Soviet Union would one day be forced to resume its imports of U.S. grain'. (3) He was proved right when the U.S.S.R. came in for two waves of major purchases of grain in the 1970s. However, all did not go well for Continental Grain during this period: even though the company was well tuned into the Soviet buying programme, they underestimated its depth.

In 1975, Continental sold 4.5 million tonnes of corn and 1.1 million tonnes of barley to the U.S.S.R. The company's traders sold short, anticipating a good U.S. harvest and expecting prices to fall before the grain had to be delivered. However, the Soviets continued to buy, and Continental ended up covering its short position at peak prices just as the market began to slide down again. When the Soviets came back for a second round of purchases, Continental declined to offer.

The company did continue to diversify, and by the time Dan Morgan published *The Merchants of Grain*, Continental was already a conglomerate with diversified businesses throughout the food supply chain. But Continental was not just investing in companies; they were also trading them, always looking for undervalued companies to redress and resell.

During the 1980s, Continental Grain remained a major player in the global grain trade, but they continued to diversify. The company also began to open up and become less secretive. In 1982, they established an independent Board of Directors, adding Henry Kissinger as a founding member.

Not everything they touched turned to gold. They had set up a subsidiary to trade in the financial markets. The company, Contifinancial, was publicly traded, but with about 75 percent owned by Continental Grain. It primarily provided commercial and residential mortgages and home equity loans – what we now call the *sub-prime market*. Continental Grain did what it could to make a success of the business, including many capital injections, but the company eventually filed for bankruptcy in May 2001. (4)

In 1997, after being with the company since 1976, Michel Fribourg's son Paul was named Chairman and CEO, becoming the sixth generation of the Fribourg family to lead Continental Grain. He had been looking for a solution for the grain business for a while, initially seeking a partner. He failed to find one and quickly decided his best option was to sell the business to Cargill.

At that time, Cargill handled about 20 percent of the U.S.'s grain exports, and Continental Grain handled about 15 percent. However, Cargill had an advantage in having mills and plants to process grains into meals, flours and oils, expanding its sales opportunities and improving its overall profit margins. Consequently, as the *New York Times* reported at the time, 'Continental Grain has been left as a middleman, buying, storing and selling grain on increasingly narrow spreads'. (5)

Because of the sale, Continental Grain freed up the huge amounts of working capital that were tied up in its grain inventories. This allowed them to better support their other businesses, among them financial services and livestock, where it was the nation's leading cattle feeder.

For Cargill, not only did the transaction take out a major competitor, but it also combined Continental Grain's six export terminals, 27 river terminals and 32 buying stations with their own 65 U.S. grain-handling facilities and 19 overseas elevators. *The New York Times* quoted an analyst from Prudential Securities as saying, 'They were always a large trader. Now they're a monster trader'.

The terms of the deal were not disclosed. *The New York Times* gave an estimate of $300 million, but the *Wall Street Journal* talked of a price of more than $1 billion, once the assumption of debt was included.

I remember asking one of the Cargill team that had been involved in the transaction what they had learned from the acquisition. 'We learned a lot about customers', he replied. 'Continental looked after their customers better than we did at the time; we tended to be more transactional. Because of the purchase, we completely rethought the way we treated our customers. This was a positive result of the transaction, perhaps even more so than the logical assets and the trading teams that we had bought. It really helped us in growing our business'.

But what did Michel, Paul's father (who died 10 April 2001), think about the company getting out of the grain trade, the business that he had cherished and built?

As discussions of the sale of the trading arm to Cargill evolved, Paul Fribourg and a team of advisers flew to Switzerland, where his father was vacationing, to present the company's options.

The father, after listening to debates over the company's direction, uncertain state of the grain market and significance of leaving behind so much of his family's heritage, asked only one question: 'What about the people? Will they be able to find jobs?' (6)

When he was convinced that there would be ample work for talented traders, Michel Fribourg gave his assent. 'It was never, for him, about making money', Paul Fribourg recalled. 'It was the people'.

Once the sale was complete, ContiGroup continued to expand into agribusinesses around the world, operating each as a standalone business. The company's website now reads,

Continental Grain continues to focus on building businesses that can deliver innovation, high performance, and long-term value creation in the food and agriculture sectors. Recent venture capital investments in sustainable food technology include Impossible Foods, creator of a 'meaty-tasting' plant-based burger, and Modern Meadow, which grows cell-based leather.

And thus ended the two-hundred-year history of Continental's involvement in the international grain business. Or did it?

Somewhere along the lines, the company quietly changed its name back from ContiGroup Company to Continental Grain Company (keeping the same initials). Meanwhile, Bunge is among the investments highlighted on Continental Grain's website. Paul Fribourg is a member of Bunge's Board of Directors and was recently appointed to Bunge's strategic review committee to study options for the company.

Playing for Barcelona – Ivo Sarjanovic

Ivo A. Sarjanovic was Vice President of Cargill Switzerland where he performed a variety of executive roles including World Soybeans Manager, Business Unit Leader of Middle East and Africa, and Business Unit Leader of Sugar. He was also CEO of Alvean, the joint venture between Cargill and Copersucar. As well as serving as a non-executive director on a number of boards, he also teaches 'Agricultural Commodities' at the University of Geneva in Switzerland and Di Tella University and Austral University in Argentina.

Could you please tell me a little about your background and how you got into the business?
I studied accountancy in university, but I was fascinated by economics. I was planning on an academic career; I wanted to be a teacher, a professor. After I finished my studies in Rosario, I won a place at New York University to do a PhD in Economics, but for personal and other reasons, I had to go back to Argentina and start working.

My great-grandfather, along with others from Croatia, immigrated to Argentina in the late nineteenth century. In 1903, with two partners, they built silos in the south of Santa Fe province around Rosario and started a business storing and selling grain. When I talked with my father's partner about joining the business, he told me that I was welcome to, but I had to be ready to work for almost nothing for two years. So instead, I joined Cargill.

My father was supportive but intrigued about my decision. The family company viewed the international grain traders with suspicion. I was used to hearing that the exporters were only middlemen that added no value, and like you, I had a hard time convincing them otherwise!

I joined Cargill in July 1989, the month when Argentina suffered its highest rate of domestic price inflation ever: 197 percent in a single month! Between the day I joined and the moment I received my first paycheck, my salary had tripled. We were paid twice a month, but when we went to the shops, we still couldn't afford to buy anything. It was terrible!

After working in Buenos Aires and São Paulo, Cargill transferred me to Geneva in 1993 as a wheat trader. In late 1994, Cargill asked me to join the soybean desk. I started as a junior trader and worked my way up to become head of the desk, a position I kept from 2001 to 2011.

I was in charge of Cargill's worldwide activities in soybeans, including the coordination of crushing activities. It was a role that combined international trading with the strategic side of the business, so it was super interesting. I loved it!

So you were head of the bean desk through the whole of the super cycle?

I first visited China in 1997 when they were buying almost no beans at all. Twenty years later, they're importing 85 to 90 million tonnes each year, which is roughly 60 percent of the world's total. Each year, it was our job to try and figure out how much they'd buy; it was a really difficult task. There was a lot of uncertainty around their imports, and this led to a lot of volatility in the market.

Although Chinese import demand was the primary driver of that agricultural super cycle, there were two others. Biofuels played an important role; we saw significant supply being diverted from feed to fuel.

The financialisation of commodities also played a significant role, with investment and pension funds entering our markets to diversify their portfolios from equities and bonds. That brought a lot of money into markets that were much smaller than the financial markets that they were used to trading in. One day, you'd wake to find that a fund had decided to allocate one or two percent of their portfolio into agriculture, and their buying would push the market higher, if only for the day. Their actions added to short-term volatility.

All of this created tremendous opportunities for the desk. I was lucky to be there at that time – and to have had the right experience and the right team to enjoy it. For me, it was like playing football for Barcelona in La Liga.

What was Cargill's share of the world soybean trade at that time?

We had maybe 15 percent. The business was extremely competitive, but not only among the big trading houses. Chinese companies soon started to buy soybeans directly from the origins and trade them to destination. I remember participating in one buying tender where I was horrified to see 20 different companies competing to sell. All the prices were closely aligned. The price range was extremely narrow. All the trading companies were pricing their offers in the same way.

Was it possible to make a margin on physical transactions at that time?

Rarely: margins were thin. Traders were often willing to discount the C&F prices to put on short positions on the freight or on the flat price or the premiums. Beans sometimes traded in negative territory. It was, and still is, almost impossible to make a return trading from FOB to C&F.

Who were the main buyers in China: were they state-run or private?

We sold initially to COFCO and other state-run provincial entities, but local private buyers quickly became more active. In addition, the international traders began to build their own soybean crushing plants within China, so they'd then sell their beans to themselves. It was a bit of everything.

Did you ever have any big defaults?

There was a massive default in April–May 2004. It was the worst experience of my professional career. It became known as the 'Red Soybeans Crisis'. Brazilian soybeans destined for seeds, for replanting, are sometimes coloured red. The Chinese claimed they found some of these red beans in cargos arriving in their ports and refused to let them into the country, declaring that the cargos were out of specification.

We had to divert some boats. It cost the industry a fortune; most of the sellers lost money. Soybean prices and premiums collapsed, as did freight rates. Some traders argued that the Chinese defaulted because they had overbought, but I don't know if that was the case.

My management within Cargill was extremely supportive; there was no blaming. Everyone worked together to try and sort it out as best we could. But it was no fun.

Talking of Cargill, you were with them when they acquired Continental's grain business in 2000.

I wasn't involved in the acquisition, but I was involved in the integration of Conti's activities and people.

Cargill bought the business at just the right time, at the bottom of the previous cycle, and we'd fully merged the two businesses in time for the super cycle that kicked off a few years later. It was a win for Cargill, but it was also a win for Continental, because it freed up capital that they could invest in other businesses.

I believe that Continental's management was keen to get into businesses that were less cyclical. They could've kept the grain operations, but they would've needed to constantly invest large sums just to keep up. They probably decided that they could get better returns, with less risk, elsewhere.

How did the acquisition benefit Cargill?

There was severe overcapacity in the sector in the 1990s, and the acquisition helped to reduce that overcapacity. It specifically helped Cargill to better manage their assets. The extra storage allowed us to better meet the growing demand at that time for identity-preserved products. And of course, by taking on their teams, we benefitted from introducing a new culture to the company. That's always a good thing!

In 2011, you moved within Cargill from beans to sugar. What prompted that move?

I'd been in soybeans for almost 20 years, and I wanted a change. I also wanted to have a position that was more managerial, more asset-based and less trading-oriented. Becoming head of Cargill's Sugar Division was a perfect opportunity for me. I jumped at the chance.

What are the main differences between the sugar and the soybean markets?

The biggest difference is the delivery mechanism. Sugar trading revolves around the delivery process against the futures market, especially the optionality that you have between different origins. Sugar is a genuine 'world' contract, as opposed to a 'domestic' one. Sugar trading revolves far more around the spreads and the differentials and less on the flat price. As a consequence, the spreads and premiums behave differently. It took me a while to come to grips with that.

What was a surprise was that physical margins were even worse in sugar than they were in beans. Traders are even more willing to discount physical prices to put on a short sales book to end destination.

In terms of origination, sugar is completely different from soybeans. Unfortunately, the grain trading companies hadn't realised this when they invested so heavily in Brazil's sugarcane sector. It was a huge misjudgement.

When you run a sugar mill, your area of sugarcane origination is strictly limited. In soybeans, you have a much bigger area; you can build a huge plant in a port and draw in beans from an ample geographical area. It's uneconomical to move cane over large distances, so your economies of scale are less. Origination is much harder in sugarcane than in beans, and this usually forces you to grow your own cane. As we know, traders don't make good farmers. The grain trading companies viewed sugar mills in the same way as they viewed crushing plants, but they're very different. On top of this, the ethanol policies of the last decade punished the sector badly.

With the benefit of hindsight, the investment by the grain trading companies into the Brazilian cane sector has been the biggest destruction of value in the history of the grain business – billions of dollars.

After a few years of running Cargill's Sugar Division, you merged it into Alvean, a joint venture with Copersucar.

Alvean was probably the best idea I've ever had professionally, combining what at that time were the two biggest traders in a market that was desperate for consolidation. Cargill had the global trading expertise, while Copersucar had the origination infrastructure in Brazil. The combination was very strong. Karel Valken from Rabobank once described it as the Uber of the commodities business.

Moving on to your current position, you now act as an advisor to trading companies on risk management.

Risk management is a journey. We can only try for continual incremental improvements. Also, I don't think there is a definitive way to manage risk; different companies have different methods.

Thirty years ago, we managed risk in terms of the size of the position measured in tonnes. We then moved on to looking at the risk in monetary terms, the value. We then began to incorporate tools that were developed by the financial industry, such as daily value at risk, or DVAR, drawdowns and stress. We combine all these tools into what we call a *dashboard*, and then we try to find a balance, a way to combine each of the various legs, such as flat price, spreads, premiums and freight positions, within limits.

It was challenging at the beginning, but most people now realise that you can't trade if you don't use those tools. Without them, you may overtrade relative to your equity and run the risk of blowing up.

Could you explain how trading companies manage risk?

Commodity merchants measure risk in terms of DVAR, or daily value at risk – the amount of money they are risking on a daily basis. Risk managers in a company will look at historical price data to see how volatile prices have been in the past to estimate how volatile they'll be in the future. Given that DVAR is a backward-looking tool, you can complement the exercise by 'stressing' the position to see how prices might move in various scenarios, especially scenarios that are at either end of the distribution curve – events that we'd call a 'Black Swan'. The amount of risk that a trader or a department will be allowed to take will be limited by DVAR and stress limits.

This number is important for two reasons. First, a trader will be judged on what multiple of DVAR that he or she achieves. Good traders should achieve a multiple of six to seven times. Secondly, the amount of risk that a trading company takes is a function of their equity. In general, equity should be closely linked with the total amount of risk that the traders in the company are taking.

Does trading a number of different commodities reduce risk?

Yes and no. It depends on correlations and seasonality. Companies may be able to even out earnings by trading different commodities: wheat may make money one year, while corn or soybeans may make money another year.

Is there a temptation to take bigger risks when physical trading margins are under pressure?

Yes, traders can get frustrated and bored when markets are quiet and then turn their attention to speculation. This is why risk management is often even more important in quiet markets than in volatile ones. But companies know that. They've learnt their lessons.

Are computers now better traders than humans?

Algorithmic traders, or 'Algos', as we call them, now trade a big percentage of the daily volumes on the futures markets. Everyone says they are the future of trading, but I'm not convinced. Considering the volumes that they trade on commodities, they don't seem to be making much money. I sometimes feel that people exaggerate the success that the algos have on the markets.

I'm quite sceptical of this. Perhaps they make money in the financial markets where you have more variables and therefore more complexity, but I don't see it happening in commodities in a structural way. Nobody seems to make money trading these days. This is valid for humans and robots. But technology could give a false sense of comfort in this area. Where I do see big room for data crunching is around processes and continuous improvement.

How much of an edge does a physical trading activity give you when trading futures?
Much less today than in the past: information is democratised and instant. Having said that, being in the physical business allows you to trade the basis, the spread between the price of the physical commodity and the price of the futures. You can't do that if you're in a hedge fund without access to the timely information of physical flows.

Having a global footprint helps, as does experience. Information itself is not the most important. What is important is how you interpret that information. But the value of the physical footprint and how big you need to be to get a return is certainly challenged today.

I get the impression that competition among physical traders is greater now than it has ever been.
I think that it's interesting to remember that now, when we're again talking about the need to consolidate the industry to restore margins. When Cargill acquired Conti's grain business, the consolidation helped improve margins for a while, but new entrants quickly came in. The sector is now as competitive, or even more competitive, than it has ever been. Part of the problem is that the cost of entry is quite small relative to other industries. It never ends!

We've recently seen Chinese state-owned COFCO entering the business, as well as the Russian state-owned VTB bank, even if on a more local scale. How do you view that state involvement?
Those companies have an advantage when geopolitics becomes important. This is the case now with the U.S. trade war with China. In addition, state-owned companies can operate on a more long-term basis, compared to a publicly quoted company, such as ADM or Bunge, that are judged on every quarter. These two elements give state-owned companies an advantage in certain circumstances.

COFCO is a global player, but will VTB originate outside the Black Sea? A narrow geography will put them at a disadvantage to the global trading companies.

Do you think that the current U.S. trade war with China will have a lasting effect on trade flows?
Yes, the Chinese will want to diversify their import origins and rely less on the U.S.

As for trading, the trade war has been accompanied by what I call bad volatility – in effect, volatility that can't be predicted. We all put a huge effort into following weather patterns, predicting crops and buying rounds, but no one can predict what President Trump will tweet tomorrow. This political volatility has resulted in trading companies reducing their risk exposure, and this is obviously affecting their profitability.

Is there anything that you'd like to add?
The grain trading companies are going through a difficult period, but that shouldn't put anyone off from joining the business. I've had – and I still have – a fascinating career in the markets, and I'd recommend any young person join the sector.

In addition to my current work, I've finally got around to doing what I had always wanted to do, and that's teach. I currently give courses on agricultural commodities at the master's level at the University of Geneva, as well as at the universities of Buenos Aires and Rosario in Argentina. I love teaching young people about our business and sharing my enthusiasm for the business with them.

Jonathan, you and I are similar in two ways. We both failed to convince our fathers of the value added by agricultural commodity merchants. And we both ended up doing what we had planned to do: you writing – and me teaching!

Thank you, Ivo, for your time and input!

Chapter Nine: Archer Daniels Midland

"Free trade in the food industry is essential." Juan Luciano – CEO (1)

The subtitle to Dan Morgan's book The Merchants of Grain is *"The Power and Profits of the Five Giant Companies at the Centre of the World's Food Supply."* Back in 1979, the five companies he referred to were André, Bunge, Cargill, Continental and Dreyfus. Archer Daniels Midland Company barely got a mention in Dan Morgan's book, and then only in a footnote describing payments made to U.S. President Nixon at around the time of the Watergate scandal.

Today, 40 years later, ADM stands second among the giants of the grain business with annual revenues in excess of $60 billion, a market capitalisation of more than $20 billion, and profits that in 2018 touched as much as $2 billion. Publicly listed on the NYSE since 1924, the company has 40,000 employees serving nearly 200 countries, 450 crop procurement locations and 330 food and feed ingredient manufacturing facilities. (2) ADM processes as much as 60 million tonnes of agricultural commodities each year.

The history of ADM (3) (4) goes back to 1902, when John W. Daniels founded the Daniels Linseed Company in Minneapolis, Minnesota. The company opened its first mill in 1903 to crush flaxseed to produce linseed oil, which at that time was used primarily as a drying oil in paint. The company soon became America's leading crusher of flaxseed.

George A. Archer, who owned half the company, became director and vice president in 1905 and the company's name was changed to Archer-Daniels Linseed Company. In 1923 the firm merged with the Midlands Linseed Products Company to form Archer Daniels Midland Company.

The company expanded steadily over the years, both geographically and across commodities. By the time ADM celebrated its 50th anniversary in 1952, it was the largest soybean processor in the U.S. The company had no bank debt and had paid a dividend every year from 1927 onward.

However, uncertainty in the processing industry in first half of the 1960s reduced earnings for ADM. In 1966 the company recruited 48-year-old Dwayne O. Andreas and his brother Lowell to the leadership team.

Dwayne Andreas was born in Worthington, Minnesota in 1918, the fifth of six children. His father moved the family to Lisbon, Iowa, where he purchased a grain elevator and raised livestock on a small farm. Dwayne began working at the elevator when he was nine. He became CEO of ADM in 1970, and then chairman, a position he kept for nearly 30 years.

When Dwayne Andreas died in November 2016 in Decatur, Illinois at the age of 98, a New York Times obituary described him as *"an executive whose mastery of the global grain trade and the levers of political power turned the Archer Daniels Midland Company into a farm products giant and pushed it to the front ranks of American industry."* (6)

Under Andreas's leadership, ADM by 1979 was the second largest soybean crusher in both the U.S. and the world behind Cargill. It was also one of America's largest suppliers of basic foods.

The company's growth in oilseed processing continued into the 1980s. Soy products soon outstripped linseed and the others, earning Andreas the nickname 'Soybean King'. But the company also grew its corn division, producing ethanol in addition to high-fructose products.

ADM made its first-ever foray into consumer food products with the launch of its *Harvest Burger* brand soy-based meat substitute in the early 1990s. In a 1993 interview, Andreas called the development of the meat-like soy product *"the most important food development of this century."*

ADM reacted to the squeeze on profit margins in the 1990s by first consolidating existing businesses, and second by diversifying into new businesses. An example of the later was their entry into cocoa: by the end of the 1990s ADM was grinding 450,000 tonnes of cocoa beans per year, about 20 percent of the world crop.

Dwayne Andreas' nephew, G. Allen Andreas was named CEO of the company in April 1997, following the downfall of Michael D. Andreas, Dwayne's son and heir-apparent, in a highly publicized price-fixing scheme involving three products derived from corn: lysine (a livestock feed additive), high-fructose corn syrup, and citric acid. ADM pleaded guilty to two counts of fixing prices for lysine and for citric acid, and agreed to pay $100 million in fines, at that time by far the largest criminal antitrust settlement in history. In addition, the company paid another $100 million to settle lawsuits brought by customers and investors. Kurt Eichenwald described the episode in his 2000 book *The Informant*, which was later turned into a film directed by Steven Soderbergh and starring Matt Damon.

In 2009, ADM named Patricia Woertz as President and CEO of the company. She had previously spent 29 years at Chevron. Her appointment placed her as the top-ranking woman on the *Fortune 500's* list of top CEOs. *Forbes* ranked her as the 26th most powerful woman in the world.

In an interview with *Fortune Magazine*, Patricia Woertz described herself as an outsider at ADM: *"I'm outside the company, outside the industry, outside the family, outside the gender expectations."*

One of her more astute moves was to increase ADM's investments in Wilmar. The two companies' relationship dates back to their days operating soybean crushing joint ventures in China. In 2006, ADM exchanged its ownership shares in those joint ventures for a 10 percent ownership stake of Wilmar, and over the years has increased its shareholding to just short of 25 percent. (8) ADM views Wilmar as 'a strategic partner' in Asia, and ADM's chief financial officer is a board member of Wilmar.

Patricia Woertz also began the company's strategic shift in direction to enter the flavouring and health-conscious food sectors. In 2014 ADM made its biggest acquisition ever when it bought the Swiss-German natural ingredient company *WILD Flavors* for $3 billion. (9) The purchase gave ADM access to a variety of flavours, seasonings and colours derived from natural sources and used in processed foods and drinks.

Patricia Woertz retired in 2015, and Juan Ricardo Luciano took over as the company's new CEO, after having spent 25 years with Dow Chemicals. Since joining the company he has further developed ADM's strategy to build a global nutrition company offering a wide portfolio of food and beverage ingredients, flavours, and solutions. Luciano also moved the company out of sectors that he perceived to be low margin and slow growth; under his leadership, ADM shed its cocoa and chocolate businesses, and the company is currently looking for strategic alternatives for its ethanol dry mills.

Some argue that given the extent of this strategic and structural reorganisation ADM should no longer be categorised as a grain merchandising company. But then, it has always viewed its (huge) commodity trading operations as a service function to its industrial processing, rather than as a standalone operation.

Having said that, this view was challenged in early 2018 when it was reported that ADM was in merger talks with Bunge Ltd. The companies never confirmed that any conversations had occurred, but any such merger would have created an agricultural trading company that, at least in terms of revenue, would have approached the size of Cargill Inc. (10)

In an interview with Reuters in January 2019 (12), Luciano downplayed the merger talks, saying, *"I cannot run ADM and say Bunge is out there, oh, I never made an analysis of Bunge. Of course we do."* He explained that ADM has looked at other industry players, but that in the end the company had preferred to pursue growth in its nutrition business through smaller acquisitions and potential joint ventures.

"We feel we don't need that monster transformational transaction," he added. Acquiring Bunge would be *"a nice optimization but I have a lot of the things that Bunge has."*

The company's actions bear out that approach. Since the WILD acquisition, ADM has added a series of bolt-on acquisitions in the nutrition space, adding capabilities ranging from savory flavors to vanilla to citrus extracts. Today, ADM is a major player in fast-growing markets like alternative meats.

In 2017, the company entered the rapidly growing personalized nutrition space with the purchase of Spanish probiotic leader Biopolis; since then, through a series of partnerships and acquisitions, ADM has significantly expanded its ability to provide ingredients and supplements that can support health and wellness. And earlier this year, ADM purchased of global animal nutrition provider Neovia, announcing its commitment to leadership in that space.

As well as expanding into the new area of food ingredients, ADM has also expanded its footprint in sweeteners and starches through acquisitions and joint ventures in Bulgaria, Turkey, Hungary, Morocco, France and most recently Russia.

And it has expanded its global logistics chain, allowing it to deliver grain directly to customers in key markets, as opposed to port to port.

Today, more than 115 years after its founding, ADM is one of the world's largest agricultural processors, but even more, it sees itself as a global nutrition leader whose purpose is 'to unlock the power of nature to enrich the quality of life'. That's not bad going when you consider that the company hardly got a mention from Dan Morgan when he wrote *Merchants of Grain* 40 years ago!

Trading with a Purpose – Greg Morris

Greg Morris is president of ADM's Agricultural Services and Oilseeds business unit and is a member of the company's Executive Council. He has responsibility for the company's agricultural origination, global trading, transportation and oilseeds businesses.

Good morning, Greg, and thank you for taking the time to talk with us. First, could you please tell me a little bit about yourself and how you began in commodities?

Good morning, Jonathan. I grew up in a small town 100 miles west of Chicago. My mom was a nurse, and my dad worked for a regional utility company. They were great role models, particularly of the importance of a strong work ethic, which I've tried to carry with me throughout my career.

I attended Illinois State University and studied finance. When I graduated, I interviewed for a number of different roles in a variety of companies. A trading role seemed to resonate with me, particularly commodity trading. When I ran across ADM at one of the job fairs, the company seemed like a bridge between where I came from in rural Midwestern America and the interests I had in markets. I joined ADM's merchandising training programme in January 1995.

Does ADM recruit mainly from universities?

Years ago, ADM primarily hired out of college, but we've evolved. The world is changing faster than ever, so it's critical to have a broader perspective at different levels –from inside the industry and from other relevant industries.

A diverse workforce is also critical to ensure we're prepared to move into new geographies and growth areas, armed with the right skill sets, and able to relate to the ever-changing consumer of the future.

Could you please tell me a little about your career progression since joining ADM?

Over the past 24 years, my career trajectory at ADM has provided me with an end-to-end view of our business. Across a variety of roles and locations, I've been able to gain a particular depth in commodity merchandising and commercial management.

I took my first managerial role when I was 27 years old, running a soybean processing plant in Mexico, Missouri, then spent time in Cedar Rapids managing our Western bean trading for NA Oilseeds. These early years taught me some of the values I've carried through my career: be organised and prioritise your time, which allows you to take on expanded roles and more responsibility.

In 2003, I moved to our headquarters in Decatur, Illinois, taking a corporate role in risk management, followed by roles in our Corn Processing Business Unit overseeing corn positions and feed positions. These opportunities gave me two very different outlooks on how to assess and manage risk – at both a corporate and divisional level.

With that experience, I returned to Oilseeds in 2006 for a divisional leadership role in our North American soybean processing business and then spent four or five years incrementally increasing that portfolio to include cottonseed, canola, sunflower seed and flax processing and eventually our specialty ingredients business.

As part of our portfolio transformation, ADM acquired WILD Flavors, a world leader in natural flavours and colours, in 2014, and I was selected to lead a new business unit focused on this full portfolio.

After a brief period in that role, the previous leader of the Global Oilseeds business unit left ADM to pursue other interests, and I was asked to take over the leadership of the business. It was an easy choice for me. Global Oilseeds was our largest business unit; it just felt natural coming back to it. I considered it an honour and a privilege to be asked to do this.

Earlier this year, I was asked to bring together our Origination and Oilseeds business units into what we call today *Ag Services and Oilseeds*, which I now lead. This new, combined business unit constitutes a significant portion of the employees, the revenues and the profitability of the corporation. Fortunately, it's also made up of some of the best talent in the company and the industry, so I'm fortunate to work with a great team every day.

Could you tell me a little about social responsibility at ADM? For example, how do you make sure that your processes and your supply chains are environmentally sustainable and don't impinge on human rights?

ADM is a company with deep roots in agriculture. We understand the importance of being good stewards of land, water and air – all of which are critical to our business and the people we serve.

We're proud of our achievements in important areas of sustainability and social responsibility. Since we launched our No Deforestation, No Peat, No Exploitation policy in 2015, we've achieved more than 98 percent traceability to mills in our palm supply chain and 99 percent traceability to direct supplier farms in our soy supply chain in Brazil and Paraguay.

We're conducting human rights audits of farms from which we source to check their adherence to our Respect for Human Rights policy. We utilise the globally recognised SEDEX platform to perform human rights audits in our facilities. And we've invested significantly in technology such as digital satellite farm maps of our soybean suppliers in the Brazilian Cerrado region so we can track adherence to our sourcing policies in our supply chain.

We also set aggressive operational goals to reduce our energy usage, greenhouse gas emissions, water usage and waste production by 2020 – we actually met those ahead of time, and today, we're setting our next generation of environmental goals.

And this year, our Board created a new committee on Sustainability & Corporate Responsibility, led by Board Member Suzan Harrison. Its remit includes sustainable practices and environmental responsibility, as well as community relations, social wellbeing and safety.

Of course, there's always more to be done. We do business in some sensitive parts of the world, and it's our responsibility to ensure that we have the right approach and that we're applying the right pressure to make progress and implement change. In a number of cases, we're dependent on our trading partners, so it's a question of always working up and down the supply chain to make sure that everyone is aligned in expectations and in terms of transparency.

What tonnage of commodities does ADM trade each year?
We process about 60 million tonnes of agricultural commodities each year. We don't disclose the tonnage that we trade, but it would certainly be bigger than that.

How do you manage the pressure of the job?
On the work side, it really helps to have a strong team that I can count on – people who trust and respect each other and who have some longevity together. You have to be able to know who is ready for more responsibility and then, just as important, be willing to hand off responsibility and give them autonomy to deliver.

On the personal side, my wife is the rock that keeps our family organised and making progress in life. The pressures of what happens at home every day are just as strong as those that happen in the work environment – and I'm truly fortunate to have a partner that can help me manage both worlds. Without her, there's just no way I'd be where I am today.

How do you manage your work–life balance?
I wonder whether you can ever really strike an ideal balance. It's situational, changing day to day, and a constant challenge. Family is certainly my priority, but work has certain demands as well, so you have to strike the balance of being both disciplined and sometimes flexible.

I try to be efficient with my day, and I'm disciplined about leaving the office on time. I thoroughly enjoy time with my family, but running a global business that operates 24/7, you can't just turn off the responsibility. Whether I'm sitting at my desk or at home with my family or on the sidelines of a baseball or soccer game, the business is still operating … which means I'm continuously maintaining flexibility on both sides of the equation.

The way we work, and how we work, has changed over time. Video conferencing and email have certainly become more accepted and allow me to keep connected with my team; it also saves on travel expenses and time away from my family.

I also take time for myself and for my health. I make exercise a priority and do it regularly, but I try and do this early in the morning, so other priorities at home or at work don't get in the way. Staying healthy is a lifelong effort, and we can all control more than what we really want to admit. It just takes some discipline and effort.

Can you give me an example of a bad trade that you made – perhaps when you first started?

There have certainly been some bad trades, but there's really not one in particular that stands out. One thing that is certain, though: bad trades teach you a lot about managing risk. Our markets are much different today than when I started in the business.

Algorithmic trading dominates the day-to-day order flow. Crop production is more dispersed now in the world, while consumption is dominated by certain countries. All of these changes impact how we manage our risk positions, and our approach to managing risk has evolved as well.

What advice would you give to a young person starting a career in commodities?

In a trading role and in the current environment, the best advice I could give would be to keep your head on a swivel. You have to pay constant attention, whether to global economics, geopolitics, the weather, currencies or the latest consumer trend. As a commodity trader, you can't read a newspaper or watch the news without naturally connecting it back to your business, because it all matters.

From a career growth perspective, it's important to think beyond whatever your current role is. I would advise any young person in this business to stretch themselves and find other ways to contribute to the corporation and develop good business management and leadership skills. Trading can be a great foundation, but don't limit your professional options.

Some people would say that ADM is an industrial rather than a trading company. Would you agree?

Many companies that operate in this space feel that their job is to trade. Our philosophy at ADM is different. We trade with a purpose. We don't trade just to trade; I think that's yesterday's model.

We trade to support higher utilisation rates in our assets. We trade to help provide products for our customers. So, no, I wouldn't say that ADM is necessarily a trading company. We trade as a critical function of managing our portion of the supply chain to serve our global customer base.

Could you tell me a little about ADM's acquisition of Wild Flavors?
When we brought the company's special ingredient businesses into my group, we put together a growth strategy for the business. This ultimately led to the acquisition of WILD Flavors, which is still the largest acquisition in the company's history. With that acquisition, we created a fourth business unit, then called *Wild Flavors and Specialty Ingredients,* and now called *Nutrition.*

Since adding WILD, we've further increased our ingredient capabilities with acquisitions of companies with offerings from savoury flavour systems to natural vanilla to gluten-free flours. Those additions have helped us build our Nutrition business into a leading global provider of ingredients that help make the foods and drinks increasingly in demand by health-conscious consumers.

Would you consider your investments in flavours and ingredients as moving down the value chain, or would you consider them as a diversification, a side road?
We consider these investments as expanding the value chain of our processing streams to create additional value for our customers. It allows us to create a stronger connection with our customer base, participate in faster-growing markets and create a more stable business.

There are the food and flavour additions I mentioned above, but we see our Nutrition business as more than that. It also includes animal nutrition; last year, we added Neovia, a global leader in value-added animal nutrition solutions. And we're expanding in the Health & Wellness space – probiotics, enzymes and other ingredients and supplements that can help improve health.

These are all important growth opportunities for ADM. Consumers are looking for healthier products that they feel good about eating and drinking or feeding to their animals. And today, ADM is a one-stop, full-service partner in creating those solutions.

Where are the future growth opportunities in the business?
In Ag Services and Oilseeds, growth in the future isn't necessarily going to come in the same way as it has in the past.

In the past, we invested capital to expand volume and to achieve incremental increases in operating profits. That works as long as new capacity doesn't exceed incremental demand, which can lead to more volumes and lower margins.

Growth opportunities in the future will be more dependent on talent and technology. Talent has always been important. Going forward, we need people that think about process improvement, understand how to strategically use data and technology, and of course, we'll always need to be able to develop the right execution strategy to navigate a complicated world.

Technology will also be a critical part of our future, leveraging sensor technology, data and analytics in our manufacturing and trading environments and embracing technology to engage with producers and customers in a more modern way.

For the organisation as a whole, we've been deliberate in expanding our ingredients and flavours businesses. These are areas that are experiencing accelerated demand growth, growth that's happening faster than GDP.

As an example, if you look at the consumer trend for meatless alternative products, you may ask who the largest vegetable protein ingredients supplier in the world is. Well, you're talking to them. We've been in the vegetable protein business for decades now, and we have the native knowledge and the capabilities to leverage those ingredients in new and different ways. It's really a great opportunity for us to work with our customers to develop new and interesting on-trend products.

Of course, our legacy businesses offer growth opportunities as well. In my own business, oilseeds crushing and refined oils continue to enjoy steady growth over time as populations grow and diets evolve.

Looking forward, we believe we can continue to deliver on our ability to 'unlock the power of nature to enrich the quality of life' through a combination of our deep understanding of the world's nutritional needs, our access to the best foundational products nature provides, and the ingenuity and dedication of our global colleagues.

Are you affected by the current overcapacity in agricultural production and logistics?
We've certainly had some challenges with the oversupply of some raw materials, such as grains and oilseeds, and this has led to margin compression. However, it goes back to having the right philosophy.

As I said earlier, we don't just trade to trade. That's just a grind. We trade to support our assets at origin and to move closer to our customers. Also, an oversupply situation on a global basis may not be an oversupply situation on a regional basis.

Recent trade policies and decisions have resulted in regional dislocations, as has the terrible weather in some of the growing areas in the U.S. Some parts of the U.S. have been badly hit by flooding; others have been relatively OK. Our global footprint has allowed us to keep supplying our customers – when we can't get something out of the U.S., we can often get it out of Europe or South America, and vice versa. That's really the critical role for our industry. Companies with global reach like ADM are the ones that can move agricultural and food products from areas of supply to areas of demand. So it's been a dynamic situation, but overall, I think we've fared pretty well in a challenging environment.

Are there any ways that the sector could better meet the challenges it faces?

Looking forward, I believe that partnerships will become more interesting for the industry as a whole.

At ADM, we've done some partnerships, as have others in the industry, to reduce the risk of an investment or to participate in a new region of the world. For example, we've recently entered into two separate joint ventures with Cargill: one called SoyVen, which owns and operates a soy crushing facility in Egypt, and another, called GrainBridge, that is developing a single digital platform for farmers to consolidate information on production economics and grain marketing activities. ADM is also a founding member of an industry initiative to standardise and digitise global agricultural shipping transactions.

Do you view your investment in Wilmar as a partnership?

ADM has built a number of crushing plants in partnership with Wilmar in China, and we took an equity stake in the organisation when it went public. We've since added to that position, because we believe in the Wilmar organisation.

Wilmar gives us exposure to the fast-growing regions of the world like China, Southeast Asia, India and Africa. Population growth in those regions has outpaced, and will continue to outpace, the rest of the world. So it's both an investment and a partnership.

Should trading companies be publicly traded?

The primary responsibility for any company – whether public or private – is to create shareholder value.

As I said before, we're a processing company that trades various markets to manage the risk in our supply chain, to maximise utilisation of our assets and to hedge our margins. One of my primary responsibilities is to try to transform our portfolio to create a more stable set of businesses and dampen volatility. For Ag Services and Oilseeds, that could be through geographical diversification so we have the right exposure to different regions of surplus, or it could be by extending our value chain, or it could be through expanding the services we offer or stabilising the execution of the overall business though more prudent risk management.

As a corporation, it could be moving further into flavours and ingredients; both are stable, predictable businesses with opportunities for growth. There's a role for us to play as a publicly traded company operating in the space we operate in, but our strategy has to match what investors want.

Investors want stability and predictability. They want an investment they can depend on. They want a strong management team, and they want a strategy that's going to provide the value that they're looking for. Each of our business units has the opportunity to deliver these.

Is there anything that you'd like to add?

I think, for me, it's important to recognise that ADM has undertaken a lot of change in the recent past, but there's one thing that has remained constant. We're proud of the role that we play in the world.

Our purpose statement says, 'We unlock the power of nature to enrich the quality of life'. We believe that's a noble cause. But at the same time, we're evolving. We're transforming our portfolio of businesses, our capabilities and the way we interact with our customers across all of our businesses. We're more process focused and disciplined, and our growth strategy includes a very robust agenda.

ADM is a much different company than the company I joined 24 years ago. We're a stronger company, and I'm proud to have been part of the evolution.

Thank you, Greg, for your time!

Chapter Ten: Bunge

'We will continue to streamline and focus the business as we position Bunge for the future'. Greg Heckman, CEO Bunge

Bunge, as it exists today, can trace its ancestry back two centuries, having been founded as an import–export trading business in 1818 in Amsterdam by Johann Peter Gottlieb Bunge. (1) The company dealt mainly in rubber, spices and hides from Dutch overseas territories. By 1859, when Johann's grandson Charles moved the company headquarters to Antwerp, Belgium, the company had become one of the world's leading commodities traders.

Charles had two sons: Edouard stayed with his father in Antwerp, while Ernesto immigrated to Buenos Aires in 1876 to expand their operations in Argentina. In 1884, Ernesto partnered with his brother-in-law, Jorge Born, to form Bunge y Born in Argentina, to trade and originate grain. In 1897, the company took on Alfredo Hirsch who, 30 years later, went on to become president of Bunge y Born, a position he kept for the next 30 years. By the turn of the century, Bunge's Argentine operations outstripped those of the parent company in Antwerp.

In 1905, the company expanded into Brazil's flour milling sector and, in 1938, into fertiliser. Bunge North American Grain Corporation was founded in New York City in 1923 to trade domestically. In 1935, the company bought its first sizable grain facility, Midway, beside a rail terminal in Minneapolis, adding physical facilities to its grain trading capabilities.

When Juan Perón became President of Argentina in 1946, his government partially took over the domestic grain trade, prompting Bunge to move further into Brazil and expanding a grain origination business in the U.S. Midwest. In the 1950s, Bunge moved down the supply chain into the retail sector in Brazil with branded vegetable oil and margarine. In 1969, Bunge inaugurated the first soy crushing plant in Latin America in Brazil.

In response to the slow markets and poor trading margins in the 1960s, Bunge took a major strategic decision in 1970 to de-emphasise grain trading and to focus instead on investments in capital assets in the Americas. In the process, the company closed most of its trading offices in Europe and Asia.

In 1975, the group moved its global headquarters to São Paulo, Brazil, and continued to invest in capital assets. The company initially turned to public financing in 1988, issuing commercial paper for the first time. Expansion and diversification, however, led to the need for more experienced executive talent. In 1992, after 175 years of family management, the Bunge Group decided to turn operational activities over to non-family professional management, its founding families participating only on the board of directors.

In 1994, Bunge y Born became the Bermuda-registered Bunge International Limited, with headquarters in São Paulo. In 1996, the company took a strategic decision to focus on agribusiness and food and exit unrelated areas. Management set out to re-establish Bunge as a major global player in agribusiness by increasing investment in North American oilseed crushing, acquiring crushing capacity in Argentina and Brazil, and creating a destination marketing capacity.

In 1998, Bunge moved its global headquarters from São Paulo to White Plains, New York, and once again refocused the company's strategy, returning to the world of commodity trading that it had shunned since the 1970s. The company called the division *Bunge Global Markets* and based it in White Plains, opening trading offices in Europe and Asia, with an important hub in Geneva, Switzerland.

The new century saw Bunge make its initial public offering of equity on the New York Stock Exchange. As a public company, Bunge continued to diversify both ways along the supply chain, opening crushing plants in China and Vietnam.

Bunge also entered the bio-fuel business with two partnerships to produce corn-based ethanol in the U.S. and biodiesel in Germany, later acquiring a biodiesel plant in Italy. Further diversification took the company into port construction and management, first in Turkey and Latvia, and then in Vietnam. In 2003, as part of its drive into retail edible oils, Bunge acquired Hindustan Lever's Indian edible oils business. In 2007, it launched consumer vegetable oil brands in Romania and acquired a German manufacturer of consumer margarines and dressings as well as a Finnish margarine business.

Bunge continued to build its footprint in the edible oils market. In 2017, the company acquired a producer of olive and seed oil in Turkey, as well as Lindemann, a supplier of oils and fats to the German bakery market. The company also acquired a business in Argentina specialising in the production and packaging of edible oils. One of its bigger purchases that year, however, was a 70 percent interest in *IOI Loders Croklaan*, a leader in the business-to-business (B2B) palm and tropical oils market, with strengths in confectionery, bakery and infant nutrition applications.

One of Bunge's biggest investments in recent years has been into Brazil's sugarcane sector. In 2007, in a joint venture with Itochu, Bunge purchased its first sugarcane mill in Brazil, and two years later, the company began construction on its first greenfield mill, as well as acquiring a majority stake of another sugarcane mill. In 2010, Bunge acquired the Moema Group, a cluster of five sugarcane mills, while selling its Brazilian fertiliser nutrients assets.

All this activity has transformed Bunge into a diversified food supply company with sizeable interests along various supply chains across the globe. These range from flour milling, soybean crushing, corn milling, biofuels, edible vegetable oils, port infrastructure and sugarcane. The company has a market capitalisation of $8 billion, net sales of $46 billion and more than 30,000 people employed in 40 countries worldwide.

Grain and oilseed trading and merchandising is an integral part of each of these activities, but Bunge long ago ceased to be a pure commodity trading company. In that respect, the company is similar to Louis Dreyfus Company – an integrated agricultural supply chain company.

Bunge and Louis Dreyfus are similar in another respect: both have attracted the attention of the commodity giant Glencore. Glencore first looked at acquiring Dreyfus in the early 2000s, but after an initial flurry of excitement, the talks came to nothing. Glencore began talking to Bunge in May 2017, and at one stage, it looked as if a deal might be concluded. Although at the time, Bunge had more than twice the net sales of Glencore Agriculture, Bunge had been weakened by their investment into the Brazilian sugarcane sector, along with a general decline in trading margins.

It is not clear whether it was Bunge or Glencore who broke off the talks, but they ended without any further public comment from either side. Glencore agreed not to make a hostile bid for Bunge for a period of one year, and things went quiet until January 2018, when *The Financial Times* (2) reported that ADM had approached Bunge about a potential takeover. Again, nothing came of the talks.

In October 2018, Bloomberg (3) reported that Bunge had reached an agreement with two activist investors, D.E. Shaw & Co and Continental Grain Co., to bring in new directors and start a strategic review. Bunge put Continental Grain's CEO Paul Fribourg in charge of the review. The strategic committee has a mandate to look for potential material mergers, acquisitions, divestitures and other key strategic transactions.

In 2019, Greg Heckman, Bunge's newly appointed CEO, found a solution for the company's Brazilian sugar mills, putting them into a newly formed joint venture with BP. The joint venture was the largest deal in Brazil's sugarcane sector since Royal Dutch Shell joined forces with Cosan to form Raízen in 2011. Bunge received cash proceeds of $775 million as part of the agreement, but also wrote off $1.5 billion to $1.7 billion related to 'cumulative currency translation effects'. (4)

A few months later, Greg Heckman announced that the company would again be moving its global headquarters from South Plains to St. Louis, on the banks of the Mississippi River in Missouri. (5)

For a brief period in 2018, it looked like Bunge might exit the grain business and sell their grain trading activities to either ADM or Glencore. The talk died down, but in 2019, it picked up again with rumours of a sale to Glencore.

However, when I first started my research on Bunge, my computer's autocorrect function kept changing Bunge to *Bungee*, as in jumping. Funnily enough, my autocorrect had a point. Over history, whenever outside observers predicted that Bunge would crash onto the rocks below, it would somehow bounce back. It's something that Bunge has repeatedly done for the last 200 years! (And I hope it continues for the next 200!)

We Feed A Hungry World - Greg Heckman

Gregory A. Heckman is Bunge's CEO and also serves on Bunge's board of directors.

He is Founding Partner of Flatwater Partners and has over 30 years of experience in the agriculture, energy and food processing industries. Most recently, Greg was CEO of The Gavilon Group. Previously, he was Chief Operating Officer of ConAgra Foods Commercial Products and President and COO of ConAgra Trade Group.

Greg holds a B.S. in Agriculture Economics and Marketing from the University of Illinois at Urbana-Champaign.

Good morning Greg. Could you briefly tell me how you got into the grain and oilseeds business, and your career path since then?

I grew up in Cerro Gordo, IL – a farming community of 1,200 people only 13 miles from Decatur. E.A. Staley and ADM were the two agricultural titans headquartered there. My father was a banker who lent to farmers and all the industries that support them. He also had a small farm. My uncle farmed a few thousand acres and was an implement dealer. I grew up involved and around all areas of agriculture.

I ended up at the University of Illinois in Agricultural Economics, after entering in LAS – Prelaw, but that is a different story! I interviewed with most of the big Ag companies. I had offers from a few, but I took a job with ConAgra as a trainee trader.

I ended up spending 24 years with them, watching the company go from $5 to $29 billion in sales, and then back down to $12 billion as the company switched their focus to food. I had a great career there, getting the opportunity to work with, and for, some fantastic people who were generous with their time and helped me develop.

I became CEO for the first time when we took the commodities businesses private in 2008, renaming it Gavilon. The team and I transformed the business to become number two in the sector.

We subsequently sold the company in two transactions in 2013, and I remained as CEO of Gavilon for Marubeni until I retired in 2015. I am especially proud of all we were able to accomplish with the teams at ConAgra and Gavilon to create value for employees, customers and our communities.

I joined the Bunge board in 2018 and was honoured to become the CEO in 2019. Bunge is a company that I had always admired because of their culture, their global footprint of assets, and their vast customer base. I felt that I could be part of creating value while continuing to learn and grow personally.

What are your biggest challenges in being CEO of one of the ABCDs?

The current global environment is the biggest challenge. The industry has been overbuilt and needs some consolidation. Technology is changing rapidly and Ag and Food have been slow adopters. In addition, consumer trends are evolving and changing rapidly.

The industry has been built on what we expected to be continued globalization and open, fair and free trade. However, we have been experiencing a move back to nationalism recently, which is causing major trade flow disruptions.

AS CEO you have found a good home for your Brazilian sugar cane assets and you are working on restoring margins by reducing your cost base. What other measures are you taking to 'right the ship'?

We are organizing our business around our customers, the assets that serve them and the people that operate those assets: where price is established, where we innovate and where we make capital allocation decisions. This will all lead to being more customer focused—on both ends of the value chains where our customers live. It will improve our speed of decision-making. The by-product will be lower costs.

At the same time, we are increasing transparency and accountability. We are also ensuring our rewards systems are aligned to creating shareholder value—maximizing the strengths of 'One Bunge' to reach our full potential.

We are exiting businesses where we don't have the right to win and can't meet our financial hurdles.

We are also streamlining our asset and office footprint.

Please describe your vision of the future for your company: where are the main opportunities?

Our vision is to feed a hungry world by connecting farmers and consumers.

We are the world's largest global oilseed crusher. We have acquired Loders Croklaan and integrated it with our legacy fats and oils business. This creates a great platform to add value to our fats and oils outputs through our offerings to customers.

We are developing a number of projects to help capitalize on and further add value to our protein outputs.

We are a regional leader in milling in the Americas.

We want to continue to develop our value chains to serve all of our customers in the feed, food and fuel markets. This means developing more transparent and sustainable supply chains, creating value from the seed through to the end products, and looking for opportunities to innovate with customers to meet consumer preferences and needs.

What is Bunge's USP?

We are one of a few 200-year-old companies! We have proved we can adapt and be a survivor and a trusted, reliable long-term partner to our customers.

We have a global agribusiness and food ingredient platform that would be difficult if not impossible to replicate.

We have the leading agribusiness platform in South America, which will be a big part of the production volume growth needed to feed the world.

We have a highly educated, trained and passionate workforce that wants Bunge's customers to be successful; and they are proud to be part of Bunge.

You recently launched a strategic review of your business. This has led to rumours that Bunge might exit grain and oilseed trading to concentrate on higher value-added businesses. How would you respond?

We are looking at everything in our business to ensure we are creating shareholder value. That being said, there will continue to be volume growth in agricultural commodities to feed a hungry world, and the majority of that supply growth won't be where the demand growth happens.

We also have a global processing infrastructure to feed and support. We are the #1 Global Soy Crusher, we have an excellent soft seed crushing franchise and a strong wheat milling franchise in S. America, and wheat and corn milling in N. America.

Our newest business is Loders Croklaan, which has given us an excellent platform to value-add our fats and oils output from our crushing.

You have made an astute investment into alternative meats. Some have described this as a type of hedge against the trend to plant-based diets. Is this trend really a threat—and what other threats do you see?

We have an internal Venture Fund that helps us stay in step with innovations that are both additive and possible risks. *Beyond Meats* fits both categories, as it could be a risk to meat consumption—and ultimately protein meal demand—or it may actually help grow overall meat and plant based protein consumption.

Bunge appears to be navigating the trade wars reasonably well, but do they remain a threat to your business model?

Absolutely, these businesses were built believing free, open and fair trade would continue to drive globalization. This needs to happen to feed a hungry world in the most low cost and sustainable way: allowing crops to be grown in the areas with the most comparative advantage, and moving them in the most low cost value chains to where they need to be processed and ultimately consumed.

Investors in publicly quoted companies look for steady growth, but grain and oilseed trading is cyclical. How do you resolve that contradiction?

We are much more than a trader and distributor of agricultural commodities. However, we do need to continue to build out our diversification, which will lower the volatility of our earnings and dampen some of the cyclicality.

The other thing we must do is to communicate our business better. We must make it more transparent and simple to understand, so that our investors can appreciate the seasonality and cyclicality, and what that means for our earnings and returns.

When you first joined the business did you ever imagine that you would end up as CEO of an ABCD?

No, I never really looked that far ahead. The team and I took on the challenge that was in front of us, conquered it and then looked for the next hill to climb. The rest of it kind of takes care of itself.

I do love leading teams though, I really enjoy putting people in the best position to succeed, putting them in a role that is their highest best use for the organization, while also being a place they can continue to develop. I enjoy seeing them be successful and do more by working together than they every imagined possible.

I also really enjoy seeing people's success enable them to do the things they want for their families - like buying homes and educating their kids and spending quality time together with family.

Is there anything that you would like to add?

I have always enjoyed these businesses in spite of their challenges of being high volume, low margin, and with volatile earnings—and with so many factors outside of your control: weather, currency, governments and so on.

This is a business and industry where people make a bigger difference than in any other. People have a bigger impact on delighting customers, managing risks and ultimately creating returns. That makes it challenging and fun to be a part of the journey.

We feed a hungry world. It's a noble vision to be part of.

Thank you Greg for you time and insight!

Chapter Eleven: Cargill

'The days of 'Hey, we're going to buy your crops, we're going to store it, we're going to play the carry'—you know, sell it at a profit—it's over'. (1)

David MacLennan,
Cargill CEO

In 1979, when I joined Cargill's training programme, I was told that the company made no money on selling grains to destination, the FOB load port to the C&F destination portion in the supply chain. Instead, the company viewed these sales as a necessary evil. The money was made upstream: tiny margins on (at that time) selling seeds, fertiliser and other chemicals to farmers, buying and storing grain at harvest time, shipping it in barges down the Mississippi, storing it again at the port and then elevating it onto the ships.

Cargill also made money by offering risk management services to farmers and even executing transactions on the futures markets. The final stage of selling and shipping the grain to the final buyer was a game that you had to play as best you could, without losing too much money on it. As Cargill and the other heavyweight grain companies knew 40 years ago, the money was in originating grain, not in marketing it to destination.

After completing my training programme, I moved to Cargill's sugar department, where I worked on the hedging desk, first in London and then in Minneapolis. Returning to London, Cargill moved me from the futures desk to the physical sugar desk. My new role was to buy white sugar from European producers and sell to the MENA (Middle East North Africa) region. Then, most importing countries bought their sugar through government tenders. I had a miserable time trying (and failing) to not lose money buying FOB Europe and selling CIF MENA. It was exactly the sort of business that the company had warned me against on my training programme.

Cargill can date its history (2) back to 1865, when William Wallace Cargill founded the company in Conover, Iowa. He had been born in 1844 in Port Jefferson, New York, the third of seven children of Scottish sea captain William Dick Cargill, who had immigrated to New York in the late 1830s.

His brother Sam joined William Wallace in 1866, forming W. W. Cargill and Brother. Ten years, later Cargill moved to La Crosse, Wisconsin, and a third brother, James, joined the business. In 1898, John H. MacMillan Sr. and his brother, Daniel, began working for W. W. Cargill. John MacMillan then did a smart thing and married William Wallace's eldest daughter, Edna.

William Wallace's son William invested company money into unrelated outside investments, including a vast irrigation project in Montana and a railroad that was said to 'start nowhere and end nowhere'. (3) The father visited Montana in 1909 to look at his son's irrigation project; appalled, he returned home, caught pneumonia and died. When Cargill's creditors heard of the outside investments, they sought repayment, and from 1909 to 1916, the company hovered on the brink of bankruptcy.

During that time, the Cargill and the MacMillan families fought for control of the company. The MacMillan family won. William Cargill was bought out with $25,000 in cash, some railroad bonds and a loan of $250,000. However, the Cargill family was not excluded completely; William Wallace's descendants still own 10 percent of the company.

Post-World War II, Cargill made a strategic decision that still shapes the company today: a move into soybean crushing. It also began to expand geographically, building grain elevators in Brazil. As Dan Morgan wrote in his book, this was territory that had long belonged to Bunge, and Cargill was signalling that the real battle to divide up the world had begun. (4)

There was logic in the way that Cargill expanded. Most of its investments had some connection to agriculture, bulk commodities, trading and transportation. For example, in the 1950s, Cargill's grain barges were returning empty from trips to the Gulf Coast. Cargill began filling the barges with rock salt for the return trip. It then bought a salt mine in Kansas. Soon, it was selling salt for family dinner tables, cattle licks, meat packaging and highway de-icing.

Cargill was still in full expansion mode when I moved to Minneapolis in 1979. In the previous few years, for example it had bought two steel companies, a turkey processing company, two flour companies, 137 Canadian grain elevators, a Memphis cotton company and a life insurance firm. It had also entered the coal business, built plants to produce high-fructose corn syrup, opened new grain handling facilities across the U.S. and started trading metals in New York.

I joined the training scheme at Cargill's European trading division Tradax in September 1978. The company's U.K. office was in Maidenhead, a pleasant but boring (for a 21-year-old) town on the River Thames. After a three-month training period, I was allocated to the soy meal desk, given a list of farmers throughout the U.K. and told to call them and sell them soy meal for animal feed. My success was limited.

When I heard that there was a position open for a trainee on the company's sugar desk in the City of London, I jumped at the chance. Along with another applicant, we journeyed to London. I can't remember the name of the other applicant, but he'd been doing quite a bit of research into the sugar business and seemed even more desperate than I was to get out of Maidenhead.

The interview wasn't much of an interview. It consisted of the head of the trading desk taking us out to lunch and getting us drunk. (Remember that this was 1978: it wouldn't happen now!) He then found an excuse to send us both back, but at different times, to the office. The other applicant left first but never made it back to the office. Somehow, I did. I got the job by default.

One Friday evening 10 months later, I was about to leave the office when I got a call from the head of the sugar desk in Minneapolis. He asked me if I could be in Minneapolis on Monday morning. I told him that I could and asked him how long he wanted me to stay. 'About two years', he replied.

I took a flight on Sunday morning and was horrified to see that nearly everyone on the plane was wearing German *lederhosen,* with duck feathers in their caps. I wondered whether everyone in Minneapolis dressed that way and was relieved when one of them told me that they were returning from a beer festival in Munich and that, no, nobody dressed that way in Minneapolis!

Cargill's head office was based in Minnetonka (also home to Tonka Toys) and consisted of the Lake Office, a lakeside mansion complete with a marble staircase and 13 fireplaces, all modelled on a French château, along with a purpose-built office complex – in the shape of a low pyramid that hid nicely in the surrounding woodlands – about a five-minute walk along an underground tunnel from the château.

The château wasn't ideal: Cargill's entire domestic grain hedging operations were managed from a tiny room that had previously been the butler's office. Besides, the company's 40 top managers were separated from the teams that they managed. Even so, it wasn't until 2016 that the top management finally moved to the main office and the château was put up for sale. (5)

Cargill typically puts 80 percent of earnings back into the business. Tensions began to mount in the late 1980s, when the company's owners began to push for an IPO. The company responded in 1993, reportedly purchasing 17 percent of the firm for $730 million from 72 members of the Cargill and MacMillan families. It used the shares to begin the employee stock plan.

Cargill had a tough time in the years following the implementation of the employee stock plan. Its financial unit lost hundreds of millions of dollars in 1998, when Russia defaulted on its sovereign debt. Meanwhile, the commodities and ingredients business, which was by then 75 percent of Cargill's total revenue, was hit badly by the 1997 Asian financial crisis. However, by 2002, the company had rebounded with over $50 billion in annual sales, twice the amount of its closest rival, Archer Daniels Midland. In 2008, Cargill's quarterly profits exceeded $1 billion for the first time.

Today, Cargill is still the largest privately held corporation in the United States. In 2018, it had revenues of $115 billion and earnings of over $3 billion. According to the company's website, Cargill employs over 155,000 employees in 66 countries. It is responsible for 25 percent of all U.S. grain exports and supplies about 22 percent of the U.S. domestic meat market, as well as, incidentally, all the eggs used in McDonald's U.S. restaurants. On any given day, the company may handle up to 20 percent of the world's food supply.

Cargill continues to pay 20 percent of its revenues as dividends and reinvest the rest in the business. That means, for example, that Cargill had $2.4 billion to invest into its various businesses in 2019. That's a huge sum compared to the company's smaller competitors, who might 'only' have hundreds of millions to reinvest. This difference could well mean that Cargill will continue to widen the gap with its competition in the years to come.

The physical grain trade has always been tough, and the grain-trading companies have continually had to reinvent themselves to thrive and survive. Whether by luck or genius, Cargill has managed to stay ahead of the pack.

Trading is an art, not a science – GJ

Gert-Jan ('GJ') van den Akker is responsible for strategy and execution for Cargill's agricultural supply chain businesses. He joined Cargill in 1987 in Amsterdam and held several positions across Cargill's agricultural supply chain businesses, including roles with palm oil by-products in Kuala Lumpur, domestic grain markets in Tokyo and corn and soybeans in Geneva.

GJ has also held leadership roles in Cargill's energy, transportation and metals businesses. He was managing director of the worldwide ocean transportation business from 2007 to 2011.

In 2013, he left Cargill to become senior head of global regions at Louis Dreyfus. He was a member of Dreyfus's senior leadership team, a member of the Dreyfus risk committee and leader of business development in the grain and oilseed sector. He rejoined Cargill in December 2015.

You spent much of your career in shipping. What did you learn from your time in shipping that helps you in your current job?

I learnt that, to be successful in commodity trading, you have to have a physical presence and a deep understanding of what's happening in the physical markets. That's clearly something that helped us as we built our shipping operations. We had good insights into the physical movement of goods; this helped us with our trading.

Second, I learned the value and importance of building customer relationships. We were an operator, not an owner, of ships, and we had to provide our customers with a better service than any ship owner could. Sometimes, it was on price, but more often, it was flexibility. I also learned the importance of having very strong supply relationships. At Cargill, we treat our suppliers as if they were customers.

What does your current position entail?

Cargill is now split into four divisions: agricultural supply chain, animal nutrition, protein and salt, food ingredients and bio-industrial. I oversee the agricultural supply chain business, what I would call the 'original' Cargill. It includes everything that relates to grain, oilseeds and agricultural products, from origination along the whole supply chain to destination and distribution. It also includes all our oilseed crushing activities around the globe and includes our sugar business, Alvean, a joint venture with Copersucar, as well as our palm oil business.

Also, I'm a member of what we call the Cargill Executive Team, a group of 10 people who are accountable for strategy and who oversee the global enterprise.

What in your career has been the most challenging, and what has been the most fun?

That's a good question. I had the most fun in the shipping business. It was such a phenomenal time. I like businesses where you can invest and grow.

Without a doubt, the position I have today is the most challenging, simply because of size and accountability. It takes a huge amount of effort to grasp and understand the complexities around the world and to manage all the different elements that impact agriculture markets. In addition, since I took on this role, we've had to make some pretty tough decisions around our portfolio of businesses. There are certainly areas where we continue to grow, but we've also taken some assets out of our portfolio. That's never fun. It often comes with job losses. Even so, although we've been managing the portfolio, our overall business has continued to grow.

Today's environment is in itself a challenging one for commodity traders. The margins are thin, so you have to be on your toes. That puts a lot of pressure on me, personally.

How have you managed the stress?

Commodity trading requires a high level of resilience. Markets don't always go in your favour, and that can be very stressful.

I've been very fortunate in that I can see the relativity of things. I can go back home in the evenings, have dinner with my wife or family, and I can let things go by. I can empty my brain of work. It doesn't always happen, but generally speaking, I can relax.

I do some exercise. I play golf. I'm a mediocre player – a handicap of 15 – but I enjoy it. I also spend quite a bit of time in the gym, although apparently, not as much as Chris Mahoney, the CEO of Glencore Ag. I love hiking. Working here in Geneva is great, because it allows me to get out into the mountains on the weekends.

Good traders only talk about their bad trades – what was your worst?

I have had bad trades, but I'm not sure that I want to recall them! Maybe I could tell you instead about what could've been anyone's worst nightmare of a trade. This was back in 2009, when I was in charge of the shipping business and we had a lot of ships chartered out. Shipping rates collapsed: Capesize (vessels that carry 150,000 tonnes) rates dropped from $200,000 per day to $5,000 per day in one month. Our market exposure was huge, and we were worried that our charterers would default. We had to manage that exposure and ensure that we got contract performance. It took a year out of my life, but by and large, we came out okay in the end.

Are markets your passion in life – or is it golf?

Neither! My family comes number one in my life, so if I have a passion at all, it's for my family. Managing my work–life balance has been one of my biggest personal challenges. It's tough to find the right balance. We've all made the mistake at some stage in our careers of not spending enough time with the family. But the older I get, the more I understand the importance of family. Even though my children are now grown up, I love seeing how they're getting on.

I'm fascinated by – rather than passionate about – markets. I always have been. There are so many different variables that impact price. I enjoy the intellectual challenge of trying to work out what variable will have the most impact at any given time.

How have the grain markets changed since you began in 1987?

Although this may surprise you, I don't think they've changed much; the business models haven't really changed. Cargill's function for the past 150 years was to be a global supply chain manager – to move food from farm to fork. Cargill has never farmed, except in the palm oil business, where we operate plantations in Indonesia and where we pride ourselves on setting the highest standards in the industry. Instead, we build relationships with farmers. We acquire grains and oilseeds from them, we store them, we trade them, hedging our risk on the futures exchanges. We transport them, and we arbitrage between domestic and world markets. That has been what we've always done, and that's still what we do!

What has changed a lot recently is the availability of new technology and data – and new ways to analyse that data. Cargill has always been at the forefront of data collection and analytics. We've always understood the value of data, whether proprietary information on the back of the businesses we're involved in or publicly available information, such as weather.

Today, there's much more data available. We have to be able to analyse it, but our basic supply-chain business model hasn't changed.

Having said that, I believe the biggest change in the grain business is yet to come. With advances in technology, the requirements to be successful will change, as will the services that you provide to your customers. The newer generation of farmers is latching onto technology in terms of production, and they now want to transact in a different way than they used to transact. That's all changing. Those relationships will change along with technology.

Is there going to be consolidation?

I think the market will consolidate to deal with excess capacity, but please don't ask me how that will happen, because I don't know. It doesn't have to be among the big companies.

The last time we were in a situation of excess capacity was in the late 1980s and 1990s. We saw two huge players exiting the market because they no longer thought that the risks were worth the rewards. Could that happen again?

Players come and go – that will never change. The way that the industry manages risk will have to change. In today's world, you need the right talent, as well as investment in IT systems. In that sense, scale is critical – along with a physical presence. It will become increasingly difficult for companies with no scale or significant physical presence to participate in this business.

However, you have to guard against bureaucracy. You can't let bureaucracy stifle trading or discourage talent. There are still things we at Cargill must do to improve, but we know that adding layers of bureaucracy adds to costs. You can't blow up the costs, stay competitive and be successful.

What are the biggest challenges currently facing the grain merchandising industry?

In the 2000 to 2010 boom, the industry built up too much capacity, too many silos. Farmers around the world have also built storage capacity. Their need for merchants of grain to store commodities and to take them off their hands at harvest time has become less. That's a significant change that challenges intermediaries such as us. We need to add value to the farmers in a different way than we have done in the past.

Another challenge that we face is government intervention; the current trade conflict is an example. Tariffs and import and export bans make it harder and more costly to move food around the world. They lead to inefficiencies and extra costs.

Ian McIntosh, the CEO of Dreyfus, recently said, 'One tweet and everything changes'. Traders need volatility, but they like volatility that is at least partially predictable.

If you trade, you need price volatility. If the price doesn't move, you can't make money. You might not lose, either, but not losing isn't enough to stay in business. By definition, traders require volatility.

However, unpredictable political volatility increases risks and costs. It becomes a casino, and then it becomes gambling rather than trading. There have been a lot of market-impacting tweets. That has made trading difficult in the past year.

But one thing I'd say is that our global scale has helped us to find solutions. Recently, trade tariffs have made it more expensive to supply U.S. beans to our buyers in China, but because of our global scale, we've been able to supply Brazilian beans instead. We couldn't do that without global scale. If you were a small regional player in the U.S., you would've been caught in that.

Can grain merchants still add value, or can the market now do without intermediaries?

There are a lot of myths around the grain trade, that traders just make money hand over fist, that they're making huge amounts of money on the backs of farmers and consumers. It isn't true. In reality, margins are very thin in the agriculture sector.

On the plus side, pressure on margins means that we're constantly looking to make the systems more efficient, to cut back costs, and to make sure that our agricultural products are moved in the most cost-effective and efficient way.

So, yes, there's a need for intermediaries, as long as we can continually reinvent ourselves to add value. We have to differentiate ourselves from our competitors and to add value on both ends of the spectrum, at origin and at destination. If you cannot add value, then there is no reason for you to be in business.

Is traceability compatible with tradability?

I don't think traceability necessarily kills tradability, but it clearly restricts it. You end up with an IP (identity preserved) product. It's a value-added product that isn't really exchangeable. A commodity is a commodity because it's exchangeable. An IP product requires segregation; it isn't a standard product.

Our objective within Cargill is for all products to become sustainable. Once that happens, the distinction between traceability and tradability no longer exists.

How has Cargill changed since you joined?

At its core, the company hasn't changed. We're still a values-driven company where ethics and compliance are at the top of who we are. That hasn't changed over 150 years, and I don't think it will ever change. It's a family requisite. The Cargill family cares about the company, about passing on to the next generation, and that will only happen if we take care of the company in an appropriate manner.

Cargill has, however, changed from a portfolio perspective. When I joined in 1987, we were still predominately a trading company. The trading part of Cargill is still a critical part of the company. We still have an active trading business. We trade actively around our assets. We're a major supply chain manager. But we've also diversified our portfolio into value-added products. We've invested heavily into animal feed, meat businesses, starches and sweeteners, and fermentation. That has diversified the revenue streams, but it has also allowed us to capture margins in the downstream supply chain just as the margins in trading were under pressure.

Chris Mahoney, the CEO of Glencore Agriculture, told me that something like 15 percent of his company's revenue comes from trading and merchandising.

It's difficult to put an exact number on it, and trading is an art, not a science. It varies from year to year. We still have a huge amount invested in people and talent to trade and position in the marketplace, and I'd guess that it's larger than our competitors today. Nevertheless, the trading side of Cargill relative to the rest of Cargill is now less than it used to be. That is simply because our portfolio on the value-added side has grown significantly.

What makes Cargill different from the other grain merchandising companies – what's your USP?
I'm not going to talk about our competitors, so I'll answer that question in terms of what I think we're good at.

Number one is our exceptional talent – our people. Number two is that we're truly global as a company; we have good assets in all the key geographies, whether at origin or destination. Number three is the way that the different businesses within Cargill work together. Number four: I believe we can differentiate ourselves by the importance we place on our relationships with customers and suppliers. We work with our end users and our suppliers to adapt to their changing needs.

Would you recommend young people to become traders, to join Cargill?
You're asking someone with a fascination for markets and trading so, yes, I'd recommend anyone become a trader. Trading will never disappear. We manage risks, and those risks will never disappear. There's risk all along the agriculture supply chain, and that risk has to be managed. To manage risk, you have to understand the marketplace.

To take that one step further, you go beyond simply risk management into trading opportunities, where you see something that the market is mispricing, and you seek to profit from that. That's how markets work. It's a fascinating business. You have global forces at play.

There's now a greater need to understand mathematics and mathematical models than in the past. Data science is becoming increasingly more important. I joined Cargill before the Internet existed. And I studied law, not mathematics. But I guess I must have some ability at maths; otherwise, I wouldn't be where I am today.

So you need to be strong in mathematics now to be a good trader, and that isn't for everyone. You also need to be able to manage stress. Your job shouldn't be at the cost of your health. It's a tough environment. A lot of people come and go. It's a performance-driven culture. If you don't perform consistently, you will be replaced. You're always at the cutting edge. Performance is quick to come and go.

Cargill is often viewed as a training programme for the industry. How do you feel about that – and how do you manage it?

I have mixed feelings about that. In one sense, it bothers me. Through our training, we're obviously feeding our competitors with talent. But at the same time, I'm proud that we recruit and train people so well. That tells you a lot about this company and the way we invest in our people. I think that's a good thing.

But frankly, there is no choice at the end of the day. We're a pyramidal structure. People are promoted on merit, and there will be people that fall out of that system. Our objective is to maintain our strongest talent. We don't always succeed. But not everyone can make it to the top, so there will always be people that seek other opportunities. I think that's OK. It's the way the system works; it's inevitable.

What would you like to read about in a book about the grain trade?

The grain trade plays a vital role in the agriculture sector, and I think that story needs to be told. The industry has a stigma that's hard to lose, but the key is transparency. We must show we're doing good, but we also have to admit to our challenges and vulnerabilities. I'm proud of the way that Cargill has evolved. We tell our story in good faith. We have very strong values, and we're in the business for the long run.

To feed a growing population, we have to make sure that our farmers receive a fair payment for their crops and that they thrive. But at the same time, we need to care for the planet. We don't want any further deforestation. There are paradoxes that we need to manage. We're in the middle of this and want to play a role. There are a lot of conflicting issues to be managed. We cannot ignore one in favour of another. They need to be handled and met at the same time.

Thank you, GJ, for your time and insights!

Chapter Twelve: COFCO International

'We want to be an international trading house like one of the ABCDs'.
Johnny Chi, CEO, COFCO International Ltd. (1)

On my first day at Cargill's head office in Minneapolis, my new boss took me on a guided tour of the offices. He was particularly keen on showing me the Lake Office, connected to the main office by a long underground tunnel. As we walked along the tunnel, my boss suddenly stopped, turned to check if anyone else was around and then opened a door into a well-furnished European-style sitting room. 'This is where we entertain Prodintorg when they come to buy grain', he told me. 'We only use it for the Russians. When COFCO visits us, we use a different room. I will show you'. He led me a little further down the corridor and showed me the 'Chinese room'. It, too, was well furnished, but in an oriental style.

'Who are the tougher negotiators?' I asked him. 'The Chinese or the Soviets?'

'Both COFCO and Prodintorg have monopolies over food imports into their respective countries', he told me. 'The traders in both these organisations are the top of the top, the smartest and the brightest in the country. Both are tough negotiators, but you'll find that the Chinese are born traders. If something goes wrong, and you fail to execute the contract correctly, then you'd better watch out'.

Unfortunately, he was proved right a couple of months later when poor weather and congestion at load port led to one of our shipments from Brazil to China missing its Bill of Lading date by one hour. We had guaranteed COFCO that the vessel would leave the load port by midnight on a certain date. Our vessel sailed at 1 a.m. the following day. The market had fallen sharply since we had made the sale a few months earlier, and we ended up paying COFCO $1 million to persuade them to still take the cargo. Although a fortune, it was still less than the loss that we would have made if we had resold the cargo on the open market.

Back in 1979, we had sold that fateful cargo to COFCO on a C&F flat-price basis, arranging the shipping ourselves. Over the years, COFCO became progressively more sophisticated in their trading. Instead of buying C&F, they began to buy FOB. They still bought on a flat (outright) price but began chartering their own vessels to pick up the commodity at load port. Soon after, COFCO evolved further and began buying their physical needs on an unpriced basis, handling the futures hedging and the price risk themselves. Regarding managing their positions on the futures markets, their traders were as good as, if not better than, the trade houses from which they were buying their physical commodities.

I continued to deal with COFCO over the 40 years that I was in the business. However, I remember in particular one meeting that I had with COFCO's top management in China in 2012. They were thinking of buying a sugar mill in Brazil and wanted to know what I thought of the idea. COFCO had already bought a sugar mill in Australia, their first foray into overseas production, and were thinking of further diversifying their origination.

They told me that the Chinese government was keen to maintain food supplies to the country's growing population. SOEs (state-owned enterprises) were being encouraged to invest in farmland and agricultural production facilities around the globe: hence, their interest in the mill in Brazil.

Chinese companies have since invested in overseas food production in more than 30 countries, and China is the largest foreign owner of agricultural land in Australia. (2) COFCO, through their acquisition of Noble, has even ended up with a couple of Brazilian sugar mills.

However, their investments into farmland and productive agricultural assets have at times caused political friction in some host countries. In addition, the assets have sometimes proved difficult to manage due to cultural differences, as well as to local government interference. Besides, it has become clear that owning farmland in a foreign country does not guarantee supply. This was highlighted in 2010 when Russia banned wheat exports.

Owning Russian farmland is useless if you can't export the wheat. Owning a global trading company can better meet a goal of ensuring supply. If Russia bans wheat exports, a trading company with a global footprint can replace Russian wheat with another origin. More recently, because of the trade war with the U.S., the Chinese government has imposed tariffs on U.S. soybeans. Having a global footprint means that you can supply China with replacement beans from Brazil or Argentina.

State-owned COFCO (China National Cereals, Oils and Foodstuffs Corporation) is China's largest food processor, manufacturer and trader. Founded in 1952, it's one of the country's largest State Owned Enterprises (SOEs), coming under the direct supervision of China's State Council. Between 1952 and 1987, it was the sole agricultural products importer and exporter operating in the country. Over the years, COFCO has developed into a diversified conglomerate, involving farming, food processing, finance, warehouse, transportation, port facilities, hotels and real estate.

Headquartered in Geneva, COFCO International Ltd was founded in September 2014 when COFCO acquired 51 percent of Noble Agri, the agricultural trading arm of Singapore-based Noble Group, for $1.5 billion. Noble Group Ltd (3) had entered the world of agricultural commodity trading with the demise of Andre & Cie in 2001, when Noble bought André's grains business for an undisclosed (but rumoured to be cheap) price.

Noble Group Ltd was founded by Richard Elman, who named his company after James Clavell's 1981 novel *Noble House*, a tale of a trading house in 1960s Hong Kong. A wave of acquisitions turned Noble into a conglomerate operating assets the world over: coal mines in Australia, sugar mills in Brazil and American fuel terminals.

Richard Elman had dropped out of school at 15 to work in his family's scrap-metals yard in Newcastle. He soon took over running the yard, developing skills in buying and selling metals that eventually took him to San Francisco, then Japan. In the early 1970s, Elman founded Metal Ore Asia in Hong Kong and then sold it to his next employer, Philipp Brothers (Phibro) (4), then a global commodity giant.

Elman left Phibro in 1986 and started Noble Group with $100,000 of his own money. Over the next ten years, he turned it into a global commodity trader, listing the company on the Singapore Exchange in 1997. The company continued to expand and at one point employed over 15,000 people. The expansion, however, was built largely on debt, and by the early 2010s, waning profitability began to make the company look less tenable.

In February 2015, an analyst group, Iceberg Research, run by an ex-employee, published a critique of Noble's accounting practices, warning some earnings wouldn't materialise and suggesting that the trader couldn't repay its debts. The company dismissed the critique, but later wrote down $1.2 billion, mostly from long-term coal contracts it had booked at an excessive price.

As its fortunes turned, Noble tried to stay afloat by selling assets, including the agriculture unit it had built on Andre & Cie's foundations. However, buyers understood the company's desperation, and the sales netted less than Noble had hoped. With $1.5 billion in debt to repay in the first half of 2018, the company had no choice but to restructure, a process completed in December that year. (5)

Just as Noble had taken advantage of the demise of André & Cie in 2001, COFCO took advantage of the demise of Noble. Having acquired 52 percent of Noble Agri in April 2014 for $1.5 billion, COFCO bought the remaining 49 percent in December 2015 for $750 million.

But COFCO didn't just buy Noble Agri. Their ambitions were much bigger. Just one month after purchasing their initial stake in Noble Agri in September 2014, COFCO paid $1.3 billion for 51 percent of Nidera, a deal that valued the Dutch grain trader at $4 billion, including debt. Nidera's founding families controlled the other 49 percent until August 2016, when COFCO bought the rest of the group for $448 million. The purchase was completed in 2017.

Nidera was founded in Rotterdam, in the Netherlands, in 1920, where its early activities centred on grain and foodstuffs merchandising in specific markets from which it took its acronym: Nederland, (East) Indies, Deutschland, England, Russia and Argentina.

At the time that COFCO took a majority stake in 2014, Nidira was trading annually around 33 million tonnes of grains and oilseeds worldwide, employed 3,800 people and had revenues of over $17 billion. By 2015, annual turnover had risen to $ 18.5 billion.

Nidera also had interests in fertiliser and agricultural chemicals, and with Nidera Seeds, it was an important plant breeder in South America. COFCO sold the seed business in 2017 to Swiss-based Syngenta, which was bought by ChemChina.

As is often the case with takeovers, however, COFCO's acquisition and integration of Nidira and Noble did not go smoothly. With the benefit of perfect hindsight, it was perhaps overambitious to acquire two large companies virtually simultaneously. Mergers are fraught with difficulties; it's hard enough for a buyer to make a success of one acquisition, let alone two.

The integration process came at a difficult time for all traders. Four years of bumper global grains and oilseeds harvests had squeezed profits at the established players. For a while, the two units, Noble and Nidera, worked independently and often competed against each other for the same business. It was probably only in 2018 that the two purchases were finally integrated and working smoothly as one operation.

The integration of Nidera was further complicated by the disclosure of a $150 million financial hole in Nidera's Latin American accounts, as well as $200 million in unauthorised trading losses on its Dutch biofuels desk. (6) At the time of writing, COFCO is in court proceedings in Holland against Nidera's previous owners, arguing that they overpaid for the company. (7)

Despite its difficult birth, COFCO International is now an agricultural powerhouse. In 2018, it was the fourth biggest soy exporter from Brazil, almost neck and neck with Dreyfus in third place with 11 million tonnes. (Bunge was first with 18 million tonnes, while Cargill was second at 12 million tonnes.) (8)

Meanwhile, COFCO International has become the second-biggest grain exporter from Argentina, behind Cargill. The company is also one of the most active trade houses in the Black Sea region. In 2018, the company generated $34 billion in revenue – four-fifths that of Louis Dreyfus. China accounts for maybe 20 percent of its sales.

In January 2019, COFCO International's chairman told the *Economist* magazine that the firm is at last in a position 'to embrace growth and development. Our strategy is to leverage our strong presence in China to grow our global business'.

Although COFCO International has now earned a place at the top table, doubts persist among some in the industry about whether the trading firm will really challenge the existing dominant players in grains and oilseeds. In the end, they suspect, the company may prioritise securing strategic food supplies for China over commercial aims in an era of rising trade tensions. One former manager told Reuters, 'It's a big machine. It doesn't think like a business. It thinks like a government'.

The company has played down suggestions that it's torn between competing objectives, unsure whether to pursue its own commercial aims or the strategic interests of its home country.

COFCO owns 48 percent of COFCO International, and China Investment Corp owns 12 percent. Other shareholders include Standard Chartered Bank, the World Bank's commercial arm IFC and Singaporean investment fund Temasek. These minority shareholders are not only looking for a return, but they are also searching for an exit strategy in the form of the IPO that the company has promised.

However, what worries COFCO International's rivals most is that the company may one day dominate direct access to China's grain market – both for strategic and business reasons – and lock everyone else out. As COFCO International tightens its grip over China's food imports, its edge could become unmatchable.

'Everything starts and ends with Chinese demand', a former trading company executive told the Economist. 'Understand what the biggest national buyer is doing, and you control the trading game'.

Unfortunately—and despite my best efforts—COFCO International declined to be interviewed for this project.

Trading is a people business—Ito Van Lanschot

Ito van Lanschot is a business developer, strategist, investor, leader, risk and commodity expert. He is founder and managing director of TRADESPARENT BV, (formerly named Commodity Services & Solutions) which is today a leader in commodity data and solutions.

Previously Ito was CEO of BayWa Agri Supply and Trade, President and COO of Reliant Energy Europe and CEO of Nidera where he was directly responsible for the international trading and processing business and operations for the grain and oilseeds complex, freight, energy business and the development and implementation of its global risk group.

You are a member of a famous Dutch banking family. Could you tell me a little about your family background?

Back in the 1400s we were originally brewers in the southern part of Holland. It was the Spanish Netherlands in those days. Later in the 1600s the family began discounting commercial debt paper, which was essentially the beginning of our banking operations. We founded the bank in 1737.

I understand that the bank has been headed by a family member right through to 1993. Why didn't you join the bank?

I did join the bank but found it boring. Our family bank was rather conservative. However, we did have quite a significant foreign exchange dealing desk including transactions for the Dutch Treasury. It was there that I got my first taste of trading, and I loved it. I was hooked!

I left the bank in 1974 to join Continental Grain in Hamburg, Germany as a trainee merchandiser. Indeed, I spent a large part of career with Conti. From Hamburg I moved first to Madrid and then to Geneva. I was then posted in Buenos Aires where I became trading manager. I moved to HQ in New York in 1980, the year President Carter imposed his export ban.

In New York, I traded both soy meal and wheat during the early 1980s, but because of the export ban the US markets were over-supplied, and margins were very thin, so we had to come up with innovative ways to make money. Conti had a significant export volume but was mainly focused on large cargo sizes – Panamax vessels. It was a very competitive market. I realized that we were not paying sufficient attention to the smaller buyers—the ones who could not buy full cargoes—and I came up with the idea of combining buyers of different commodities to various countries in the Caribbean and the South American Pacific Coast into combo-shipments of smaller Handysize vessels.

It took a while to convince the Senior Management to go down that route as it required substantial amounts of trade financing. But with the creative support from our finance team, the business took off and we built up an extended network of bonded warehouses all along the South American coast and in the Caribbean. It became a very profitable business in a separate division that we called 'Conti Latin'. When the Fribourg family sold their grain trading assets to Cargill, they kept Conti Latin and still run it successfully. I am quite proud that I was at the origin of that business.

In 1990 I moved back to Spain where I became Managing Director. I had previously worked at Conti in Madrid as trader and 10 years later I came back as their MD. That was the great thing about Conti—you got great opportunities. However, one year later, I was headhunted to join Nidera.

So, you lived through the whole boom and bust of the 1970s and 1980s.

Yes, I did, but I was only a trainee during the Great Grain Robbery, so I lived more of the bust of the 1980s than the boom of the 1970s. However, we did hear the stories, and we heard all about Mr. Fribourg and his sales to the USSR. I am a proud 'ex-Con'. It was a tremendous experience. The Fribourg family left us a lot of leeway in our daily dealings— as I said before, they gave us lots of space to operate and create opportunities.

What was it like moving from Conti to a smaller company like Nidera?

Both were family-owned and controlled companies, so there were similarities. It was a similar culture.

Nidera consisted of two companies: Nidera Handelscompagnie BV (NHBV) in the Netherlands and Nidera SA in Argentina. The family shareholders ran them as two separate companies. NHBV was a major player in the international vegetable oil business at a time when the bigger companies did not commonly trade vegoil.

I was asked to take over from Mr. Salzer-Levi as chairman of the management board of NHBV. Mr. Salzer-Levi was a member of one of the three families that owned Nidera. They had a strong and profitable vegoil team, and they wanted me to grow their Grains & Oilseeds business into a profitable global portfolio.

To what extent did the three owner-families get involved in the daily business?

The three families were all, in some capacity involved in the business. Mr. Salzer-Levi was retiring from actively managing NHBV and became the chairman of the supervisory board. We developed a good relationship; I slowly gained his trust and he gradually gave me more and more freedom and support to build the business. It was his deep understanding of the industry, the trust and understanding between the two of us that was the basis of the company's success.

But if I understand correctly you left Nidera for a first time in 2000.
That is correct. I was asked to join Reliant Energy, an American power generation and wholesale business, as President and COO of Reliant Energy Europe. The US company was based in Houston and was expanding rapidly, riding the wave of the power market liberalization that had begun in the early 1990s. It started in the U.S. with the liberalization of gas and power industry, and then came to Europe. Various governments, starting in the UK, began to sell their utility companies, which were either government owned or controlled

Reliant bought one of the largest Dutch utility companies (UNA) and asked me to help them convert it into a commercial company. That meant applying commodity-trading skills, disciplines and expertise to develop a fuel and power-trading platform. It was a tremendous challenge. We had power generation plants that had to be adapted to run in a liberalized power market. Excellent modelling, structuring and risk management disciplines were created, supported by sophisticated technology systems in order to support the trading platform and to optimize the operations of the plants in an immature gas and power market. Exciting times in a dynamically developing energy industry.

I stayed with Reliant for three years until the demise of Enron, when the whole industry imploded. Capital markets were no longer willing to support the power-generation sector, and Reliant sold the business.

So, you went back to Nidera?
When I left Nidera in 2000, Mr. Levi had asked me to join the company's supervisory board. I accepted, and I ultimately became chairman of it. So, I had kept in close contact with Nidera through my Reliant years.

But you became CEO of Nidera in 2006.
Yes, I rejoined Nidera as CEO at the request of the shareholders. The results of the previous few years had been disappointing, and they asked me to help them put things back on track.

The first thing I did when I went back to Nidera in 2006 was to establish a risk department. I had become convinced that risk management and data technology as a structured discipline was the only way to manage and optimize a business portfolio, and to invest in new technology and systems for the front office. In the few years thereafter, we were able to capture a few of the best results the company had in its history.

When I left Nidera in 2010 I started my own business, Commodity Services & Solutions, which in 2016 became Tradesparent. My objective was to use my experience in both power-generation trading and agricultural commodities trading and processing. My time in the energy industry, which was run mainly by engineers, gave me new insights into trading and processing, particularly in terms of risk and margin management.

Managing the dynamics and volatility of the Power and Gas industry with its structured and sophisticated approach could be a good example for the agri-trading and processing industry. Both industries manage physical commodities, which is a different skill then to, for instance, managing financial products or derivatives.

In addition, they are different worlds: engineers run the energy business while traders run the grain business. Merging the two disciplines meant that we have the opportunity to change the way we looked at risk within the agri-commodity business.

It was very gratifying that we were successful from day one, and that our first client is still actively using our concepts and system with great results.

Could you tell me about Tradesparent?

As a general rule, buyers drive markets; producers and processors have a poor insight into them. This was particularly the case during the super-cycle of 2006-2008, but it was also the case during the period of high price volatility from 2008 to 2010. At that time, traders were making huge profits, but processors were suffering. Processors are traditionally concerned with adding value by turning a raw material into a processed product, but they have difficulty doing that in such volatile markets. The volatility had a negative impact on their margins.

Tradesparent introduces processors to trader concepts and disciplines, a holistic risk and margin management being a major component. The Tradesparent team consists of industry experts and technology specialists who developed a concept called Dynamic Margin Management where we use proprietary data and analytics technology to tie dynamically raw material prices with the prices of the processed products along the forward price-curves of the various margin components.

Engineers run processing companies, just as they ran Reliant's energy business, but they lack the mindset to cope with, or profit from, price volatility. We work to improve their margins through better insights and trading the volatility, but within a strong risk management process.

You left Nidera again 4 years before COFCO acquired a 51 percent stake. While you were CEO, had you already started to look for an equity partner for Nidera?

Indeed, as the company had grown tremendously, and financing became an issue—how do we finance future expansion? Markets were volatile and prices were rising; high prices mean that you need more trade finance. Banks were willing to lend, but they increasingly looked at Nidera's solvency ratio. Equity was important, and we needed more equity. We started to look around for equity partners to take a 10 to 15 percent in the company

Why did the families decide to sell the whole company rather than the initial 10 or 15 percent?

As I said, I left Nidera in 2010 so I was not involved in the transaction. I can only speak from what I have heard second-hand. While our initial intention had been to find an equity partner, the families also wanted a strategic partner to help grow the business. They found that strategic partner in COFCO.

COFCO was interested in acquiring the origination assets that Nidera had in Argentina and Brazil. Nidera was interested in COFCO as a strategic partner. The 51 / 49 percent deal that they eventually agreed was in line with that logic. The idea was that Nidera's managers would continue to run Nidera with an assist from COFCO.

Nidera posted its first loss in five years in 2015 after a rogue trader incurred losses of around $200 million in the biofuels market. How did that happen, and why didn't risk management controls catch it earlier?

I was the last CEO of Nidera who had a trading and risk management experience. A financial manager took over after me, and ultimately a gentleman from Unilever. As often seen in the various trading industries, it is difficult to manage traders, you can have the best governance structure and control systems, but you always have to keep your eyes open for anything that looks out of the ordinary. So, I believe it is easier for an experienced trader to understand and to know what is not right. It takes a trader to catch a trader.

Someone recently told me that they thought it a mistake for COFCO to buy Nidera and Noble at the same time, and that they should have just bought Nidera. Do you agree?

Agricultural commodity trading depends more on knowledge and expertise than on assets. The right assets help if you are a skilled and experienced operator/trader, but assets on their own are not enough. At Nidera we started with people, with knowledge, with a network. We then added the assets.

Agricultural trading and its supply-chain is a people business; assets help, but the key is having the right people. In fact, technology is more important than asset-ownership in success in trading. You have to understand and anticipate commodity flows. At Nidera, it was only once we understood those that we invested in assets.

With all due respect to Noble, they were originally scrap-metal, not agricultural commodity traders. Richard Elman's philosophy was to buy assets and to build an agricultural trading business around those assets. Noble Agri never proved that they could do that.

COFCO had a clear mandate from their government to ensure and guarantee the origination of agricultural commodities for China, and to be less dependent on the ABCD+ group of companies.

To achieve that they bought the two companies at the same time but then had a huge challenge in integrating them, first between the two acquisitions, and second into their own organization, combining it with their way of thinking and their culture. The challenge in a trading business is to give your traders enough space to thrive, while at the same time manage the risks. I don't think it was in COFCO's culture to give traders the freedom they needed to operate.

So yes, I believe they should have only bought Nidera. Noble had assets: some were good, others less so. Many were newly and expensively built. But the people were not as experienced or skilled as at Nidera where the assets were more opportunistic and the focus was more on skilled trading expertise.

If you had been running COFCO what would you have done differently?

Culture is the biggest challenge. COFCO is managed centrally, but they acquired two organizations that were totally decentralized.

I would first have spent time making sure that the two organizations were standing on their own feet and taken time to understand them. I would not have started merging and integrating them before fully understanding their different cultures.

I would therefore have started to integrate the two back offices, but I would have run the two front offices separately. And I would have looked to see how COFCO could help those two separate operations better originate and manage the flows into China.

By merging the two operations they caused havoc, and they rapidly lost their best people.

COFCO International is now trying to compete with the ABCD+s in trading globally, but they still have many challenges to deal with.

If I were COFCO I would concentrate on China's imports and try to optimize these flows. But to be fair, even the biggest and the best—and the longest established—international traders are struggling to make a return at the moment. So, you can see the challenge that COFCO is facing.

Would Nidera still exist if it hadn't been purchased?

That is a good question. I told the shareholders at the time that it wasn't possible to continue the company in the hands of a few shareholders. We needed more capital to support growth. Some family members were willing to sell, others less so.

So no, I don't think Nidera would exist today without a strong strategic or equity partner.

Do you think there is still a role for small trading houses in today's market?

You have to be highly specialized to operate in a trading market. With the strength of the farmer and the strength of the consumer, the trader has to have a very defined role and to add value. I find it hard to believe that the smaller traders can add value unless they have something really unique in their product offering. And the markets are so transparent that this is unlikely.

The large guys are struggling as well. Our whole industry is going through a period that is similar to the time after the Great Grain Robbery of the 1970s. It was difficult to make money in the 1980s and 1990s, and it is difficult to make money now.

And when the margins aren't there, there is a tendency to over-speculate. This is something that needs to be dealt with.

Another problem is that costs are too high. I am optimistic that Blockchain will help to reduce costs and improve margins. The future is technology, but senior management needs to drive it, not the IT department.

What are the greatest risks or challenges that the trading houses face today?

The biggest risk a manager has is in taking decisions on reports based on incomplete or incorrect information. It is a real struggle for companies to collect the correct data in these fast moving and complex markets. Senior management needs to drive this effort and embrace technology themselves, and not leave it to their IT-staff alone.

In the past, trading companies had margins, so they could get away with taking the odd bad decision; everyone makes bad decisions from time to time. But today there are practically no margins in the business, and you are punished immediately for a bad decision.

What mistakes did Nidera make?

When Kuok Khoon Hong began Wilmar, Nidera was asked to partner with him. We then made a big mistake of not pursuing that opportunity. ADM took our place.

It happened a little before I joined. Asia was at that time an unknown for Nidera's shareholders; their focus was on opportunities in Europe and South America. The shareholders missed out completely. Later we tried to re-enter the market and prepared a plan for an investment in palm oil production, but it was a step too far for the shareholders.

What about Russia – Nidera was also too slow there.

If you talk about silos and port infrastructure, then yes, Nidera was too slow, too conservative. But we did develop a trading operation inside Russia, buying sunflower seeds in the interior and exporting them. It was a good business and we expanded it into Ukraine and Kazakhstan. The shareholders liked the trading part but were reluctant to invest in hard assets.

From 2014 to 2016 you were CEO of BayWa's International Trading activities, a subsidiary of BayWa AG, a large German services group. Do you think agricultural cooperatives have a role to play in international grain merchandising?

BayWa used to be a cooperative, but it is now a diversified publically quoted company. In 2012, BayWa bought the Dutch supply-chain company Cefetra B.V. as well as a majority holding in the northern German company Bohnhorst Agrarhandel GmbH. These acquisitions were the gateway to global grain markets for BayWa, and the CEO Prof. Klaus Josef Lutz asked me to join him to help him build an international trading portfolio.

I proposed that BayWa build a major presence in the European market: a supply chain and specialty business. They had a strong origination base in Germany and Austria and together with Cefetra, they could expand the supply-chain across Europe as they understood the flows. They were successful. However, for a traditional cooperative, it is much harder.

Do you have a parting message?

Yes, two! First, information is data, which is the key in running any business, but it is essential in commodity trading. You have to get to the data, clean and organize it. Only then can you start using analytics and business solutions to make informed and solid decisions.

Second, markets are becoming increasingly complex and large trading companies often struggle to manage a global portfolio with a large number of trading units and different products. You have to have the right technology to deal with that complexity.

Thank you, Ito, for your time and insights.

Chapter Thirteen: Louis Dreyfus Company

'We're the supply chain'. **Ian McIntosh, CEO Louis Dreyfus Company**

Léopold Louis-Dreyfus was born in 1833 to a farming family in Sierentz, in the French Alsace region, just a few kilometres from Basel, Switzerland. He had twelve older brothers and by the age of 16 he had probably realised that his future prospects on the farm would be limited. Trying his hand at grain marketing, he transported some wheat from his farm's harvest across the border to Basel where he sold it at a profit. The following year, 1851, Léopold began buying wheat from his neighbours, selling it in Switzerland. (1)

Léopold was too young to incorporate a company under his own name, so he set one up under his father's, Louis Dreyfus, in Berne Switzerland. Some time later Léopold changed his own surname to Louis-Dreyfus, with a hyphen. However, the company is still called Louis Dreyfus—without a hyphen. (I had always wondered why the family name was hyphenated while the company's name wasn't. Now I know!)

Nearly 170 years later, the company Léopold founded still exits. It originates, processes and transports approximately 80million tonnes of agricultural goods annually, accounting for about 10 percent of the world trade in agricultural products, and enough to feed and clothe 500 million people on earth. The company has approximately 18,000 employees and operates in over 100 countries. What is perhaps even more surprising, the company is still under the control of the Louis-Dreyfus family.

By the time Léopold died in 1915, leaving the business in the hands of his two surviving sons, Charles and Louis, the company he had founded was, along with Bunge, the biggest grain merchandiser in the world. But perhaps Léopold had the good fortune to die when he did, without seeing all of his company's Russian assets confiscated in the Bolshevik revolution two years later.

Despite this setback, Léopold's two sons continued to expand into new markets. They also shifted focus a little away from trading towards transportation, building up a significant shipping fleet.

Following the Second World War, the family rebuilt the company around grain trading and shipping, but margins were thin. Their competitors diversified into other sectors of the value chain, in particular processing and crushing, but Louis Dreyfus stuck to what they knew. As a result, the company went from being first of the world's five major grain-trading companies to the fifth.

Gerard (or William, as he often confusingly called himself) Louis-Dreyfus took over as CEO of the company in 1969, at the age of 37. He quickly realised that the company's strength was in arbitrage, and that those strengths could be used outside the grain markets. In 1971, the company went into property development, as well as into non-grain commodities. It also became skilled at arbitraging companies, selling slow-growth sectors and entering faster growing ones. In that sense, Louis Dreyfus essentially developed into a hybrid venture, private equity and hedge fund.

Interestingly, this was a model that Continental Grain was to follow a few years later. Unlike Continental, however, Louis Dreyfus kept their grain merchandising operations.

In 1976 Gerard laid out the strategy in a letter to his staff. It read (2)

"Louis Dreyfus is today in a wide variety of businesses as diverse as restaurant operations in France, irrigation systems in the Middle East, hotel ownership in Brazil, glass manufacture and wood products fabrication in South America, and office building development in United States and Canada. We have diversified and will continue to do so where opportunities are found which can be integrated into and supportive of our existing activities."

In 1986, Louis Dreyfus became one of the first companies to trade energy products, including oil and gas, as commodities, launching a subsidiary called Louis Dreyfus Energy Corporation.

The parent company also diversified into processing, buying in 1988 an orange processing plant in Brazil. It then expanded their orange juice business into Florida, buying 25,000 acres of orange groves and a processing capacity of more than 250,000 tonnes of orange juice concentrate per year.

In 1996, Louis Dreyfus Energy becoming one of the first companies to trade electricity in the U.S., expanding its business to Europe a couple of years later. In 1998 the company launched LDCom Networks and began constructing its own fibre optic network in France. By 2003 it was among the top three telecommunications companies in France.

In 2006 I was in London visiting clients and I had arranged to have dinner with the Louis Dreyfus traders. At that time their office was in Old Burlington Street in the heart of Mayfair, opposite the site of the *Legends* nightclub that I had frequented in my youth. Louis Dreyfus had a reputation for austere, low-key offices, and it was a surprise to everyone when they moved their central London headquarters to such a chic (and expensive) address.

I walked into their office building shortly before 7pm, following behind a rather disheveled gentleman in baggy blue jeans and blazer, both of which had seen better days. He shuffled towards the reception desk where the evening security guard asked for his name.

"Louis-Dreyfus," he told him.

"Yes sir," the guard replied politely. "This is Louis Dreyfus. Who would you like to see?" The man said something that I missed, and the guard again asked for his name.

"Louis-Dreyfus," the man repeated, this time with an edge of frustration in his voice.

"I am sorry sir," the guard replied with authority. "I have to have your name before I can let you enter the building."

"Louis-Dreyfus," he repeated just as firmly, but without any explanation. The security guard looked at me, a slight glimpse of panic in his eyes.

"This is Robert Louis-Dreyfus," I told the guard. "He owns the company. I think you had better let him in."

"I am sorry sir," the guard said. "I didn't recognize you."

Robert turned to see who I was. He saw that I wasn't anyone important and shuffled off into the building.

Born in 1946, Robert was Léopold's great-grandson. He was not great at school—he failed his baccalaureate twice—but he excelled at poker, eventually funding his way through Harvard on his winnings. 'Cards in hand, I came alive', he was quoted as saying. 'I forgot all my hang-ups.' (3)

Robert joined Louis Dreyfus at the request of his father, Jean, who owned about half of the company. Once there, Robert focused on Brazil, turning around an edible oil factory. (4) By the early 1980s, however, he had become increasingly concerned he'd never be more than a junior executive in the company. He left and made a reputation for himself as a 'turnaround specialist', first as CEO of U.S. pharmaceutical company *International Medical Services*, then with the British advertising company *Saatchi & Saatchi*, and then *Adidas*, where he stayed until 2001.

In December 1996, (5) the mayor of Marseilles asked him to work his magic at *Olympique de Marseilles*. Robert spent a reported €200 million on the football club and went through 19 coaches. While there, Robert was investigated for €22m of illegal payments made during the transfers of players. He was given a suspended prison sentence of three years and a fine of €375,000, commuted to 10 months and €200,000 on appeal.

After two decades outside the fold, his family asked him to rejoin the company as chairman of Louis Dreyfus's telecommunications unit. He became CEO of the entire company in 2006. He increased his own stake in the company to 61 percent by buying out cousins, including former CEO Gerard Louis-Dreyfus, father of Julia, the American actress. He also sold the shipping unit, Louis Dreyfus Armateurs based in a Paris suburb, to his cousin Philippe.

Three years later, at the age of 63, Robert died from the leukemia that he had been fighting for thirteen years.

He had been married twice. After divorcing his first wife in 1989, he married his second wife Margarita in 1992, and with whom he had three sons: Eric, Maurice, and Kyril. On his death, Robert made Margarita promise that she would keep the company in the family for their three common sons.

When Robert had first become ill with leukemia he set up a family foundation called *Akira* in which he put his 61 percent majority stake in LDC. He placed the management of the foundation in the hands of Margarita and his two closest associates. The management trio did not work well together, and a power struggle ensued. Margarita won, becoming the new chairman of the board. However, her battles were far from over.

As part of his preparation for his death, Robert had put in place a mechanism that would allow his two sisters, along with two cousins, to sell their shares in the company to the family foundation. The first of these put options was exercised in 2014, increasing the foundation's shareholding from 60 to 80 percent. The remaining shares were tendered in 2018, bringing Margarita's holding to 96.6 percent. (The other 3.4 percent belong to a cousin of Robert who has good relations with Margarita.)

Some have referred to Louis Dreyfus Company as a "company in crisis", (6) and accused Margarita, or MLD as she is now known within the company, of leaving the company short of cash by drawing out excessive dividends so as to buy out the shares of the other family members.

Although that is true, it is clear that her overriding objective has always been to maintain and strengthen the company for her three sons. In that process she has churned through a number of CEOs, and many senior managers and traders have left. Some of the original Louis-Dreyfus family shareholders have even started up in competition, opening a grain-trading company called 'Sierentz', named after the village in France where it all started.

In addition, LDC's troubled Brazilian sugarcane subsidiary Biosev continues to weigh on the results and seems to be in permanent need of financial support from its parent, the Akira Foundation. This support totaled more than $1 billion in 2018. (7)

Biosev is quoted on the Sao Paulo Stock Exchange with a market capitalization of $380 million, maybe a tenth of the sum that LDC has invested over the years. This oversized Brazilian sugarcane footprint, along with the parent company's accumulated debts, makes it harder for LDC to restructure itself to fulfill its ambition of becoming an integrated food company. However, it is trying.

In early 2016, as part of its reinvention, the company changed its name from Louis Dreyfus Commodities to Louis Dreyfus Company—a symbolic change perhaps, but one that gives a clue as to the future direction of the company.

The company now is looking to focus on its core business while at the same reducing debt. As part of this process, Louis Dreyfus offloaded its Africa-based fertilizers business as well as selling—for $466 million—its profitable metals unit to China's Natural Resources Investment Fund. (8)

In addition, the company is expanding its footprint in Asia. In 2018, LDC opened a new oilseeds processing plant in Tianjin, China (9). The plant's bottling, filling, packaging and storage facilities will allow LDC to go downstream in the supply chain by introducing packed oil, another strategic thrust.

In 2019 the company set up a food innovation division (10), part of the commodity trader's efforts to expand its business further down the food chain.

Forty years ago, Louis Dreyfus Company was looking to diversify its activities outside of its traditional agricultural merchandising business, while at the same time strengthening and consolidating agricultural merchandising the length of the supply chain. What LDC is doing now is no different to what it has always done: stay strong in its core merchandising activities to take advantage of boom times when they come, but at the same time to diversify into other sectors to help maintain profitability when the commodity markets are slow.

We know where we're going – Ian McIntosh

IAN joined Louis Dreyfus in 1986 as a trainee on their domestic grains desk in Norfolk, U.K. He traded grains in London, Paris and Melbourne before moving back to London to take over as manager of the global sugar trading operation, sequentially adding coffee, cocoa, rice, ethanol and grains. In 2008, he left LDC to run Edesia Asset Management, a new company created within the LD group. LD closed Edesia at the end of 2017, and Ian was asked to return to LDC, where he became Chief Strategy Officer before taking over as CEO in September 2018.

Good morning, Ian, and thank you for agreeing to this interview. First question: How has the market changed since you joined the business in 1986?

It has changed completely. I remember when I went on my first business trip to Russia; counterparts there didn't even have fax machines, let alone Reuters screens or iPhones with instantaneous price discovery. Digital disruption, for want of a better expression, is a reality. Both consumers and producers are far better informed, and more rapidly informed, than ever before.

But traditional trading companies still have an edge in their deep understanding of production and consumption economics, the value chain and the associated timing. Detailed supply and demand analysis still works. Price convergence in over- and under-supply markets still creates traditional responses, whether it's on the flat price and in time spreads or physical premiums.

The advent of algorithmic trading systems is just one of the changes that the sector has experienced: market price moves to constrain supply and stimulate consumption in over-supplied markets, and vice versa. However, the path to that convergence has become ever more volatile.

Markets now arbitrage information instantaneously. Market price always reflects consensus. If there is a divergence between that consensus and what we consider reality, the question we now must ask is, what route will the market take to achieve that convergence?

This is made harder because discretionary capital in the futures markets has declined relative to non-discretionary capital. We now have a dominance of long-only products, high-frequency traders or macro-capital – which, to be fair, can be discretionary – that creates a distorting effect. If the fair value is x but the money flow pushes the price to x+10 or x-10 it amplifies the convergence requirement. These force – and I think markets are still evolving – a rethink of traditional risk management techniques. The old-school 'We're right, and we'll wait to be proven right' – well, it just doesn't work anymore.

More importantly, the intermediary's traditional role in commodity markets has largely disappeared – or at least, materially changed. A significant disintermediation has taken place. This has many different, but already widely discussed, drivers.

In the past, most trading houses have had an origination focus – and some of the new entrants into the business are still origination-centric. We at LDC see our role as value-chain managers; we're mandatory value-chain participants. To succeed today, a trade house must be integrated along the value chain and become less of a trader in the conventional sense.

And you think LDC can still be relevant [and]... still add value to the supply chain?

Very much so. Take protein for example. It's a well-known story that the primary growth of protein consumption is in Asia; in particular, the rate of growth in China of meat demand exceeds China's ability to produce the raw materials necessary to produce it. The rationale for this is well documented: a combination of GDP and population growth, urbanisation and a dietary shift towards more Western diets. The reality is that, as people get wealthier, they eat more. This creates a systemic and material growth in protein consumption, leading to a protein gap.

It's easy in the West to have a preconceived view of China, but when you become immersed in the country, you realise that China is jumping over many Western developmental steps. There is a clear desire to ensure that food can be traced – that consumers can be confident that it's safe. There have been a number of examples of food contamination because of the lead time between the production and the consumption of the food. Many emerging countries are not used to the Western supply chain model. If your food is coming through a semi-industrialised chain, people must be certain that what they're eating is safe.

As a global commodity participant, LDC can supply complete traceability where appropriate – or close to complete traceability, where it's more difficult. In some cases, we're ourselves the producers, and in other cases, we're the direct link to the first producer. We not only handle the logistics but in some cases, we're also the industrial transformer.

It's different sector by sector within the agri-supply chain, but for a trading company to succeed, it needs that integration. The margin is to be found in integrating the whole supply chain, not any section of the supply chain. It's hard to make the statement today that the money is in originating beans or in trading beans. The margin is in the full value chain. It sits within the value chain. This move up and downstream is not discretionary. It's mandatory. To fail to do that risks disappearance.

But when you have a traceable supply chain, you lose flexibility and tradability.

Not necessarily. Once you have built the conduits for traceability, that traceability is transferable. But we not only have to make sure our commodities are traceable, but we also have to ensure that they're produced sustainably. This is something we take seriously. The rate of adoption by the end user of the dual concepts of traceability and sustainability has been really rapid. It has become mainstream. To fail to do that results in marginalisation.

So, once you put in place the conduits that ensure that your commodity is both traceable and sustainable, the flexibility is still there. For example, if you're selling Brazilian sugar into Indonesia and freight rates change, you can flip that cargo to another destination while maintaining both sustainability and traceability. If a company is well structured, you can then transfer that traceability – it isn't lost.

It's this multi-geographic footprint that's important. One of the things that trading companies are realising is that size really does matter. A trade house's geographic footprint matters. I think trade houses with an insufficient geographic footprint lose that flexibility.

Looking at your competitors, Glencore Agriculture says that 85 percent of their profits come from distribution and logistics and only 15 percent from trading. Cargill is making a big move into protein, and ADM, into ingredients and higher-value foodstuffs. Olam has done a successful move into what were once considered niche areas, but on such a large scale that they are no longer niche. Has LDC identified a particular focus area?

Yes, very much so. There are four pillars to our strategy.

The first is to build on and improve our traditional merchandising function. We recognise that traditional merchandising has changed, and we need to ensure that we have the correct geographical footprint and the correct information base to understand price evolution to maintain the flexibility that has always been a core element of profitability. That means maintaining the origination base. It also means increasing our consumptive footprint, where appropriate. This can mean getting closer to the consumers in the case of coffee or sugar or going further downstream in the case of oilseeds and grains. That plays into the logistics element.

The second is to recognise that disintermediation is real and that we either need to be closer to the consumer in an integrated value chain or be a consumer ourselves. We see vertical integration and, particularly, vertical downstream integration as core to our activities. An example of that is the new crushing plant that we've opened in Tianjin in China. This takes us down the animal protein route. It may mean going even further downstream, into bottled edible oils or other branded products or whatever is appropriate.

The third pillar, which follows from that, is to move more into ingredients as an active participant in the food sector. We're already in that business. For example, we produce glycerine and lecithin as an adjunct to the soya business or citrus oils and essences from our orange juice business. These were traditionally considered byproducts. Clearly, there's an opportunity here to identify cross-commodity areas.

Our fourth pillar is innovation, not necessarily in technology, but in food. We're looking at the future of food, alternative proteins and ingredients, and working to be ahead of the curve in supplying consumer needs.

So, we know where we're going. In five years' time, LDC will be a diversified food and nutrition company in addition to being a traditional commodity merchant. We have the strategy, and the roadmap is clear. It's my task now to successfully implement that strategy.

What is LDC's USP (unique selling point)?

LDC is differentiated by its long family heritage, the diversity and geographic spread of its agricultural product portfolio and the degree of integration across its value chain. Together, these factors give the company a unique identity and ability to leverage opportunities and mitigate risk over time.

It's interesting to see the way that the different trade houses are evolving, the different paths they're taking.

People tend to lump the ABCDs, as well as Glencore, COFCO and Wilmar, into the same basket. But commodity companies now have different focuses; direct comparisons are no longer valid. The acronyms are no longer valid.

The Brazilian sugarcane industry has been exceedingly challenging for companies such as yourselves and Bunge. Can you see any end to the tunnel?

The Brazilian sugarcane industry has all the ingredients for both economic and environmental success. However, the sector has suffered from government intervention. Successive governments have kept gasoline prices below their economic and environmental cost; this has made it difficult for ethanol to compete and resulted in losses for the sector. The country's new president seems supportive of their domestic ethanol industry, and we're optimistic that this situation will be changed going forward.

Having said that, there are still a lot of questions over long-term sugar consumption trends as well as over ethanol policy globally.

Continental Grain sold their agricultural merchandising business many years ago to Cargill. They apparently felt at the time that the risks weren't worth the rewards. How difficult is it for a company like LDC to move these massive quantities of foodstuffs around the world while managing the associated risks?

That comes back to an earlier point. When Continental Grain sold their trading business, most trading companies were trading in a traditional way. The current trend towards disintermediation makes it easier for us to manage our risk. It mitigates risk rather than increases it. If you're your own consumer, you're taking your own credit risk.

It's also clear that diversification does have a clear benefit. A number of the companies that have either left the business or been consolidated were relatively narrow sector. The correlation across commodities varies. Some are highly correlated, but others aren't. For example, the correlation between coffee and corn is low. The risk management benefits of a portfolio approach are significant, as too are the benefits of a diversified global footprint.

It's true that you have a different type of risk the further downstream you go and the more you immerse yourself in developing economies. Back in the 1990s, you were mainly concerned with market risk. Now, you're concerned with market, geopolitical, country risk and company risk. Having an integrated approach mitigates that.

Trading conditions have been tough recently for the grain trading companies. To what extent do you think this is structural and to what extent cyclical?

Grain is a simple commodity, with relatively low barriers to entry. It has an animal nutrition component and a human nutrition component. It also has a biofuel component through corn. Companies that are successful today in grains participate in all three sectors. The value proposition today is integrated logistics across geographies, with links to oilseeds.

Having said that, a combination of oversupply and competition means that the grain market is currently difficult, but that's part of the cycle. All commodities are the same in that sense.

How do you see technological change affecting the business into the future, particularly blockchain?

Blockchain is part of a broader move towards digital documentation. New technologies like blockchain can mitigate a number of risks and work well with traceability and the integrated value chain approach that we're pursuing. They represent a significant move in the right direction in making the agricultural supply chain appropriate to the requirements of consumers. LDC did the first-ever blockchain transaction in agricultural commodities – a cargo of soybeans to China – and we intend to remain at the leading edge of technology.

Having said that, I don't see blockchain as revenue transformative. I see it as a mandatory evolution of the value chain. Overcoming the challenges of integration, interoperability and industry standards will create a more robust, efficient and transparent way to manage our flows and reduce operational risk. It will also improve the credibility of the supply chain. In addition, it will lower barriers to entry and potentially bring more liquidity to our market.

About 30 to 40 percent of food is wasted between farm and fork. How can LDC help to reduce that wastage?

Most food waste occurs outside of the supply chain in which we operate. In most cases, LDC is not a food producer, so our ability to reduce waste at the farmer level is limited. At the other end of the chain, the fact that supermarkets sell goods with defined sell-by dates – that may or may not be appropriate – is not something that we can control. That isn't to say that we have no desire to control it, but we have no interface with that. It's therefore wrong to say that the solution to food waste sits within the commodity-merchandising sector. There's virtually no waste in what we do, and quite often, what we do regard as waste is a by-product, which is further used.

Glencore recently opened their agricultural commodity unit to outside capital. Is this something that LDC would consider?

That's a decision for our shareholders and Akira B.V., the Louis-Dreyfus family trust that has a majority shareholding in LDC. Our chairperson, Margarita Louis-Dreyfus, has said on several occasions, including recently, that Akira wishes to keep all options open, with the interests of the company always as a priority. She has said that this could be in many forms, including strategic partnerships. So, no options are excluded. We're also looking to grow different parts of our business through joint ventures, partnerships, acquisitions etc.

Would you recommend that a young person enter the business today?

Yes, very strongly. We operate in a unique sector – and it's more unique now than ever – where you can combine an interest in geopolitics with economics, with logistics, with financial elements and at the same with industrial activities and with agriculture. It's the most multi-faceted business that I can think of. That's what attracted me to commodities in the first place.

One of the areas where a young trainee can come in and really make a difference is in how the world is nourished and how farmers can not only survive, but thrive. In addition, there's the whole area of traceability, sustainability, human rights…it's a hugely multi-faceted sector. For any young individual with an ambition to be part of a global business, it's a great career.

Is there anything that you'd like to add?

What I really want to stress is that preconceived notions of what a trade house is and does no longer apply. Those notions are outdated.

I would also like to emphasise the importance of adaptability. The companies that succeed are the ones that rapidly recognise change and then adapt their structures and staff accordingly.

I started life as a 'commodity trader', and I've never lost that trader's DNA; it runs through everything I do. However, we as a company and I are much less traders than we were thirty years ago. And that trend will continue.

People still use the term 'trade houses' to describe us, and I think it will be hard to change that. However, I don't think there's such a thing as a trade house anymore. We're all supply chain operators within the agricultural sector, but we're also nutrition companies. And we're all moving in our different directions. But it'll take a while for old mnemonics to change.

Ian, thank you for your time and insights!

Chapter Fourteen – Glencore Agriculture

'It's the chain that makes the money'. – Chris Mahoney, CEO Glencore Agriculture

Glencore –an abbreviation of 'Global Energy Commodity Resources' – traces its history to 1974, when the legendary, controversial commodity trader Marc Rich founded the eponymous Marc Rich & Co. AG. London's *Financial Times* newspaper once described Marc Rich as 'one of the wealthiest and most powerful commodity traders that ever lived'.

Marc Rich was born Marcel Reich in Antwerp but fled the Holocaust with his parents via Morocco to the United States. In 1954, at age 20, he started in the mailroom at Philipp Brothers, then the world's largest trader in raw materials. He worked his way up on to the trading floor in New York before moving to head up the company's Madrid office, where he started trading oil. Some observers credit Marc Rich with inventing the spot crude market; previously, all oil was traded on long-term fixed price contracts.

Philipp Brothers, now Phibro, traces its origins back to 1901, when Julius Philipp founded a small metal trading company in Hamburg, Germany. Eight years later, Julius's younger brother, Oscar, established a metal trading company in London under the name Philipp Brothers. Julius continued to run the German operation from Hamburg.

In 1914, Siegfried Bendheim, a minor partner in the London operation, moved to New York City, where he established Philipp Brothers, Inc., while Oscar Philipp continued to run the London office. In 1934, Julius moved Philipp Brothers' German operations to Amsterdam due to the rise of Nazi Germany. Even so, he perished in 1944 in the Bergen–Belsen concentration camp. The New York office at 29 Broadway eventually became Philipp Brothers' headquarters.

In 1960, Phillip Brothers merged with Minerals and Chemicals Corporation of America (MCCA) and became publicly traded. By then, the company had become the world's largest metal traders and were particularly active in tin, handling most of Bolivia's exports. In 1967, Philipp Brothers/MCCA merged with Engelhard Minerals and Chemicals (EMC). Two years later, Anglo American acquired the newly merged company. In 1981, it spun it off as Phibro Corporation. Later that same year, the newly independent company bought Salomon Brothers, at that time the world's largest investment bank and bond dealer, for $550 million.

It's perhaps surprising to a modern reader that a commodity trading company could have taken over a bank, especially one as big as Salomon Brothers. However, by the end of the 1970s commodity boom, commodity traders were the cash-rich kings of the business world. They flew first class, ate in the best restaurants and stayed in the best hotels. I was lucky enough to catch the tail end of this: my first business trip was to Paris, where I stayed a week in a suite at the Hotel Georges V, one of the best hotels in the world.

By the mid-1980s, commodity traders had become the paupers of the business world; investment bankers and bond dealers were at the front of the plane, commodity traders, at the back. (1)

In 1986, Phibro Salomon dropped 'Phibro' from its name. In 1997, the bank was acquired by Travelers Group, which merged with Citicorp to form Citigroup in 1998. With the merger, Salomon became an indirect, wholly owned subsidiary of Citigroup. In 2009, Occidental Petroleum acquired Phibro from Citigroup, estimating its net investment at approximately $250 million, and it 2016, it was purchased by Energy Arbitrage Partners for an undisclosed sum. (2)

But Marc Rich was long gone. He had grown frustrated that Phibros was not aggressive enough; he resigned in 1974 to set up his own trading company in Zug, Switzerland. He chose Switzerland because of its low tax rates and the fact that Switzerland was neutral. Back then, it wasn't even a member of the United Nations.

Marc Rich & Co. was spectacularly profitable from the start and, by the end of the 1970s, had 30 offices around the world. The five partners divided themselves between New York (where Marc Rich himself worked), London, Madrid and Zug.

In 1983, however, U.S. authorities charged Marc Rich with evading taxes and trading with Iran during the Iranian hostage crisis. He fled to Switzerland, where he lived as a fugitive for 17 years.

In *The King of Oil* (3) by Daniel Ammann, Marc Rich admitted to buying oil from Iran during the embargo, supplying oil to apartheid South Africa and bribing officials in countries such as Nigeria. He argued that all this was legal at the time. He contended the bribing of foreign officials was legal in the United States until the passing of the Foreign and Corrupt Practices Act of 1977. It remained legal in Switzerland until 2000. And as a non-U.S. company based in Switzerland, Marc Rich & Co was legally (if perhaps not morally) exempt from the embargoes on Iran and apartheid South Africa.

U.S. President Bill Clinton officially pardoned Marc Rich on his last day in office in January 2001. The pardon was highly controversial, but according to Mr Ammann, it resulted from Israel's intensive lobbying. Throughout his career, Marc Rich had given large sums to the country and worked closely with Mossad, their security services.

A member of the Swiss Parliament once referred to Marc Rich as a 'bloodsucker of the Third World'. Daniel Ammann takes a more balanced view, writing:

> Most commodities come from countries that are not beacons of democracy and human rights. The 'resource curse' and 'the paradox of plenty' are the terms economists and political scientists use to describe the fact that countries that are rich in oil, gas, or metals are usually plagued by poverty, corruption, and misgovernment. If commodity traders want to be successful, they are forced – much like journalists or intelligence agents who will take their information from any source – to sit down with people that they would rather not have as friends, and they apparently have to resort to practices that are either frowned upon or downright illegal in other parts of the world.

By the early 1990s, the legal case against Marc Rich was taking its toll. A difficult divorce and the death of his daughter added to his woes, and the company's partners began to worry about their company's future. Marc's legendry feel for the markets deserted him, as did many of his key traders. A failed attempt to corner the zinc market left the company with $172 million in losses, and the firm was struggling. After first resisting, Marc Rich finally sold his 51 percent majority share in the company in a managerial buy-out for an eventual total of $600 million.

The first thing that the new owners did was to change the company name to Glencore. The company went public in May 2011 and now has a market capitalisation in excess of £42 billion. Marc Rich himself died on 26 June 2013 at age 78. Despite his pardon, he never returned to the U.S.

Glencore Agriculture can trace its roots to 1980, when Marc Rich formed Richco Grain. A year later, he purchased the international assets of Granaria, a Dutch grain trader, leveraging his Middle East connections to become a nearly exclusive supplier of barley to Saudi Arabia.

Glencore Agriculture's transformational deal came in 2012, when it saw the opportunity to buy Viterra, Canada's largest grain handler. Viterra Inc. was (and still is) Canada's largest grain handler, with its historic roots in prairie grain-handling cooperatives, among them the Saskatchewan Wheat Pool. The company's grain handling and marketing operations are now located primarily in two of the world's most fertile regions: Western Canada and South Australia. Viterra owns and operates grain terminals in Western Canada, along with grain handling and storage facilities in South Australia.

Viterra was also one of the largest agri-product retailers in Canada, with a network of more than 250 retail locations throughout the Prairies. As part of that activity, Viterra owned a 34 percent interest in Canadian Fertilizer Limited CFI, a large urea and ammonia plant. The company also operated several processing businesses, including the Dakota Growers Pasta Company and 21st Century Grain.

In 2012, Viterra was generating $2.4 billion in revenue and $244 million in profits. When Viterra came on the market, Glencore outbid ADM in a friendly deal that valued the business at $6.1 billion.

The acquisition of Viterra transformed Glencore Agriculture into a major player. Before the deal, Glencore was handling about 45 million tonnes a year of grains and other agricultural products a year. Viterra pushed the number to 70 million tonnes.

Today, Glencore Agriculture, with Viterra, has 274 grain storage facilities in 17 countries. It has 36 processing and refining plants in a dozen countries, and 23 port terminals in eight countries. Rounding out the portfolio is a charter fleet of 180 ocean-going ships and almost 2,000 rail cars.

Shortly after Glencore acquired Viterra, falling prices of oil, copper, nickel, coal and other commodities sent Glencore shares and shares in the wider commodities sector crashing from a high of £3.50 in 2014 to under £1 in 2015. The company launched a massive deleveraging exercise, which included the sale of some non-core assets to reduce debt.

Glencore had long thought about bringing in partners to help it increase its agricultural footprint, and they quickly accelerated this process, selling 40 percent of Glencore Agriculture to CPPIB (Canada Pension Plan Investment Board) for US$2.5 billion and 9.9 percent to BCIMC (British Columbia Investment Management Corporation) for $624.9 million. The transaction valued Glencore Agriculture at U.S.$6.25 billion. The share sale created a new company (Glencore AG) with its own balance sheet, but not guaranteed by Glencore itself.

Glencore AG currently has 14,000 employees, and its products include grains, oilseed products, pulses, cotton and sugar. With crush plants in different parts of the world, the company supplies sunflower seed oil, rapeseed oil and soybean oil for the food and biofuel industries. The company processes rape methyl ester and soya methyl ester mainly in Europe and Argentina for biodiesel markets all over the world. Glencore AG operates the world's biggest soybean processing and crushing plant, with an annual crushing capacity of 11 million tonnes.

The company is also the world's largest direct originator and handler of pulses – including dry field peas, chickpeas, lentils, edible beans and lupins. In addition, it sources cotton from the major exporting countries, with origination offices in the U.S., Australia, Brazil, India and West Africa giving direct access to producers.

Glencore AG has big ambitions. In 2011, just before Glencore Plc's $10 billion IPO, it explored a merger with Louis Dreyfus, but the companies were several billion dollars apart. In 2018, Glencore AG approached Bunge about a merger or acquisition. Nothing came of the talks, but later that year, there are rumours that Glencore was in negotiations to acquire ADM's grain-handling business. Nothing came of those talks either, but at the time of publication, there is talk that Glencore AG is studying the possibility of acquiring Bunge's grain trading operations.

Other trade houses have turned to food processing and specialist ingredient activities to reduce their dependence on traditional grain trading, but Glencore remains committed to infrastructure and logistics.

Emptying a Silo with a Shovel - Chris Mahoney

Chris Mahoney joined Glencore in 1998. In 2002, he became director of the Agricultural Products business segment, responsible for both strategy and operations. In 2016, following the formation of Glencore Agriculture Ltd, he became Chief Executive Officer. Before joining Glencore, Chris spent 17 years with Cargill in the UK, the USA, Singapore and Switzerland, and held various management positions in sugar and grain. He graduated from Oxford University.

Good morning, Chris, and thank you for taking the time to talk with us. First question: You rowed in the Oxford & Cambridge Boat Race from 1979 to 1981 and are a four-time winner at Henley Royal Regatta. You won the silver medal in the eight at the 1980 Moscow Olympics. What lessons did your rowing career teach you that have been useful to you as a commodity trader?

Sport for me is a microcosm of life, especially business life. As in everything, the more you put into it, the more you get out; the harder you work, the better you become. So the things that you need to do to succeed in sport are the same things you need to do to succeed in business: effort, focus, discipline and dedication. The beauty of sport is there are little politics. If you're fast, nobody can deny it. There is no quick fix. It takes years of effort and hard work to do well in sport. It's the same in business!

When the Canadian Globe and Mail interviewed you in 2016, the journalist wrote that you looked like you 'could empty a grain silo in about 10 minutes with a shovel'. How do you keep so fit, and how does it help you bear the pressure of the job?

I probably exercise five times a week, including cycling at the weekends. When I cycle, I go at it hard. And in the gym, I don't sit on the rowing machine for 45 minutes. I do interval training, for example five times 1,000 metres. That' not only better for you but is also less boring! Also, I time and record everything, and I wear a heartbeat monitor.

Ivan Glasenberg, the CEO of Glencore, was a champion racewalker for both South Africa and Israel. Is physical fitness actively encouraged at Glencore?

I believe Ivan runs or swims every morning with a group from the office. I know, because I've tried and failed to keep up with them when I've been in Baar. We used to run together when we were travelling. I think it's part of the culture, although not for everyone. When you're exercising hard, you're not thinking about anything. In fact, if I'm not suffering, I find it less relaxing!

Marc Rich once famously told his wife when they got married that he could spare the family 30 minutes on a Saturday and 45 minutes on a Sunday. How do you manage your work/life balance?

That's absolutely not the case with me. There was one big transaction, the Viterra transaction, which was an exception. It was an intense six- or seven-month period during which I spent many weekends in Canada. That period aside, I believe I've always been able to balance my family and my work. I virtually never travel on the weekend – I make a point of that. My family is very important to me.

When you were at Cargill you 'invented' the model of modern sugar trading, levering large physical positions against futures positions and then making big profits on the futures. That was very innovative, although the model has pretty much run itself to death now. You could've ended up running Cargill. Why did you leave?

I don't know that I could've ended up running Cargill. I started in sugar, which was relatively independent, and a little apart from corporate Cargill. Working in the sugar division of Cargill at that time was a little bit like running your own company. There was no real interference from above, but at the same time, the financing and the corporate support were there. It was ideal.

Cargill likes to rotate their senior managers, and in the mid-nineties, I was transferred to the grain division in a regional management role. There are a lot of people in Cargill who know something about grain and, good company though Cargill is, there were too many opinions at that time for my liking. Perhaps unreasonably, I found it restrictive and missed the trading, and so I left, probably more my fault than Cargill's.

Didn't you at one stage trade coffee?

Yes, you're right, but for only a short period. Every morning, we had to taste different grades of coffee, and one day, my colleagues played a trick on me and slipped in two cups of tea. I couldn't tell the difference! Let's say I was not the best coffee taster in the world!

When you first left Cargill, you worked for a short while at Phibro?

Yes, in Westport Connecticut with Andy Hall, who incidentally also rowed for Oxford against Cambridge, but a few years before me. I made the easy choice – which probably wasn't the right choice – to go back to what I knew: to go back to the sugar business in a pure trading role.

When I joined them, Phibro was part of Salomon Smith Barney, but a few months later, they were bought by Travellers Group, and then three months after that, they merged with Citibank. These were two big bank mergers, and commodities didn't fit their plans. Andy told me I could stay on, but that I would have to keep the business small and focused entirely on futures and derivatives. I already believed that a pure derivatives trading business was never going to work in sugar. It had to have a physical base with origination, sales and a distribution book. Guessing whether the market was going to go up or down was never going to work, or at least it was never going to work for me.

So you joined Glencore in Rotterdam. You'd moved from Geneva to Westport and after only a few months moved back to Europe. What did your wife think of that?

She was not very happy. My wife is American – she'd been excited about going back to the U.S., and that was one of the reasons why I accepted the position with Phibro. I remember promising her that this would be our base and this was going to be our life. We bought a nice house in Connecticut, one of those old colonial houses. Our daughter was born there.

But eight months later, we talked it over, and both realised that the opportunity with Glencore was just too good to turn down. She was very supportive. We agreed to give it a go for a couple of years and that, if it didn't work out, we'd come back to Connecticut. That was 21 years ago. We moved to the Hague. She found it tough for a few years, but stuck with it. The Dutch are easy to get on with, and it's a lovely place to live – great for kids. We love it.

I joined Glencore in 1998 as number two with geographical responsibilities for South America, the FSU and Africa, and became head of Agriculture in 2002.

In 2011, your cotton-trading department lost $300 million, wiping out your total profits of that year. Would you like to briefly explain what happened and what you learned from it?

We had a large long position in non-U.S. physical cotton hedged in the U.S. futures market. It was a basis, or premium, position – not an outright position – so we believed our risks were limited. The physical market was tight at that time – both in the U.S. and globally. Our position expressed the view that world cotton was undervalued compared to U.S. cotton.

One of our competitors decided to take delivery of the U.S. cotton futures. They had specifically sold U.S. cotton to their customers and wanted U.S. cotton to cover their sales. The problem was that they wanted to take delivery of more U.S. cotton than was physically available for delivery. Rather than swap U.S. cotton for other cheaper origins, which was the economic thing to do in my view, they maintained their long position in U.S. futures, and the market went sky high. Non-U.S. origins also went up in price, but to nothing like the same extent. A huge differential opened up between U.S. cotton and non-U.S. cotton.

You were head of Glencore agricultural at that time, so the problem ended up on your plate?

I was responsible for setting up the cotton desk, so it more than landed on my plate. It was my plate. It was clearly my responsibility. We had hired a team from outside, because we didn't have a cotton business. Clearly, with hindsight, we should have looked to have developed a cotton team from within, supplemented with outside expertise. Glencore in Switzerland was not happy, of course, but Ivan supported me in a way that I never forgot.

How important is corporate culture, and if it's important, does it make it hard for mergers to work in the trading business?

Corporate culture is critical, and that's one reason why it's challenging to acquire trading businesses. Acquiring assets – a logistics business and supply chain management – is easier. There's also the issue that, unless you're willing to double the risk – double the size of the VAR – then one plus one doesn't necessarily equal two. We also do not feel we need to buy trading expertise, as we already have it.

Could you tell us a little about the Viterra acquisition and how it happened?

It was a complicated transaction, and at that time, I had little experience in major M&A. Canada and, therefore, Viterra became a focus for us because the Canadian Wheat Board's monopoly rights were about to be rescinded by the government. We were also already a big trader of wheat, barley and canola, and these were key exports from Canada. It was complementary. We began by looking at the business as a whole, and we identified the businesses that we didn't want. We presold the fertiliser production and distribution to Agrium and CF Industries. We presold a smaller piece of the fertiliser business and some of the grain handling assets to Richardson. If the transaction hadn't gone through, those sales would've been unwound.

We presold those businesses in part to help with financing the acquisition, but also because we either didn't want them or because we wanted to involve Canadian companies in the transaction. There wasn't an anti-trust issue, as we didn't already have a business in Canada, but we had to get approval as a foreign company taking over a strategic Canadian company. Pre-selling parts of the business to Canadian companies helped us enormously in getting Canadian government approval.

We also sold off quite a number of businesses post the acquisition, like the pasta, malt business and the petroleum distribution business. We ended up keeping only about 50 percent of the company. The enterprise value of the total acquisition was $7.3 billion. At the time, it was the biggest acquisition in our space – and still is.

The deal was finalised in Toronto. The Viterra people were in a building, and I was in a restaurant with the rest of the deal team, just over the road. At one stage, there was a long silence, and we thought we had lost it to ADM. There was a bit of 'toing and froing', during which I was on the phone with Ivan Glasenberg, Agrium and Richardson deciding whether we should pay more – and how much more. That was one of the beauties of working for Glencore and particularly with Ivan, whom I reported to directly. For such a large company, there was almost no bureaucracy. You could make big decisions incredibly quickly and easily. It was a huge advantage.

Glencore is somewhat more structured now than it used to be, but to some extent, it has to be given the growth of the business post the merger with Xstrata. It's still the same people, though. And the company is people. It's only as good as the people that run it.

Why did you keep the Viterra name?

In Canada, Viterra had a long history and a well-respected name, appreciated by the farming community, so we had no reason to change it. In Australia, Viterra itself had only bought the business three or four years earlier. Glencore already had a sizable trading business in Australia, headquartered in Melbourne. The Viterra business was headquartered in Adelaide, and it was a separate non-trading business providing handling services to third parties as well as to Glencore, so it made some sense to keep the two separate.

Glencore Ltd has transformed itself from a trading company into a mining and trading company. Is Glencore Ag planning any similar transformation, or did the Viterra acquisition already do that?

I think we've largely already done that. Something like 80 percent of our earnings now comes from non-trading. But the asset businesses of Glencore Ag are quite different from the mining businesses of Glencore PLC. Even where we have a dense set of assets such as in Canada – 65 country elevators and five port facilities – we're buying from the farmer and selling to customers around the world; nothing is entirely back-to-back. So these are asset-based businesses with strong elements of trading running through them. As I said, this type of business now constitutes 80 percent of Cargill Ag's earnings.

You mean Glencore Ag's?

(Laughs.) Yes, sorry. You know, I still sometimes answer the phone 'Cargill!'

Trading has become more difficult for reasons that are well known to everyone. This will not change. The transformation to an asset-based company, both in Glencore as a whole and in Glencore Ag, bought Glencore PLC to where it is today, with an annual EBITDA of $14 to $15 billion. This would obviously be quite impossible as a trading company. Already in the early 2000s, we could see that pure trading was going to become increasingly challenging.

Other trading houses are moving both ways along the supply chain. Cargill has moved into proteins; ADM and LDC, into ingredients. Is Glencore Ag planning to do something similar?

No. I think that's very difficult to do. If you're Cargill and you started to do that 40 or 50 years ago, as they did, that was the right move. They can continue in that same direction. It's a natural progression. For us to transform ourselves now from an upstream procurement, handling, oilseed-crushing company into a company that captures the full value chain – that includes refining, bottling, milling, branding, ingredients, feed – is very difficult.

I say that for a simple reason: we originate about 80 million tonnes per year, and it's much easier to capture those big flows upstream, as you're dealing with fewer origins. For example, Russia exports 40 million tonnes of wheat each year through five or six port facilities. Argentina supplies almost 50 percent of the world's soybean meal through just a few export corridors. You can capture big flows in relatively few countries moving through big facilities. The business is much more fragmented on the consumption end. Egypt, the world's biggest buyer of wheat, imports 10 or 11 million tonnes, and there are multiple importers and, in turn, numerous millers.

One of the mantras that you hear in our business is that you have to capture the full value chain. We can't possibly do that now. It would cost billions to build downstream businesses of a tonnage that was even remotely relevant to the tonnage that we secure upstream. That isn't viable from where we are today. Instead, we have to look at improving the core business by deploying capital in the right places.

What do your Canadian shareholders add to your business – and do you think that, at some stage, Glencore Ag will spin off as a private company?

Glencore Ag is already a separate company owned 50 percent by Glencore and 50 percent by our two Canadian shareholders. They add financial muscle. They're in for the long term. They bring certain insights and observations as an outsider in terms of analytics, finance and a global investment perspective that's valuable.

Are you still looking at mergers and acquisitions?

I still believe that the industry requires consolidation through mergers or acquisitions. Moving downstream is not tackling the problem. What I believe we need to do is stick to our core business, focus on developing the broadest geographic footprint to spread the crop and event risk, increase our economies of scale and take a disciplined approach to organic expansion. The industry is still underpinned by good demand growth, and seaborne trade will grow at a faster rate than consumption itself. Technology does not threaten our handling and processing businesses, as it can't replace the assets themselves.

Where is there overcapacity?
In the north of Brazil…in the U.S. Pacific Northwest…in the U.S. Gulf…in the Ukraine…on the east coast of Australia. There was only limited overcapacity in Canada on the west coast, but with recent investments in the port of Vancouver, there will now be more overcapacity for a number of years.

Not only is there overcapacity, but also the existing installed capacity has become a lot more efficient, largely because transport has become more efficient. Trains and trucks are getting bigger, and operators have expanded their terminal input capacity. For example, the railroad in Canada and barge system along the Amazon are increasingly more efficient. Efficiency gains are, of course, effectively capacity gains.

What is preventing M&A activity in the sector?
A number of things. You'd think that pressured margins would encourage acquisitions. The industry has had a difficult two or three years during which potential acquirers have had their own earning issues and were obviously less bold. Things were potentially cheaper, but the buyers were more careful. On the other hand, sellers are reluctant because they think the industry will get better. It hasn't, yet. Anti-trust and foreign control regulation are also a potential hurdle to some combinations.

Half of Brazil's cane is used to make ethanol. Do you believe biofuels have a future?
People blow hot and cold on biofuels. Politicians were positive on biofuels 12 years or so ago, and they set up structures to support them: either mandating their use or providing tax advantages or both. This propelled ethanol production in the U.S. and Brazil, and biodiesel production in Europe.

In 2007–8 and again in 2012, we had periods of high crop prices, and people became rightly concerned about the competition between food and fuel. When you look at the amount of food that gets processed into fuel, it's clear why this is an issue. We should be concerned about using food to produce fuel when people don't have enough food. The other issue is, when you look at the carbon footprint of biofuels and consider fertiliser, water and diesel use, you question whether they're really that good for the environment. That issue hasn't been completely resolved. This turned the politicians off, and the political support was pulled.

However, I think there has been something of a rethink. Food prices have come down, and we have surpluses again. When that happens, biofuels can help support prices for farmers. Over 40 percent of U.S. corn production is used for ethanol, and over 50 percent of EU rapeseed oil is used to produce biodiesel. If you took away that demand, prices would collapse along with farm incomes.

How involved are you in biofuels?

We have three biodiesel plants in the E.U. Margins were low for three to four years with static demand and production overcapacity. In the past few years, no new capacity has been added, and some capacity has been taken out. Demand has increased a little. Meanwhile, the drought last summer put some plants out of action, as they couldn't get their barges up the rivers. At the same time, the E.U. blocked SME imports from Argentina and, in some circumstances, PME from Asia. Margins have improved considerably, and the business has been good for the past year.

Biofuels are a good example of optionality in Ag assets. There's an embedded optionality in Ag assets.

So, assets are your biggest asset, so to speak!

An asset base is essential today, but in addition to their asset portfolios, what distinguishes companies is their people, their culture, the way management and employees interact and treat each other – the respect they show for each other. What kind of a company do you want to make it? In the end, any company can hire bright people, but it's the steps it takes to build a motivated, hard-working, entrepreneurial, fast-acting team that's important for success. People spend the greatest part of their lives at work; they don't do it only for the money. The Glencore culture is a strength, I believe, certainly helped in the early days by private ownership. It's something that must be nurtured to ensure that, despite growth, it isn't lost.

Thank you, Chris, for your time and insights!

Chapter Fifteen: Wilmar

'China and Indonesia were the foundation of our group' - Khoon Hong Kuok, CEO Wilmar

Wilmar International Limited was founded in 1991 as Wilmar Trading Pte Ltd in Singapore with an initial capital of $100,000. It is now Asia's leading agribusiness group with a market capitalisation of US$16 billion and a turnover in 2018 of nearly $45 billion. That's not bad for a relative newcomer in what is traditionally considered to be a slow growth industry. But then, Khoon Hong Kuok, the company's co-founder and CEO, comes from excellent breeding stock.

Khoon Hong was born in 1949, in the seaside village of Mersing in Johor, Malaysia, the second of four children. His uncle, Robert Kuok, known in the company as RK, had founded Kuok Brothers in 1949 in Johor Bahru, Malaysia, as a small family business trading rice, sugar and wheat flour. The company expanded and moved its headquarters in Singapore in 1953, where it developed its business internationally, especially in sugar. RK quickly became known as Asia's 'Sugar King'.

In 1974, RK had an opportunity to make a big sugar deal with China, but the Chinese wanted him to move his company headquarters to Hong Kong. He took the next plane out of Singapore to Hong Kong and went straight from the airport to a lawyer's office where he bought an off-the-shelf company that the lawyer had previously set up. The lawyer was Irish, and the company's name was Kerry Trading.

The company expanded quickly into China's food sector, particularly vegetable oils, transport and shipping. RK used some of the profits to found and build the Shangri La hotel chain, and his company also became a major property developer in the Asian region.

I had the good fortune to interview RK for my book *Sugar Casino*. He told me, 'I have a simple motto in life: every single material thing that I have in life can be traded. It's for sale. It's a question of, when, where, to whom and price. The first three are more important. If you like a person, the price becomes unimportant'.

Khoon Hong's father, Hock Swee, was RK's cousin. By Chinese tradition, RK referred to Khoon Hong as 'nephew', and he called RK 'uncle'. After completing a Bachelor's Degree in Business at the National University of Singapore, Khoon Hong went to work for his uncle's flour milling business in Malaysia in 1973. He quickly became what RK called the 'driving force' of the company's expansion in agriculture business.

He expanded the group's activities into feed milling, corn and palm oil trading, copra, palm kernel and soybean crushing and palm oil refining, steel drums manufacturing and consumer pack edible oils. He also started and built the first modern edible-oil refinery in Shenzhen, China, expanding the oils business horizontally, vertically and geographically.

As RK wrote in his memoirs, 'For the first time, I saw in one of my nephews a businessman who was at least as capable as myself. It appeared that in Khoon Hong I had the most capable Kuok ever'. (1)

Khoon Hong left the Kuok Group in 1991 and partnered with an Indonesian Chinese, Martua Sitorus, to form Wilmar. Their first project was a small Sumatran oil palm plantation. Later, they expanded into edible oil refining in Indonesia, then China and (through a joint venture with the Adani Group) in India.

In 1994, Khoon Hong met the then-chairman of ADM, Dwayne Andreas, and ADM subsequently acquired 20 percent of the company. ADM has since increased its shareholding in Wilmar to just below 25 percent.

Over the following decade, Wilmar expanded exponentially in palm plantation, oil refining, oilseeds crushing, shipping and fertilisers. Wilmar became the biggest palm oil player in Indonesia, while his uncle's company was the biggest in Malaysia. In China, Wilmar became the biggest oilseed crusher and oil refiner, while the Kuok Group was the biggest in consumer pack edible oils.

In 2006, Wilmar International launched an Initial Public Offering on the Singapore Stock Exchange with a capitalisation of S$2.38 billion. Shortly after, RK invested US$15 million in the company via a share placement. He then approached his nephew about buying 10 percent of Wilmar; his nephew suggested a merger of the two companies agricultural businesses.

RK writes in his memoirs that he instructed his team at that time, 'Get this (merger) done with no hiccups and no small-mindedness. If you think he's getting a slightly better part of the deal, give in. We've got to back this horse. Khoon Hong is the most fantastic businessman you can team up with'.

During my own interview with RK, I asked him if he considered himself a businessman who started as a trader. Or was he a trader who applied his trading skills to business? He replied:

> I've been asking myself that question for the past 50 years. Let's take soccer as a parallel. You can train someone to play football, but you never produce a Pele, a Ronaldo or a Messi. You have to have natural verve. We are not born equal. You either have that attribute in you, call it genius if you like, but of course, different degrees of genius, and then circumstance or fate gives you the playground to exercise your skills. If you are born in the wrong community and your parents force you into the armed forces, well, then, how do you become a trader? But traders are born, not taught.

If RK is right – and I believe he is – Khoon Hong is a born trader. Wilmar International's business today includes oil palm cultivation, edible oils refining, oilseeds crushing, consumer pack edible oils processing and merchandising, specialty fats, oleochemicals, biodiesel manufacturing, grains processing and merchandising, and sugar milling and refining. It has over 90,000 people working in more than 500 manufacturing plants around the world, as well as in an extensive distribution network covering China, India, Indonesia and some 50 other countries.

Wilmar is one of the world's largest oil palm plantation owners, with a total planted area of 230,409 hectares, of which about 67 percent is in Indonesia, 25 percent in East Malaysia and 8 percent in Africa.

Through joint ventures, Wilmar owns palm plantations in Uganda and West Africa of about 46,000 hectares. The company also directly manages 36,000 hectares under smallholder schemes in Indonesia and Africa and 149,000 hectares under smallholder and out grower schemes through joint ventures and associates in Africa. Besides plantations, Wilmar also owns palm oil mills that process fruits from their own and surrounding plantations.

Wilmar owns and operates several vertically integrated tropical oils processing plants in Indonesia and Malaysia that produce tropical oils and related products. The company also owns processing plants in China, Vietnam, the Philippines, Sri Lanka, the USA, South Africa and Ghana. Through joint ventures, Wilmar also has interests in processing plants in India, Bangladesh, Singapore, Russia, Ukraine, Ivory Coast, Nigeria, Uganda, Tanzania, Zambia, Zimbabwe, Germany, the Netherlands and Poland.

The company's oilseed crushing division operates worldwide, including in China, India, Vietnam, Indonesia, Malaysia, Philippines, Russia, Ukraine, South Africa, Zambia and Zimbabwe. It crushes a wide range of oilseeds, including soybean, rapeseed, groundnut, sunflower seed, sesame seed and cottonseed, into protein meals and edible oils. The protein meals are mainly sold to the animal feed industry, while the oils are largely sold to the company's own Consumer Products and Oleochemicals businesses.

In July 2018, Wilmar announced that it would expand its soybean crushing capacity in China, despite a drop in feed demand due to Asian Swine Fever. (2) The company said it was confident that feed demand would pick up, with an increase in poultry feed demand offsetting some of the losses from hogs. Poultry feed consumption in the country was expected to grow 20 percent in 2019 because of ASF and as people ate more chicken and duck.

As of 2018, Wilmar already had a total annual oilseed crushing capacity of 20 million tonnes in China, putting it second to COFCO, their biggest competitor in the country. By comparison, Cargill has a crushing capacity in China of 5.4 million tonnes, Bunge 4.3 million tonnes and Dreyfus 3.5 million tonnes.

Wilmar's grains business includes flour and rice milling as well as the production of rice bran oil. The company is one of the largest wheat and rice millers in China and owns flourmills wholly or through joint ventures in Malaysia, Indonesia, Vietnam, Thailand and Papua New Guinea.

Wilmar also has a significant sugar business that began with the acquisition in 2010 of Sucrogen Limited (known today as Wilmar Sugar) in Australia and PT Jawamanis Rafinasi – a sugar refiner in Indonesia. In 2011, the company bought a second refinery in Indonesia as well as Proserpine Mill, the fifth-largest sugar mill in Australia. In 2013, Wilmar bought what is now a more than 30 percent stake in Cosumar S.A., the sole sugar company in Morocco. The company operates a port-based refinery in Casablanca and seven beet and sugar cane mills in Morocco. It's the third-largest sugar producer and the second-largest refiner in Africa.

In 2014, Wilmar invested into Shree Renuka Sugars (SRSL), the leading sugar company in India, with seven sugar cane mills, two port-based refineries and the country's leading national sugar brand, Madhur. In March 2018, SRSL became a subsidiary of Wilmar when Wilmar increased their stake to 58 percent as part of a comprehensive debt restructuring exercise.

Also in 2014, Wilmar established a joint venture with Great Wall Food Stuff Industry Company Limited, the leading sugar company in Myanmar. The joint venture operates two sugar mills.

Wilmar is one of the largest fertiliser players in Indonesia, with a production capacity of 1.2 million tonnes geared towards the oil palm sector. Customers for the fertiliser are also the company's suppliers of fresh fruit bunches, crude palm oil and palm kernel. In 2015, Wilmar expanded their fertiliser operations into Malaysia through an acquisition.

As part of the company's integrated business model, Wilmar owns and manages 65 tankers and dry bulk vessels with a total tonnage of about 2.3 million tonnes.

RK wrote in his memoirs, 'Khoon Hong is a master of business. He has mastered strategic and tactical skills and has the ability to translate his vision into action. …He is a hands-on manager, …working 16 or more hours a day, every day of the year'.

All this hasn't happened without its fair share of criticism and controversy, especially around palm oil production, but the company has been working hard to improve its practices. In 2013, Wilmar committed to a 'No Deforestation, No Peat & No Exploitation Policy' for both its own operations and third-party suppliers. (3) It promised to stop buying from suppliers who cleared forest, drained peat land or exploited locals. (4) This was lauded as a transformational step towards responsible and sustainable palm oil development. (5) In 2015, Wilmar was hailed for being the first major palm oil player to step up to ensure its supply chain was de-linked from any forest destruction and human rights abuse. (6)

The company is conscious of its responsibilities. As RK wrote in his memoirs, 'Oil palm is the most economical and efficient producer of vegetable oils, especially in terms of land use, and it's important for the industry to conform and work within society's expectations, the most important aspect being sustainable development'.

Master of business - A conversation with Khoon Hong Kuok

Khoon Hong Kuok is the co-founder and CEO of Wilmar, an Asian powerhouse in the agricultural commodity business. I met him at the Kerry Centre Hotel in Beijing, where he told me that this was the first interview he had ever given. I explained my book project and he admitted that he had once been given him a copy of *Merchants of Grain* but he had never read it. "Too busy!" he explained.

I began the interview by asking him how he had got into the business. He replied:

I graduated from university in 1972. I did not want to work for the family firm, so I looked for a job outside the business. After several months of looking, I got a position as an executive trainee with a supermarket group in Singapore. The problem was that I was a Malaysian and the job was in Singapore, and I needed a work permit. At that time the relationship between the two countries was not good, and my application for a work permit was rejected.

I took about two months off for travel with my parents after graduation and didn't want to waste any more time looking for a job, so I decided to do a post graduate course in chartered accountancy. It takes time to apply to universities and then wait for the term to start, so in the meantime I went to see Robert Kuok and asked him for an internship in his companies. I wanted to see what real life business was like. He got his assistant to arrange for me to go to a flourmill for one month, then to a sugar refinery for one month, and then to the sugar plantation for another month.

RK's brother-in-law was Chairman of the flourmill. When I went to see him, he told me that instead of an internship he would like me to join the company as a wheat buyer. Prior to 1972, wheat prices hardly moved because of the huge government stocks in the US. To operate a flourmill profitably, one only needed to concentrate on production and sales. This changed in 1972 when the Russians came into the market and bought huge quantities of wheat. I told him I was not interested, as I had already decided to go for further studies.

I went to the flourmill office in Kuala Lumpur for one month where I learned technical knowledge about flour milling, wheat and flour quality. When I went to see the Chairman after a month to say 'good-bye' to him, he again asked me to stay. This time I accepted. In the meantime I had met my wife-to-be in Kuala Lumpur. I was in love, and wanted to stay there!

I was assigned to handle wheat buying, but as the flourmill was small there was little internal knowledge in the company about the wheat market. I was sent to the sugar-trading department in Singapore to learn about commodity trading. I was there for about two months before I was sent to Tradax Geneva for two weeks and Louis Dreyfus in the U.S., also for two weeks to learn about the wheat market.

In 1972, Bogasari Flour Mills, a joint venture between the Kuok Group and the Salim Group, commissioned its flourmill in Jakarta. Piet Yap, a senior Kuok Group director in charge of Indonesian business, managed it. They signed a 300,000 tonne wheat purchase contract with the Australian Wheat Board and Mr Yap needed someone to help him execute it. Since I had just had some training in the wheat market, RK suggested to Mr Yap that he give me for the job. I began buying wheat for Indonesia and Malaysia.

Bogasari's capacity increased rapidly and after a few years we were probably the biggest commercial wheat buyer in the world. This enabled me to learn a lot about the business. I could call up the top wheat trader in any company and he would teach me anything I wanted to know. I also learned about logistics and shipping as we were chartering about one hundred vessels a year, each of about 20,000 tonnes.

The first Kuok Group flourmill in Malaysia was in Port Klang near Kuala Lumpur. The original Australian owner had built it on a shoestring budget. The mill had a small flat warehouse for wheat storage, so most of the time we'd either run out of storage space or run out of wheat. When the Kuok Group started a new flourmill in Pasir Gudang, just opposite Singapore, the general manager decided to build a bigger storage capacity: 22,000 tonnes for a 230 tonne/day mill.

One day, one of RK's good friends retired and joined the Kuok Group as an advisor. RK sent him to look at some of his company's businesses and he wrote a report on the flourmill. In the report he said that the man in charge of the new mill had wasted money by building such a big storage capacity for such a small mill. I was then tasked to see how we could utilize the excess storage capacity.

Corn is the main raw material for animal feed at about 50-55 percent. At that time Thailand was the main supplier of corn to Malaysia, imported in bags. In the northern part of Malaysia the corn was imported by rail. In the central part it was imported through Malacca, and in the Southern part it was imported through Singapore. When a ship came into port in Singapore and Malacca the corn was offloaded into barges, brought to shore and discharged either directly into trucks or into warehouses on shore. If a seller didn't sell all the corn directly onto trucks, he would incur additional storage and handling costs. Similarly if a buyer didn't buy directly from the barges, he would have to pay a higher price once the corn was stored in warehouses.

Buyers and sellers continually had to evaluate the situation and see who would give in first. I decided to use the silos at our flourmills to import corn in bulk. The fob price, freight and discharging costs for bulk corn were cheaper than for bagged corn. And as storage in our own silos was free, I wasn't forced to sell when a ship arrived. This gave us bargaining power. I also gave our buyers one month to take delivery of the corn in bulk or bags. This saved them storage and interest cost. Given our advantages, within two years we had become the biggest corn trader in Malaysia.

After corn, the second most important raw material for animal feed is soybean meal. So I started trading some soybean meal. At that time, a grain major would bring in a 20,000 tonne shipment from South America, anchor it in the outer roads in Singapore, get hundreds of workers to bag it on board, then bring it on shore in barges and send from there to Malaysia. I began by buying a few hundred tonnes, selling them to my corn buyers.

All the animal feed mills in Malaysia were located inland, and they had to buy all their raw materials in bags. I decided to build feed mills next to our flourmills so that we could use our silos to bring in corn in bulk—and also use our flourmills' by-products in bulk. The savings were considerable and in seven or eight years we became the biggest animal feed manufacturer in Malaysia.

Later I decided to build a soybean crushing plant next to the flour and feed mill in Pasir Gudang to take advantage of the cost savings from operating all three factories in one complex. The soybean plant was 400 tonnes a day, which produced about 70 tonnes of soybean oil. The volume was too small for an efficient refinery but I wanted a refinery that had the flexibility of selling crude or refined soybean oil. I decided to build a 200 tonne refinery that could refine both palm and soybean oil. That is how I got involved in soybean crushing and oil refining.

How long after joining the group did you build the crushing plant and oil refinery?

I started with the Kuok Group in 1973. The soybean plant was commissioned in August 1980 and the refinery in February 1981.

Refining margins were excellent in the late 1970s, sometimes more than US$ 50 a tonne, but it was too easy to build a refinery and capacity overexpanded. By 1981 margins had become negative.

Most of the other refineries were trading 'back to back', buying at the same time as they sold; they didn't take many positions. The Kuok Group had a trading culture. RK made a lot of his money from his sugar refinery not by trading back to back but by taking positions on sugar. As the oil refining margins were negative, we had to put a lot of effort into trading. It enabled us to survive the negative refining margins, make some money, and expand our capacity.

And then you went into palm plantations?

The Kuok group went into a palm oil plantation in Malaysia, buying a plantation that the state government wanted to sell. I became of a director of that business, and learned about the plantation business.

When you go into palm oil production you take a piece of land, say 10,000 hectares, but you first have to build the roads, housing, a nursery, and then clear land for planting. The seedlings take about one year to grow before you can plant them in the field. The first year you might plant 500 hectares, the second year you might plant 1,500 hectares and the third year you might plan 3,000 hectares and so forth.

The palm oil tree is like a mango tree; that's the best example. When you plant a mango tree, it starts bearing fruit only after a few years. At first there are very few fruits, and the fruits are small with not much juice. Every year there is more fruit and the fruit get bigger and juicier.

It is the same with palm. You start to get fruit after about two and a half years. The first year you may get seven tonnes per hectare; the second year you may get 13 tonnes; the third year maybe 20 tonnes and the fourth year maybe 26 tonnes per hectare. So when you start a new plantation you bring in more acreage each year, and the trees mature to produce more fruit. The production curve of a new palm oil plantation is exponential.

This means that a refinery in a new location may run at low capacity due to a shortage of crude palm oil. However, just a few years later, it will need to expand the capacity to cope with more than enough supply. We bought a refinery in Sandakan in East Malaysia that was not doing well because they did not have enough supply of palm oil. Production quickly expanded and the refinery became highly profitable a few years later. The East Malaysian refinery had a big advantage in supplying China because the cost of palm oil and freight was much cheaper than from West Malaysia. This helped make the Kuok Group the biggest supplier of palm oil to China.

Did you also sell to India?

At that time the country's State Trading Company (STC) controlled all palm oil imports. After starting the palm oil refining business, RK sent me to be the Sales Manager of the Malaysian flourmill based in Kuala Lumpur. The general manager who took over from me at the palm oil refinery sold STC a 6,000 tonne cargo of palm oil at $600 C&F and a week later a second cargo at $660 per tonne. The problem was that he sold the two cargos short, expecting the price to fall. It didn't. It shot up to more than $1200 per tonne.

There was a shortage and everyone knew we were short. We were caught. It was a real crisis for the company: we were losing $600 or $700 per tonne on 12,000 tonnes. I came back from Kuala Lumpur to take direct charge of the oil refinery and of the short position.

I flew to India to see the STC and told them that we couldn't deliver because there was a shortage. I explained that Kuok Group was a reputable company and there was no question of us defaulting. I asked them to allow us to deliver soybean oil, which was normally at a premium to palm oil, but was then trading at a discount. I offered to pay them an agreed price difference.

I was only 35 years old. I knew that I would lose a lot of money but I wanted to fulfil the contract to make sure that I didn't damage the company's reputation. I had decided that once I had fulfilled the contract I would quit the company, and my career in commodity trading would be over.

The negotiations were long and difficult, but in the end the STC offered me an extension for one month at a 4 percent discount in the price. I was really lucky. During that month the market crashed and I ended up making money on the contract.

But while I was in India trying to sort it all out I began to understand how the STC planned and organized their purchases. Most people had access to their buying schedules, but they took them at face value. I learned to check their plans and began to forecast their supply and demand myself. I started selling to STC and became one of the biggest sellers to them. I also became an expert on India. That knowledge, together with my knowledge of China, helped us make a lot of money on palm oil and become the biggest palm oil trader.

As well as trading you also invested in assets.

A few years after Deng Xiao Peng started economic reform in 1978 China began to allow the import of edible oils but not grains. When oil was first imported, it was in drums as the quantity was small. Even as the economy developed and imports increased, most of the imports were still in drums; only Shanghai could discharge oil in bulk. We used to drum the oil in Singapore, which had a big petroleum industry and drum factories for products like lubricants. We brought palm oil from Malaysia to Singapore and soybean oil from South America to Singapore for drumming. Our volume became very big and we decided to build a drum plant in Pasir Gudang as land, labour and oil transport costs were much cheaper there than in Singapore. All this gave us a $10 per tonne advantage over our competitors who were shipping to China out of Singapore.

Controlling the whole supply chain also let us control the quality. The traders in Singapore were buying the cheapest oil each time, whereas we made sure we maintained the quality of the oil we supplied. As a result our brand began to command a premium because of the quality of our oil and the better condition of our drums. At one time we had almost 100 percent of all the sales of drum palm oil into China. That and our East Malaysian refinery is how we became strong in China.

Tell me about your brand in China.

The brand for our drum oil was *Neptune*, the king of the sea. It dominated the drum oil market.

Before and in the early years of the economic reform, the Chinese were consuming mainly semi-refined oil. Refined oil was trading at a premium of $70-80 per tonne, but there wasn't much demand for it. Most consumers couldn't afford it. And as for consumer packs, only small quantities were sold in Southern China supplied from Hong Kong. It was too expensive for Chinese consumers.

Despite that, I decided to build a 300 tonne per day refinery, a drum and a consumer pack oil plant. China at that time had about 1.1 billion people, and I reckoned that if only 0.1 percent of the population used our oil then we would be able to sustain the factory. So we went ahead. It cost $11 million to build. We made our investment back in eleven months.

In those days in China every salary was fixed by the state. So when a company made money, it could not pay its workers more than the official wage. So what companies did was to give 'welfare'—goods instead of money during festive seasons. Many companies started giving their workers our refined cooking oil as welfare.

When you cook with semi-refined oil it fills the kitchen with smoke. The Chinese had tiny kitchens and there was quite a lot of lung cancer. Suddenly the Chinese found they could cook with refined oil—a beautiful golden colour—and there would be no smoke. People started buying it with their own money. Demand really began to take off. Every year we expanded capacity.

Palm oil is no longer sold in drums, but our consumer pack brand *Arawana* sells about four million tonnes a year.

But then you left the Kuok Group.

I left in 1991. I had some differences with my uncle, but it wasn't acrimonious. I left and went to Indonesia and decided to go into palm oil plantations and, later, refining.

Why palm—and why Indonesia?

Palm oil demand was growing rapidly in both China and India. It is the cheapest and most versatile oil. Soybean oil is suitable for salads, but not good for deep-frying. You can't use soybean oil for making soap, and you need to hydrogenate it to make margarine and shortening. You can use palm oil for stir-frying, deep-frying, margarine and shortening, soap and oleo chemicals. And the best thing was that it was the cheapest oil in the world to produce.

At that time in Indonesia it cost $120 per tonne to produce. You fractionated it, refined it and sent it to China and it cost less than $200 per tonne. Soybean oil cost a lot more.

Indonesia has a huge land mass and you could buy good land for $100 per hectare then, much cheaper than in Malaysia. Labour was also cheaper as most Malaysian plantation workers came from Indonesia. At that time Indonesia was trying to encourage farmers to use fertilizer, mainly for paddy. The government subsidized it, so that was cheaper than in Malaysia.

Where does the name Willmar come from?
My founding partner's name is Martua Sitorus. He had formed a company in Singapore with a friend called Wilson to manufacture rubber gloves in Indonesia. The business never took off and the company was dormant, so when we started on our own we used his company. Many people thought my name was William, or Wilson or something like that. Maybe the company should really have been called Marhong or Hongmar!

How did you get the financing at the start?
In 1991, it cost about US$1,500 to develop one hectare of oil palm plantation in Indonesia. As a rule of thumb, you need 40 percent equity, 40 percent loan and 20 percent recurring income from areas planted earlier. So for 6,000 hectares you would need about US$3.6 million over a few years.

An oil palm plantation takes many years before it starts producing income. When we started we didn't have much money so we couldn't develop the plantation business in a big way. We had to depend on trading and refining profits to grow the business. We were fortunate when our refinery was commissioned in 1993 as refining margins were good and it was also quite easy to make a profit trading. We also went into shipping to take advantage of arbitrage opportunities between Indonesian domestic and export markets. The profits we made enabled us to expand in Indonesia and overseas, in addition to developing out plantations.

In 1991 Indonesia produced about 2 million tonnes of palm oil. Now it produces more than 43 million tonnes. This enabled us to expand our refining and palm oil related industries and trading in a big way.

NGO's have criticised Wilmar over sustainability and the environment. How would you respond?
In the old days palm oil plantations were burning forests to clear land and some even discharged effluents in the rivers. Today most major plantation group adopt sustainable practices. The NGOs have been a force for good in this.

The problem comes when NGOs just want to attract attention to attract funds. The biggest companies attract the most attention and we are the biggest player in palm oil. So even though we stopped planting oil palm in new areas many years ago—and we were among the earliest to adopt sustainable practices—the NGOs still criticised us for buying palm oil from other producers who were burning to develop new areas. The NGOs attack the big names like us, not the smaller producers who sell to us. We decided to adopt sustainable practices because we believe big corporations must be socially responsible. Having seen the deterioration in the environment due to burning and other irresponsible practices of some plantations, we decided to take a lead even if we had to sacrifice some business.

The accusation that palm oil is not environmentally friendly is no longer fair.

What about labour issues?
Palm plantations bring good jobs deep into inland areas far from the towns. You need engineers, agronomists, and accountants—a lot of people. We need about 0.2 people for every hectare of palm. So if you have 10,000 hectares you need about 2,000 and if you include their families, it supports a lot of people. To attract and retain staff, you have to build good housing for your employees, as well as schools and clinics. In those rural areas the government does not usually provide good facilities.

I have been told that you could increase palm oil production without increasing the area...that with better trees you could double production. Is that true?
With better seedlings, technology and management, the yield of new palm plantations today is much higher than the past. This is especially so in Africa where production can be increased significantly by re-planting the old plantations, thus minimizing deforestation.

Going back to Wilmar, to what do you attribute the company's success?
Right time, right place and plenty of luck.

Asia didn't export any major agriculture commodities before palm oil came along; they needed them all to feed the growing population. Palm oil production in Malaysia and Indonesia increased from 9.0 million tonnes in 1991 to 62.5 million tonnes in 2018. It became a globally traded commodity.

China imported 136,000 tonnes of soybeans in 1991 and 84 million tonnes in 2018, becoming the world's biggest soybean importer. Population and economic growth in Asia increased per capital consumption of agricultural commodities as well as the quality of the processed agricultural commodities that they consumed. These developments enabled us to become a major palm oil trader and a major agricultural commodity processor.

Could you tell me about your partnership with ADM?

About two years after I started Wilmar, a trader from Toepfer, a German trading company who was buying palm kernel expeller from us, asked me why we didn't expand into China. I told him that I would love to, but I didn't have the money or the people to do it. The trader told me that ADM, their major shareholder, had recently set up an Asian Pacific office in Hong Kong and he knew the V.P. there. He suggested I talk with him. 'ADM are good people,' he told me.

The V.P came to Singapore to meet me about a week later. He called me a few days later to say that his chairman Dwayne Andreas had invited me to go to Decatur to meet him. I took a flight to O'Hare airport and then flew in a company jet to Decatur. It was the first time I had ever taken a private jet. At that time Wilmar was not even worth $10 million, ADM was a $12 billion listed US company, and Dwayne Andreas was very powerful, friendly with Gorbachev and Reagan and all that. I was 34-35 years old, starting a company.

I went into a meeting with him—there were six or seven people there, their top people. He asked about what we were doing and my vision for Wilmar. After that we had lunch in their canteen, and that night he put me in a small guesthouse next to his house. I was later told that Gorbachev had also stayed there. That evening Dwayne held a cocktail party for me, followed by dinner in his house. The next day I had breakfast with him. When I went to see him to say 'goodbye' we sat together for another 10-15 minutes. He told me, 'Young man, let's make money together, and not from each other'. And that is what we did.

Dwayne Andreas was a visionary. ADM was the world's biggest soybean crusher and therefore the biggest soybean oil producer. Palm oil was becoming important. Asia, especially China, was becoming increasingly important. Andreas decided that ADM had to be part of it. But ADM didn't know how to do business in Asia. Most other big companies would have gone it alone, but Andreas wanted to do it in partnership. He was brilliant in assessing business opportunities and assessing people's characters.

I offered Andreas 20 percent of a new integrated grain and oilseed project near Shanghai, along the Yangtze River, which we were starting with COFCO. He agreed to take the stake, but he also wanted 20 percent of Wilmar. I countered 10 percent, but I eventually agreed to sell him 20 percent.

I rarely saw him after that. It was about 3 years later, when I wanted to expand crushing in a big way in China. He asked me to meet him in Decatur and told me that he didn't think it was a good idea. He said it was better to crush the beans in the U.S. or South America and then ship the meal and oil to China. I disagreed. 'Can you imagine when China eventually buys 30 million tonnes of beans?' I asked. 'How can you import efficiently 24 million tonnes of meal and 5 million tonnes of soybean oil? It is better to bring in soybeans and crush them there'.

Two days later he came back and agreed to join my project. When ADM bought into Wilmar, we had no shareholder agreement, no joint venture agreement, but the best security for a joint venture is to make it very profitable. We went on to do dozens of projects together. It was a wonderful partnership. ADM today holds 24.9 percent of Wilmar.

In 1995 China imported about one million tonnes of soybeans. In 2017 they imported 94 million tonnes. The market grew 94 times in 22 years. This enabled us to increase our crushing capacity in China massively and today our China crush capacity is bigger than ADM's crush capacity in the U.S.

Could you tell me a little about the merger with the Kuok Group?

While we were launching the IPO, RK asked a nephew who was in charge of his shipping business to contact me to ask whether I would offer him some Wilmar shares. I said 'sure', and eventually the Kuok Group took US15 million shares.

Soon after listing, RK learned that we were looking to place 10 percent of Wilmar's shares with a large U.S. private equity firm in Hong Kong. He called me while I was doing a presentation in Goldman Sachs' Singapore office. He said that it wasn't a good idea to raise money from a private equity fund because they have to exit after a few years. 'If you need support', he told me, 'I will support you'.

I thanked him for the offer but said I was in a meeting and would be leaving for London that evening to spend a few days with my family before flying to the U.S. I told him that I would think about his offer and send him a mail in a few days. I didn't wait a few days. During my flight to London, I wrote him an email listing Wilmar and Kuok Group's agriculture operations. I suggested that we merge the two groups.

He called me in London the next day to tell me he liked the idea, and asked that I see him in Hong Kong as soon as possible. A few days after I returned from the U.S., I went to Hong Kong to meet him. He had gathered his two sons and a nephew to meet me. He told them to discuss the details of the deal and to go to him if there were any disagreement.

The meeting with the cousins didn't take long. I suggested that the Wilmar and Kuok Group each forecast their next three years profit and take the same P/E valuation. It was a very fair proposal and the deal was concluded in a short time, without any intervention from RK. The following week, the financial team of both groups met and finalized the details. The deal was completed in less than a week without any investment bankers involved. The Kuok Group's edible oil, trading and oil palm plantation assets were merged into Wilmar in return for about 33 percent stake in the company. Kuok Group is now the biggest investor in Wilmar. ADM is the second biggest with 25 percent.

How important for you was the merger with the Kuok group?
When I started Wilmar I had decided not to compete directly with my old company, but to try and grow in different areas and sectors. The result was that the two companies were complementary. As a result, the synergies of the merger were enormous: one plus one equalled not two, but three or four.

With the growth of your business in China, why didn't you move, like your uncle did in the 1970s, to Hong Kong?
Until the last couple of years, China was about 40 percent of our business, Indonesia was around 40 percent and the rest of the world made up the other 20 percent. China has risen now to about 55 percent, but it is still better to manage the China business from Shanghai and the palm business from Singapore. I spend between a quarter and a third of my time in China.

Why haven't you expanded in the West?
We have a strong position in Asian and African countries with over 4.5 billion people. The population and economic growth of these countries are among the highest in the world, and per capita consumption of agri-commodities is increasing. The population of North, Central, South America and Western Europe combined is less than 1.5 billion and per capital consumption is not increasing much.

We do not have the financial resources, brands and distribution network of the food giants in the West. We don't want to go to markets where we have no comparative advantage.

Would you ever consider buying a Western commodity trading company? It might help you to originate commodities.
It would only be worthwhile for us to buy a Western commodity trading company if we could integrate it effectively into our operations to bring up the synergies. To do that, I would have to spend a lot of time in the West. I am already 70. There are better opportunities in Asia and Africa for me on which to spend my energy.

How do you see the Chinese market developing?
The Chinese are the fussiest people in the world when it comes to food. China will soon become not only the biggest but also the most sophisticated food market in the world.

Even though it cost us more we have always built our processing plants with high factory and food safety standards. In the past, this put us at a disadvantage over plants with lower standards and costs. But now the government has become very strict on this, and our competitors have to install the same systems as we do. The same applies to pollution controls. This levels the playing field.

To succeed in a very competitive country like China you have to produce, market and distribute the best quality product at the lowest cost. Our integrated plants mean that our production costs are lower than our competitors, and our bigger volumes and multiple locations give us lower marketing and distribution costs.

You once said that you would like to become the Unilever of Asia.
No, I want to be an integrated agricultural commodity company involved in crop cultivation, processing, trading and downstream branded products.

Unilever is really only downstream now. They used to have good plantations and processing plants, but they sold them all because they only wanted to stay in the high margin businesses. We believe that an integrated model is much better.

Your uncle told me that you were working 16 hours a day, and that he was trying to persuade you to delegate more. How do you manage to grow from a small business to such a big business but still maintain control over it?
I work 16 hours on some days but not every day. I always tell people that if I were to drop dead tomorrow our existing business would continue successfully. It is the new projects that keep me busy. Do we go into rice? Do we go into sugar? Who do I put in charge of it? How do I structure it? What is the right business model for that business? All that takes a lot of time and I am probably the best person to do the job.

People think I spend a lot of time running our existing businesses. I don't. The time I do spend is to ensure we have sound risk management, to ensure we have good people managing it and to make sure our operations work closely with each other to bring out the full synergies of our group. For example, if Indonesia increases the duty on crude palm oil, China will import more refined products instead of making them in China. Our teams look at the total profit of the group and not at the profit of individual units.

It is not that difficult to manage our existing operations. We set manufacturing standards to ensure production is well managed and I just control the purchasing of raw materials and pricing of the products. Of course, selecting good people to manage the operations is the key.

You have three sons and one daughter. Have you tried to persuade one of them to come into the business?
I believe that you must let your children pursue their interests. Our job is pretty tough; you have to have a passion for it. If you have a passion you can work 16 hours a day and not feel tired. If you have no passion you work nine hours and you are tired. And you will not think from morning to night about the business because you will find it boring.

I told my children that if they were interested in other businesses then they should go ahead and I would give them the money to get them going. But if they're interested in my business they are very welcome to come and join me if they're good enough.

The decision in my case is simpler because I don't have a controlling interest in Wilmar. My children do not have the birthright to take over from me. They can only do so if they are good enough.

Last question: do you consider yourself a trader or a businessman?
I do not believe in pure trading because the Internet has made information flow too fast and too transparently to still make back-to-back profits. I believe in building manufacturing and logistics infrastructure that can help trading; you can trade on the raw materials and products of the plants. When you have a lot of factories and a lot of products it can create many trading opportunities.

Trading also helps identify manufacturing opportunities. I would not have bought the East Malaysian refinery or built the first refinery in China if not for knowledge gained from trading. So I would consider myself both a businessman and a trader.

Thank you Khoon Hong for your time and insights!

Chapter Sixteen: A Competitive Future

'The commodity trading industry is on a path that's not sustainable. The typical margin for a trading company is about 0.5 percent of turnover. The trend will continue. It is not cyclical; it's structural'. Marco Dunand, CEO Mercuria Energy (1)

Back in 1979, when *Merchants of Grain* was published, the ABCCD group of companies (André, Bunge, Cargill, Continental and Dreyfus) dominated the global grain trade. Shortly before the book's publication, another 'C' (Cook Industries) had gone into liquidation. During the ensuing 40 years, André and Continental also left the business, ADM become the 'A', and there was only one 'C' left. To the delight of journalists and management consultants, the 'ABCD' acronym was born.

Like the 'BRICS' acronym for Brazil, Russia, India, China and South Africa lumps together five countries that little resemble each other, the ABCD acronym lumps together four companies that, although in the same business, are very different in many ways. That also applies to the ABCD+ category that includes COFCO International, Glencore and Wilmar. They're all different animals.

In addition, the ABCD+ group still account for 'only' about 50 percent of the world trade in grains and oilseeds. Who accounts for the rest?

In 2017, Olam, an Asian commodity-trading giant, took a strategic decision to exit the mainstream grain business and concentrate on the more niche sectors of the food supply chain. However, they've recently once again become active in Brazilian soybean exports, especially to Asia. Although publicly quoted, they're majority owned by Temasek, Singapore's sovereign wealth fund. (2)

CHS Inc., an agricultural cooperative based in Minnesota, is also active in the international trade of grain and oilseeds. It owns and operates various food processing and farm supply businesses, and is a co-owner of Ventura Foods, a vegetable oil processor. The cooperative can trace its history back to 1931 with the founding of the Farmers Union Central Exchange in Saint Paul, Minnesota. It later became Cenex, from the combination of the last two words in its previous name. In 1998, Cenex merged with Harvest States Cooperatives to form Cenex Harvest States, and in 2003, the cooperative changed its name to CHS Inc. Employing more than 11,000 people, CHS states on its website that its purpose is 'to create connections that empower agriculture'.

Gavilon, based in Omaha, Nebraska, is the second-largest grain handler in North America based on storage capacity and employs 2,000 people around the world. Besides grain and oilseed merchandising, it also trades fertiliser. The company dates its history to 1874, when the Peavey Company built its first grain facility. In 1982, Peavey was acquired by ConAgra Foods, Inc., and later became part of ConAgra Trade Group, which was sold in 2008 to become an independent company, Gavilon.

Marubeni Corporation purchased Gavilon's agriculture assets and businesses in 2013. The purchase strengthened Marubeni's grain flows into Japan and Asia, and Marubeni became a major soybean exporter to China, particularly to the country's private buyers.

Other Japanese companies, such as Mitsui, Mitsubishi and Itochu, are also active participants in the grain trade, originating in the Americas and exporting to Asia. ZEN-NOH, a federation of 1,173 agricultural cooperatives in Japan founded in 1972, is particularly active in originating from the U.S. The cooperative is one of the Japan's largest importers of animal feeds and agricultural fertilisers. ZEN-NOH is also involved in the production of farming equipment, primarily tractors.

Engelhart Commodities Trading Partners, commonly known as ETCP, was spun off from the Brazilian investment bank Banco BTG Pactual SA in 2013. The company made headlines in 2018 (3) for racking up almost half a billion dollars of losses over the previous three years. Because of those losses, ECTP exited the physical trading of energy and most metals, plus its cotton-trading business, but kept grain, coffee and sugar trading. (At the time of writing, they're exiting coffee trading.) BTG Pactual still owns a reported 15 percent of the trading house, while the management own another 15 percent.

Concerning regional players, Amaggi (4) in Brazil is the world's largest private producer of soybeans and is also a large exporter in its own name. The company is controlled by Blairo Maggi, the governor of Mato Grosso state and a former Brazilian Minister of Agriculture. Amaggi employs 3,100 workers and has a total soy crushing capacity of 2.4 million tonnes per year from three plants in Brazil. In 2019, Amaggi entered into an agreement with Marubeni to supply soy and other grains to Japan and China.

In Argentina, Vicentin, (5) founded in 1929, has a significant market share in Argentina's soybean crushing and exports. Aceitera General Deheza, (6) founded in 1948, is also active in origination and exports, as is Molinos Rio (7), Argentina's largest branded food company.

Although the ABCD+ grain trading companies have developed a strong foothold in the Black Sea region since the end of the U.S.S.R., they face strong competition in the region from local trading companies.

In 2018, the number-one exporter of wheat from Russia was RIF, founded in the southern Russian city of Rostov-on-Don in 2010 by an ex-Glencore employee. (8) The company's trading operations were originally based in Lausanne Switzerland, but have since moved to Dubai.

Glencore was the second-largest grain exporter from Russia in 2018, but the third-largest was Aston, which owns its own terminals and is a major trans-shipper from the Sea of Azov. Besides being the country's third-largest exporter of grain, Aston is Russia's largest exporter of vegetable oils and the leading processor of oilseeds. In 2018, ADM bought into Aston's starch and sweetener operations in Russia, and the two companies now run the business as a joint venture. (9)

The largest grain exporter from Ukraine in 2018 was Kernel (10), a major Ukrainian agro-industrial company founded in 1995 with 15,000 employees spread between Ukraine and Russia. The company owns significant farmland in central Ukraine and operates grain export terminals, silos and trans-shipment services. Kernel also owns a small offshore trading company, Avere, based in Geneva. (11)

Nibulon was the second-largest grain exporter from Ukraine in 2018. Founded in 1991, the company produces and exports grains and oilseeds. According to the company's website, (12) Nibulon owns 388 silos and over two million tonnes of grain storage, along with a network of 25 trans-shipment terminals.

Agroprosperis, founded in 2007, is also a major exporter of Ukrainian grains and oilseeds. (13) The company is owned and managed by NCH Capital, a $3 billion private equity firm based in New York. NCH Capital also owns Agro Terra in Russia, which together with AgroProsperis in Ukraine makes it one of the largest agribusinesses in the world, with nearly 700,000 hectares of land, producing over four million tonnes of grains, oilseeds and sugar beets. (14)

In 2019, VTB, a state-run bank, began building a position in the Russian grain market by taking control of two of the three port silos in Novorossiysk, as well as the railway locomotives and logistics company Rustranskom. At the time of writing, VTB is also in talks to buy 50 percent of the Taman silo. If they are successful, the bank will control half of the Black Sea silo capacity.

VTB is also building their own agricultural trading company, using its assets as a base. To this end, the state-owned bank acquired MiroGroup Resources, which works closely with Solaris Commodities S.A., a grain trading company based in Morges, Switzerland. At the time of publication in 2019, Solaris had become the third-largest trader of Russian wheat in the current 2019–2020 season.

Some traders are concerned that the Russian government wants to take centralised control of grain exports. The grain business had been largely under the Russian government's radar since the end of the U.S.S.R., but as export volumes have increased, the government may now be considering grain as a foreign policy tool. This could add a new non-commercial competitor to Black Sea trade flows, perhaps mimicking Chinese government-controlled COFCO International.

There is a concern that the Russian state will become one of the major offtakers of Russian grain through their control of export assets. If they do, they'll exercise control over the price at which grain is bought internally and would also have a significant influence on the world price of wheat. In a few years' time, will VTB be as well known in the international grain trade as COFCO is now?

But then even, COFCO is not without its own Chinese competitors. Many other Chinese companies are now importing both grains and oilseeds into China, some of which are competing on the FOB markets in both North and South America. In 2019, the Chinese government told five Chinese companies that they could apply for exemptions from the 25 percent tariffs on U.S. soybean cargoes arriving before the end of the year. (15)

Within Africa, ETG (16) promotes itself as 'the African trading company', and it's indeed a major player across the continent. In 2018, Mitsui bought 30 percent of ETG. Mitsui is also a minority player in ENERFO (17), a company that is fast expanding, trying to establish itself as the main regional trader for SE Asia.

All these smaller companies continually challenge the bigger traders in regional markets. Said Soren Schroder, a former CEO of Bunge, 'It's very clear that there are too many, too many trying to do the same thing with a small margin'. (18)

They're all trying to make their money in two ways: first, by moving a physical commodity along a supply chain, earning tiny margins each time they transform it in space, time or form. Second, they use their skills and information flows to take risk positions on the market. These can be flat price positions, but they're more likely to be on the differentials, betting that the market is incorrectly pricing the different costs involved in the trade houses' basic business of transforming commodities.

The first activity is often labelled as 'commercial', and the second, 'speculative'. The media, general public and legislators tend to view commercial activities as a good thing in terms of feeding the world and generally adding efficiencies to the food supply chain. They tend to view speculative activities as a bad thing, adding no value but driving up food prices for consumers and driving them down for farmers. As one of my wife's good friends once told me, 'I don't want a speculator between me and a farmer!'

The grain trading companies have largely – and historically – built their businesses around commercial activities, buying grain from farmers and then storing, marketing, transporting and processing it. At various times, traders have added other activities such as financial services, agricultural inputs and distribution (including retail product branding). However, speculation has always been, and will always be, an integral part of their business model.

It's impossible to grow or distribute food without some degree of speculation. But more than that, trade houses couldn't remain in business if they solely lived off the tiny margins that they earn moving commodities from one end of the supply chain to the other. Speculation is not the icing on the cake; it's one of the cake's ingredients.

The low margins currently being experienced by grain trading companies are a function of both cyclical and structural factors. In down cycles, prices are less volatile, and trade flows are more constant. This makes it harder for trading companies to add value. Trade houses make more money when markets are disrupted.

When physical trading margins are under pressure, there is a temptation for traders to turn to speculation to maintain revenues. This sometimes leads to over-speculation; historical examples include Ferruzzi, André and possibly Continental Grain (but in Russian bonds).

Besides excessive risk taking, trade houses are reacting to margin pressure by cutting costs. However, there is a tendency for cost cutting in a commodity supply chain to lead to increased supply, and this often results in lower prices. Acting alone, an individual player in the supply chain might increase his or her margins by cutting costs. However, if everyone does it, the resulting extra production could result in a fall in price that negates costs saved.

One way cost cutting can work is through consolidation: if done properly, it can lead to a rationalisation of the sector and the removal of excess capacity. It can also widen an individual company's global footprint and result in increased optionality between origins. It can also prompt economies of scale. Unfortunately, if not managed correctly, mergers can sometimes lead to value destruction rather than value addition.

In addition, as Chris Mahoney so rightly pointed out, company owners are more reluctant to sell during downcycles, making both diversification and consolidation harder. During upcycles, potential acquirers no longer see the need or urgency to diversify or consolidate. Sellers back away during downcycles; buyers back away during upcycles.

Meanwhile, banks are reluctant lenders, and investors are reluctant investors during downcycles. It is, therefore, easier to diversify a business with internal funding than with borrowing. This could give an advantage in the future to Cargill and ADM, who are better positioned debt-wise compared to, say, Bunge or Dreyfus.

Over the past couple of years, there have been rumours that Glencore was trying to buy the grain merchandising assets of Dreyfus or Bunge (or even of ADM) and that COFCO was looking at merging with Dreyfus. Partly for the reasons described above, nothing has yet happened on either front. As in comedy, timing is everything in trading.

Another reason for the lack of consolidation has been fear of intervention by the competition authorities. The argument goes that the big grain traders are, well, big; it would be difficult (if not impossible) for governments to allow them to get bigger.

But how big, really, are these grain trading giants? If you ignore the three biggest (Cargill, ADM and Bunge), the (estimated) combined market capitalisation of the remain four adds up to a meagre $25 billion. Compare that to the market capitalisation of, say, BP at $120 billion. Rather than giants, grain-trading companies are relative dwarfs in the wide world of business.

Even if the seven dwarfs aren't allowed to merge, they can still find pre-competitive areas where they can collaborate. Technology is one such area, and the major trading companies are already cooperating to build an industry-wide blockchain trading process. (19) Sustainability is another area, with traders all participating in individual commodity round tables. However, areas for pre-competitive competition remain limited, and the business remains fiercely competitive. This makes diversification even trickier.

Moving along supply chains – vertical integration – can cut costs, lead to better risk management, reduce counter-party risk (because you trade more with yourself) and move your company into more value-added activities closer to the consumer. This can enable one to shift a business from low-margin commodities to higher-margin ingredients. 'Ingredients' have higher pricing power than 'commodities'.

One problem of moving up or down a supply chain is that one can end up competing against one's own suppliers or customers. Another problem is that one can end up in unfamiliar businesses. Growing sugarcane requires a different mindset to trading sugar. And processed food companies are largely brand management companies: the value is in the brand. Brand management is a different skill than commodity trading.

As Glencore saw with their initial venture into cotton trading, diversifying into other commodities can also be tricky. In addition, the commodities that one wants to start trading can often be just as competitive and low margin as the commodities one is already trading. By moving into them, you're making them even more competitive.

Sometimes, the trading companies have diversified into completely different areas, such as property development, media, telecommunications or whatever was hot at the time. Some, such as the Kerry/Kuok group, have been spectacularly successful, as was Dreyfus in telecommunications and energy distribution. Other companies have had less luck.

It's a difficult choice to make: should I diversify into new activities or concentrate on my core businesses? However, one advantage that trading companies have is that they are good at trading. They can trade assets and companies as well as they can trade the underlying commodities.

One diversification that the trade houses have recently been making – and continue to make – is into alternative meat products. The trade houses make a considerable percentage of their income from animal feed, especially corn and soybeans, and this business is threatened by the consumer trend away from meat. Admittedly, the trade houses are well placed to supply the necessary vegetable inputs for these new meats, but the order of size is significant. Remember that, in an average feedlot, it takes 10 calories of feed to produce one calorie of beef. It only takes one calorie to produce one calorie of plant-based meat!

The agricultural trade houses are well aware of this and are investing in alternative meat ventures, partly as a hedge against the threat of a drop in feed demand. In the second quarter of 2019, Bunge reported $135 million in net unrealised gains resulting from their shareholding in Beyond Meat. This gain represented 36 percent of Bunge's profits that quarter and 80 percent of the profits made from the company's oilseeds business unit.

Growth in alternative meat is strong, but it's starting from a low base of less than one percent of the market for real meat. However, investing in alternative meat also allows the trade houses to better understand a consumer trend that threatens their business models. Cargill has invested in both cultured (lab-grown) and plant-based meat, while ADM is also investing in alternative meat supply chains.

Apart from alternative meat, what strategic decisions have the grain traders taken – and in what direction are they heading?

ADM is aiming to build its value-added businesses such as nutrition and flavours. Simultaneously, they are selling off what they consider non-core activities. ADM continues to view agricultural merchandising as a core activity.

Bunge is strengthening internal risk management, cutting costs throughout their businesses, putting their Brazilian sugarcane assets into a joint venture with BP and investing further into downstream oil and fats. There is still some talk that the company might exit grain trading, but currently, Bunge remains a global leader in oilseeds and crushing.

Cargill is consolidating their early mover advantage in animal nutrition and protein, including aquaculture. They are seeking to maximise economies of scale, while expanding partnerships to increase destination sales. The company has a heavy focus on innovation in IT and AI, as well as on new products and processes in food and feed.

COFCO International is expanding their global origination footprint to increase sourcing optionality for their parent company in China, particularly considering the trade wars with the U.S. The company is still bringing together their two acquisitions, Nidera and Noble, and an IPO planned for 2020 is likely to be delayed.

Dreyfus is refocusing on Asia, while moving closer to the consumer, especially through innovations in food and feed. An IPO or straight sale is off the table, but the company is searching for partners in strategic areas and activities.

Glencore's objective is acquiring physical assets at origin while exploring options to increase destination sales.

Wilmar is consolidating their advantage in palm and oilseeds, while making supply chains more sustainable and traceable. The company is increasing its focus on consumer food products. An IPO of their Chinese businesses is planned for 2020.

Time will tell how each of these strategies works out, but to finish the book, one of my interviewees asked what I would do if I were running a trade house. His question took me by surprise, and I deflected it by replying that no one would be stupid enough to hand me the reins. (And they wouldn't!)

Having had the chance to think about it, I'd now reply that, in the short-term, I would hope for market disruption to boost commercial margins and provide more opportunities for speculation. However, hope has historically never proved to be much of a business plan.

In the long-term,, I believe that the only way for the trade houses to regain profitability is by recapturing the market power that they have lost over recent decades. How can they do that? Although it may be presumptuous of me, here are five suggestions:

Stay in the game. The world needs you, and it will need you even more in the future. Some of the problems that you face are structural, but many are cyclical – and cycles turn. As part of your daily activities, you must continue to educate politicians and the public on the important role that you play. In the past, you didn't need the public's support, but you do now. And for the moment, the public 'just don't get it'. The public will have to 'get it' for you to maintain your social licence to operate.

Consolidate responsibly. When demand is stagnant, try to lower costs through consolidation, not through increased production. Perhaps you'll have to close your smaller, less efficient facilities and concentrate production and throughput in bigger ones.

Innovate, and innovate again. The food supply chain has a history of innovation, but to be effective, innovation should be in the form of new products and processes, rather than simple cost cutting. Blockchain can reduce costs, but if it lowers costs across the whole sector, it may just result in lower prices for the consumer. That's a good thing, but a better thing would be new products or ingredients your customers might be willing to pay more for.

Transforming commodities into ingredients is one way now to shift pricing power from consumers back to producers. Some commodities, such as coffee and cocoa, are already losing their commodity status and are differentiated by origin. End consumers are already willing to pay more for gluten-free, lactose-free, organic, non-genetically modified or locally produced food. And as ADM has discerned, big brands are willing to pay more for specific food varieties that fit their particular recipes. And perhaps you could do even more with the by-products of your processing activities.

Diversify across and along supply chains. Some of the most successful companies in the sector currently are the most diversified across commodities; if you trade enough in enough markets, at least a couple will make money each year. They won't be the same commodities each year, but hopefully, winning commodities will make more than losing ones. It can be tricky for a company to shift focus from its core competence, but it can be worth the effort. Many of you are already turning yourselves into diversified food companies. Keep going!

Manage risk. In difficult times, it can be tempting for companies, especially individual traders, to take excessive risk by speculating on future price moves. This has been disastrous in the past and could be disastrous in the future. So, perhaps the most important advice I could give any trading company now is to strengthen risk management.

In the play *The Leman Trilogy*, Mayer Lehman, the youngest of the three brothers who founded Lehman Brothers, asks a certain Isaac Newgass permission to marry his daughter Babetta. The year is 1858, and the three brothers are based in Alabama, where they're building their first fortune in the cotton trade, acting as cotton 'factors', buying from local plantations and shipping raw cotton to Northern mills. Rather like my own father, Isaac Newgass is having difficulty understanding what Mayer does and how he makes money.

'So, you are a middleman!' the future father-in-law finally exclaims.

'We are not middlemen', Mayer angrily replies. 'We are businessmen!'

Over 150 years later, grain merchants are still trying to lose the middleman nomenclature and to be known simply as business people!

The new normal – J–F Lambert

J-F is a former banker with a banker's DNA. He spent most of his career in international banking and trade finance, with stints in Greece and Asia. He was originally with Crédit Commercial de France, or CCF, and then with HSBC, when they took over CCF. He moved to London, where he built their structured trade finance activities, and then the global commodity finance activities for the group. J-F is now a consultant on trade and commodity finance and strategy for banks, companies and funds. He also teaches commodity market dynamics at Sciences Po in Paris and regularly lectures at the London Business School.

What, in your view, are the biggest challenges facing the agricultural trading houses?
The biggest challenge is that everyone has access to, and shares, the same information with regard to trade flows and physical supply and demand. This means that the only time an agricultural commodity trading house can really make money these days is when a market is dislocated. But even the dislocations are becoming easier to anticipate and manage.

Commodities traders are struggling in this environment to make a difference – to create what I would call *differentiating factors*.

The world went through a commodity supercycle from 1998 to 2008. We know how it changed the world and in particular how commodities became a financial asset class. But when you look at the numbers from 1992 to nowadays and adjust them for inflation, you find that food and agricultural commodity prices have remained largely flat – unchanged over the past 30 years.

That's an extraordinary phenomenon. When I was born, there were 2.7 billion people on this planet, with probably a maximum of 350 million people in the middle class. We now live in a world where there are 7.6 billion people, soon to become nine billion, and with a middle class that is likely to reach five billion in the next decade or so. That's a huge increase in food demand, especially when you add in the crops grown for biofuels. And yet, supply has kept pace through technology: hence, flattish prices.

Looking forward, global climate change means there are potentially huge dislocations around the corner. However, I suspect – and, of course, hope – that supply will again be able to anticipate and adapt to these challenges – as it has done so far.

The second challenge has been the financialisation of commodities. In the past, futures markets supported and facilitated physical commodity trading. Nowadays, the futures markets are much bigger than the physical flows and have become much more sophisticated with the dominance of automated trading. The CFTC reported in March 2019 that the share of automated futures and options transactions in grains and oilseeds had reached 70 percent of total trades! This makes it much more challenging for physical traders to use the futures markets to hedge or to structure a trading strategy. They'll now almost always find somebody ahead of them, anticipating their order and taking advantage in a micro-second of a mispricing. It's a huge challenge.

The trade houses are trying to meet these challenges in different ways.
Well, let's start with the basics. For a trader, logistics are absolutely paramount. The only added value of the trader nowadays lies with the efficiency and the smoothness with which he meets the needs of the destination by sourcing at various origins, come rain or shine. In that respect, logistics plays an essential part of all trading houses' toolkits.

Although everybody is investing in logistics, Glencore is differentiating itself through a strategy of size. They believe that, through size, they can reduce costs and perhaps even become a price setter rather than a price taker.

When you talk to ADM or Cargill, they tell you that they don't trade commodities, but they are an integrated supply chain from farm to fork. Their profits are not coming from trading; their profits are coming from sophisticated supply chain management. They also endeavor to generate commercial margins by producing and selling value-added products downstream.

Cargill has been doing this for many years now, shifting focus to animal and fish proteins. This certainly makes sense when population is increasing and the middle class is growing. The world needs more protein, and Cargill's investment into the verticality of the protein supply chain is paying off handsomely.

ADM is a different animal. Let's not forget that the original 'A' amongst the ABCDs was André, not Archer Daniels Midland. What I mean to say is that ADM is, by and large, an agri-industrial company, not a trading house. It has developed into trading, but the bulk of their money is spent and earned on the industrial part of the business.

If you ask Dreyfus, they'll tell you that they're no longer a trading house and that they're now supply chain managers. However, Dreyfus is probably one of the last true large trading houses left in the market. Unfortunately, that's not by choice, but because the industrial bets that they've made in the past are now backfiring on them.

For example, Dreyfus integrated a highly efficient supply chain in concentrated frozen orange juice. Is there much upside there? Nobody wants frozen orange juice anymore; most restaurants don't even serve it even for breakfast. Then, of course, there's their investment in Brazilian sugarcane, which is struggling.

For now, therefore, Dreyfus still relies more on trading than their peers, and its financial capability to move into more added-value business is quite limited. That's quite a challenge in a market where the odds of making money through trading get slimmer.

Bunge is somewhere in between Cargill and Dreyfus. There's more trading at Bunge than at Cargill, but Bunge is keen to complement their upstream capabilities with downstream access, in search for commercial margins. Their aim is to lower their reliance on trading and become more of an agri-industrial company. Their recent acquisition of Loders Croklaan (1) in the Netherlands is an example of this move to industrialisation.

The fact is that trading bulk commodities is no longer a sure way to make sustainable money. To generate recurrent profits, the big trading houses have to evolve into a more integrated process. But can they all afford to do it? And even when they can, how can they be sure to choose the right supply chain to integrate?

Making the right choice is not easy, and time is of the essence. Pure trading struggles for profitability but warrants nimbleness. Successful integration can be profitable but can prove to be a riskier option; the industrial cost base is high and unforgiving in a downturn.

What about COFCO or, rather, their trading company COFCO International Ltd? You once said that its role was to feed the dragon.

COFCO International is a game changer in the world of agricultural commodity trading.

There has recently been some restructuring inside China between COFCO and Sinograin, with Sinograin's soybean crushing assets being transferred to COFCO. (2) Both are SOEs, State-Owned Enterprises. This comes after Chinatex was taken over by COFCO. (3) The government clearly wants to create a juggernaut to optimise agricultural commodity sourcing. However, as China is no longer self-sufficient in food, trading expertise at origin becomes critical.

This is where COFCO International has an important role to play: the procurement of food and agricultural commodities.

COFCO International was created out of the acquisitions of Noble Agri and Nidera. It wasn't a smooth or easy journey, but the combined company is now becoming truly efficient. The question is whether the company will become a fully fledged large trading house playing with a wide number of optionalities, at destination and at origin.

I believe their true mission is to optimise sourcing at origin and ensure a smooth and efficient supply for the Chinese market. Their grip on China as a destination is already strong and will only get stronger. This is a major issue for the ABCDs, as the price discovery in China will get more difficult to read. COFCO International will master the prime destination, so the real agenda is at origin. This has become critical amid the spat between the U.S. and China.

What's happening between the U.S. and China is not a short-term phenomenon. I believe the rivalry between the U.S and China is a new normal. If that view is correct, COFCO International's role becomes even more important. It must restructure the sourcing and origination of China's food imports to lower China's dependency on the U.S. To deliver, COFCO International needs to become more efficient and nimbler at origin – in Latin America, Asia, Europe and Africa. COFCO International has been assigned a strategic geopolitical role. To fulfill it efficiently, I expect there could be further acquisitions and alliances down the road.

There has been talk about COFCO and Dreyfus seeking partnerships in different areas.

As I mentioned, Dreyfus is currently in the weakest position amongst the five. It relies more on trading than its peers, but its expertise at origin is clearly undisputed. As a result, Dreyfus is probably in the most strategic position vis-à-vis the Chinese.

Given the current trade wars, the Chinese can hardly turn to U.S.-based trading houses for assistance. Nor can they turn to Glencore, as the company currently has a complicated agenda with the U.S. authorities. As a result, oddly, Dreyfus's relative weakness may become a decisive strength in an alliance with COFCO International.

I had been looking at the industrial investments that the trading companies have been making as a diversification away from their trading operations. However, the way you describe it, they're not diversifications but vertical integration.

As I said earlier, the pure trading of bulk commodities is no longer viable unless you have a hugely dominant role in one single commodity. This is the case, for example with Dreyfus in cotton. Dreyfus makes good money in cotton because of their global footprint and because they're the dominant player in the cotton industry.

The only way for large trading companies to make recurrent money is by creating commercial margins. If I'm efficiently sourcing a commodity, transforming it and then morphing it into a consumer product, I can take advantage of attractive commercial margins to complement dwindling trading profits. If I'm efficient, the margins further downstream will support my work at origin. This is where I see complementarity. This is a development, which makes me question whether down the road we'll still have pure traders of agricultural bulk commodities.

Another path taken by most large trading houses is to complement their trading business by risk management and trade finance activities. ADM, Cargill, Dreyfus, Bunge and COFCO International have developed financial engineering capabilities. Figures aren't disclosed, but all five are making profits out of these activities, some quite handsome. The idea for these groups is not only to support their customers and suppliers through market and credit risk management solutions, but also to market packaged risks predicated on trade flows to third-party investors and, therefore, generate profits without weighing on their respective financial resources. In this sense, the large trading companies have become investment bankers of some sort. Of that game, Cargill is certainly the master.

Do you believe that traceability is an integral part of that new model?
Yes. Consumers in sophisticated markets are now more aware and more demanding. Traceability isn't a luxury; it's a must have. I think that part of the process of industrialisation is to efficiently support the traceability requirement. For now, consumers in developed countries are the most demanding, but with emerging urban middle classes around the world, requirements for traceability will only rise and spread. Soon, no party will be able to be active on any food and agri supply chains without demonstrating total control of qualities and origins and providing reliable and certifiable information about their trades.

There seems to be a growing trend for banks to link finance to sustainability and human rights objectives.
Banks' strategy in that respect is very much the result of the zeitgeist: societies at large, in developed markets notably, became concerned about environmental issues and human rights objectives. As corporate citizens – and because reputational risk is on top of the agenda for most banks' CEO and boards – banks are keen to do the right thing. Bankers are, therefore, eager to attract and support sustainable trade flows.

For example, when my former shop was financing the palm oil industry in Indonesia or Malaysia, we were restricting our dealings to producers certified by the Round Table on Certifiable Palm Oil, or RSPO. But at the time, very few if any, of these producers could guarantee that 100 percent of their production was sustainable. Only a portion of it was.

One way for us to entice palm oil producers and the trading houses to channel sustainable palm oil flows into the bank was by lowering the margin that we earned; other banks did the same. This was really not satisfactory, as capital requirements for lending to these customers remained unchanged, whether the flows of goods we financed were sustainable or not. It was like shooting yourself in the foot. It was unsustainable from the lender's perspective!

But as this issue gets more sensitive, I see a future – not too far away – where at least the large banks will eventually only finance sustainable production. This is the trend. If you look at the coal business, not a single international bank will finance a new project in coal-fired power generation. So, I think that banks will have to exit non-sustainable agribusinesses. Not doing it would merely be unacceptable to the society at large, and the reputational risk incurred would be too high.

Will any of the big trading companies exit their bulk commodity trading operations to concentrate on higher-value parts of the supply chain?

Trading companies will not 'quit' trading. It's their core expertise and their culture. However, trading as a standalone is no longer generating profits in line with the risks undertaken. All large trading companies, therefore, are endeavouring to complement – or rather, enhance – their trading capabilities by capturing what they have identified as the higher-value parts of the supply chains. This is easier said than done.

First, you need to identify the right supply chain and the right portion of it: upstream or downstream. Bunge and Dreyfus made bold bets with sugar in Brazil, for instance which proved with hindsight not so timely. Cargill has chosen the animal nutrition chain, which looks to be the right move. However, the new normal between China and the U.S. might create a trickier environment for them. Bunge has invested in palm oil processing in Europe, which may prove somehow challenging as European consumers are growing more hostile to palm oil, both as a fuel substitute and food ingredient.

Second, investing in supply chains is costly, and companies need the financial strength to do so. Bunge paid almost $1 billion to acquire Loders Croklaan. Dreyfus had to recapitalise Biosev in Brazil, and it cost them $1billion to do it. (4) Cargill has invested more than that in building its animal nutrition supply chain.

Not every player can afford the combination of risks and costs involved. This leaves them with two alleys: partnerships and mergers amongst equals.

Agri-industrials that seek the flexibility and adaptability that trading brings through the management of optionalities at origin will be interested in building partnerships with trading houses. They could, of course, try to poach individual traders or even acquire a trading desk, but partnerships are probably a safer route, as trading requires totally different skills to running manufacturing or industrial processes.

Mergers amongst trading houses to create critical mass are another possibility. However, notwithstanding tricky issues of managing likely overlaps and multiple systems for trading platforms, the current environment is not conducive to this.

U.S.-based trading companies will need to reconsider how they still can safely develop their business with China. Glencore, a non-U.S. company, would possibly be interested in acquiring trading and logistic assets in North America – they once disclosed their interest in Bunge, for instance. But they'll first have to solve their legal issues with the U.S., and that might take some time. Besides, any major acquisition in North America will also raise anti-trust issues.

So, the market has simplified. If you're in the U.S., there's little you can do unless you're buying an independent South American player. But even if you do that, how easily are you going to take advantage of it? I fear that it will get increasingly difficult for an American company to sell to China.

Okay, so no mega-mergers on the horizon, just some shuffling of assets.

Correct. You'd have an antitrust issue if ADM, Glencore, Bunge or Cargill tried to do something. And because of the trade wars, Bunge may not be able play ball anymore with the Chinese. Nor ADM.

All this leaves us with the most likely partnership: between Dreyfus and COFCO International. The owners of Dreyfus need money, and Louis Dreyfus Company needs a model. COFCO International would not buy Dreyfus outright because Dreyfus isn't for sale, but I can see partnerships being initiated which would create value for Dreyfus and where Dreyfus could bring its expertise to COFCO International's procurement strategy.

Do you think that trade houses should be publicly quoted?

A listed company has to have a growth story to tell, year after year, to investors. This doesn't fit well with the cyclical nature of the commodity business. But I'll go one step further. As I already said, commodity traders are currently struggling to make money, and I think that they'll continue to struggle in the years to come. So I doubt we'll see any commodity traders listing in the next 10 or 15 years.

You'll have noticed that most of the commodity companies listed during the supercycle. Glencore was the exception, but their game plan was to accumulate capital to diversify from trading. It ended up with what was really a reverse takeover of Xstrata, the mining group.

Whether the existing listed companies will remain listed is a good question. However, if you look at Wilmar and Olam, you'll see that there is little to no float anymore; the general public holds few of their shares. Temasek have effectively taken Olam private, while the Kuok family largely own Wilmar, with a minority interest from ADM.

Being listed has made the life of Bunge's management considerably tougher as they endeavor to overhaul the company's strategy. The company is in a stage of transformation. Whether they can achieve that transformation over the next few years under their new management will be interesting to follow. ADM is, as I said, an industrial company: by and large, its profits are made out of the industrial part of the business. Their trading profits are made up mostly through their participation in Wilmar.

Does their recently announced JV with BP solve Bunge's problems in Brazil?
The problem for Bunge's new management is that they have losing cards in their hands. Unless sugar and ethanol prices improve, their investments in the sector will continue to be challenging.

The JV is a smart move, as it allows the deconsolidation of a large part of its sugar mills' exposure in Brazil. The JV will carry the assets, but Bunge will still be in a position to offtake the sugar whenever it makes business sense, whereas BP will handle ethanol production. Bunge moves from an asset-heavy position to a much less risky asset-light strategy, and the company gets leaner upstream, where trading profits have dwindled.

Profits lie with added value downstream or, as Cargill has done with animal nutrition, through the full integration from farm to fork. However, both downstream and integrated strategies remain risky because of the potential consequences of the U.S. trade war with China and the corresponding reshuffling of China's sourcing strategy for the U.S.-based ABCDs. Times are tough, and geopolitics don't help!

Is there any solution to Dreyfus's sugarcane assets?
I think that they'll just have to grin and bear it until they find a buyer or until prices rebound. The problem is that the profitability of the ethanol is directly in the hands of the Brazilian government. It's not that Dreyfus is unable to manage these assets or that someone else could manage them better. It's just they're stuck in an unattractive business.

Would you recommend a young person now join one of the big grain trading companies?

There's no better school for someone to learn about markets and discover how the world works. Commodities are about history, demography, geography, economy, finance and geopolitics! It's fantastic training for young people, even if they intend to move on to other activities.

Let's compare a trader in a bank and one in a commodity-trading house. The former gets to master capital markets, while the latter, in addition to the financial market dimension, gets to understand how physical flows work in real life, as well as how to handle shipping and commercial negotiations, often onsite! Tell me, what matches this?

Thank you, JF, for your time.

A bid is an offer made by a trader to buy a commodity. It stipulates both the price the potential buyer is willing to pay and the quantity to be purchased at that price.

Bid/Ask spread
　　The difference between the price that is bid and the price that is asked for a commodity. Sometimes called a bid/offer spread.

Bill of lading (B/L or BoL)
　　A document issued by a carrier (or his or her agent) to acknowledge the receipt of cargo for shipment. A bill of lading is negotiable and serves three main functions. It acknowledges that the goods have been loaded, details the terms of the contract of carriage and serves as a document of title to the goods.

Buffalo
　　Someone who is neither bullish nor bearish but thinks that prices will stay in a range.

Bull
　　Someone who thinks prices will increase.

Bull market
　　A market where prices are rising.

Calendar spread
　　An options or futures spread established by simultaneously entering a long and short position on the same underlying asset but with different delivery months.

Call option
　　The right to buy something sometime in the future at a predetermined price.

Carrying charge
　　A market structure where a commodity for nearby shipment is less expensive than for later shipment; also known as **contango**.

Capesize
　　Cargo vessels with a capacity over 150,000 tonnes, but can carry as much as 400,000 tonnes or more. They are primarily used for transporting coal and iron ore.

Cash against documents (CAD)
　　Payment term for a transaction where an intermediary, usually a bank, holds documents that specify the terms of the transaction. When payment is remitted, the bank releases the documents showing the buyer can take ownership of the product.

Cash settled
　　A futures contract under which no physical deliveries are made.

Certificate of origin

A document issued by a certifying authority stating goods' country of origin.

Charter party
The contract between the owner of a vessel and the charterer for the use of that vessel. The charterer takes over the vessel for either a certain amount of time (a time charter) or for a certain point-to-point voyage (a voyage charter).

Circuit breaker
A mechanism that automatically halts trading on a futures market if prices move too far too fast, allowing time for market participants to react and place offsetting orders.

Collective goods.
In economics, a collective or public good is a good that individuals cannot be effectively excluded from using and where use by one individual does not reduce availability to others.

Commodity broker
A person or entity that puts together a transaction between a buyer and a seller of a commodity for a commission: a broker does not own the commodity at any stage and does not take any price risk on the commodity.

Commodity Futures Trading Commission (CFTC)
An independent agency of the U.S. government that regulates futures and option markets.

Commodity trader
A person or entity that takes a price risk in the process of transforming a commodity in one of three ways: in space, time or form. A trader is a contract principal on the deal – at some stage in the process, he or she will actually own the commodity involved in the transaction.

Commercial
An entity that uses futures contracts for hedging, as defined by the CFTC. To qualify, a commercial trader needs to be engaged in the physical-commodity supply chain.

Common Agricultural Policy (CAP)
The agricultural policy of the European Union that implements a system of agricultural subsidies and other programmes.

Contango
A market structure in which a commodity for nearby shipment is less expensive than for later shipment, also known as a **carrying charge**.

Convergence
As a futures contract month approaches expiry, futures and physicals' prices converge. At expiry, futures and physicals delivered against the contract are worth the same.

Cost and freight (named port of destination; C&F or CFR)

Whereby the seller pays for the carriage of the goods up to the named port of destination. The seller is responsible for originating costs, including export clearance and freight costs for carriage to the port of destination. The title (ownership) of the goods passes to the buyer when he or she has paid for them.

Cost, insurance & freight (named port of destination; CIF)
Similar to C&F, with the exception that the seller is required to obtain insurance for the goods while in transit to the named port of destination.

Commitment of Traders (COT) report
A report published each Friday detailing the share of the open interest in a futures market held by the different categories of market participants.

Crop year
A period of twelve months during which all of a country's production is included in statistics: crop years obviously vary from commodity to commodity and from country to country.

Default
A situation where one party to a contract fails to fulfil their contractual obligations.

Deficit market
When the demand for a physical commodity exceeds the supply of that commodity at a particular period of time.

Delivery period
Under a FOB contract, the delivery period refers to the dates within which the buyer must present the performing vessel for loading. The seller must have the goods ready for loading during these same dates. The vessel can complete loading under a FOB contract after the end of the delivery period

Delta (of an option)
The amount that the price of an option moves relative to the price of the underlying asset.

Delta hedging (of an option position)
A strategy that aims – by offsetting long and short positions – to reduce, or hedge, the risk associated with price movements in the underlying asset.

Demurrage
The charges that the charterer pays to the ship owner (or the FOB seller pays to the buyer) for the extra use of a vessel after the period normally allowed to load and unload cargo (laytime). Officially, demurrage is a form of liquidated damages for breaching the laytime set out in the charter party.

Despatch

The opposite of demurrage. If the charterer requires the use of the vessel for less time than the laytime allowed, the charter party may require the ship owner to pay despatch for the time saved.

Documentary credit. See **letter of credit.**

Elevator
A facility to stockpile or store grain or other dry agricultural commodities in bulk. It can also refer to a bucket system or conveyor belt that carries a dry commodity from a lower level a higher level, in a silo or other storage facility or onto a vessel in a port. It has become a generic term for port loading facilities for dry commodities such as beans, grain or sugar.

Equilibrium price
The price at which the marginal supply of a commodity equals the marginal demand for that commodity.

Exchange for physicals
A mechanism whereby two parties exchange a position on a futures exchange for a physical contract; sometimes called **against actuals**.

Ex works (named place) (EXW)
The seller makes the goods available at his or her premises.

Fair average quality (FAQ)
Used to describe a commodity that is of an average quality for that crop year.

False messaging
Sending incorrect price signals to market participants, usually refers to activity in a futures market.

Federation of Oils, Seeds and Fats Associations (FOSFA)
This is the main trade association for the oil, seeds and fats industry that regulates legal contracts in the trade/industry.

Firm bid or offer
When a trader makes a firm bid or an offer for a specified quantity (with all terms previously agreed) for a specific time period, he cannot withdraw that bid or offer during that time period. If the other party wants to book him before the end of the specified time period, the trader must complete the deal. This is a fundamental part of the trading system: a trader's word is his bond.

Flat price
The outright price of a commodity, usually expressed in dollars, or dollar cents per tonne, bushel, pound or kilogram.

Floor/ring/pit
Where open-outcry trading takes place.

Food and Agriculture Organisation (FAO)
This is a specialised agency of the United Nations that leads international efforts to defeat hunger.

Force majeure
A common clause in contracts that essentially frees both parties from liability or obligation when an extraordinary event or circumstance occurs that is beyond the control of the parties, such as a war, strike, riot, crime or an event described by the legal term *act of God* (hurricane, flood, earthquake, volcanic eruption and so on) and prevents one or both parties from fulfilling their obligations under the contract.

Forward market
The over-the-counter physical market in contracts for future delivery, so-called *forward contracts*. Forward contracts are personalised between parties (that is, delivery time, quantity and other terms are determined between seller and buyer). Standardised forward contracts are called *futures contracts* and traded on a futures exchange.

Free on board (named loading port; FOB)
The seller must load the goods onboard the ship nominated by the buyer and custom clear the goods for export. The buyer pays the cost of marine freight transport, insurance, unloading and transportation from the load port to the final destination.

Front running
Buying or selling in front of a customer order.

Futures commission merchant (FCM)
An individual or organisation that solicits or accepts orders (or both) to buy or sell futures and options contracts and accepts money or other assets from customers to support such orders.

Futures market
A *futures or derivatives exchange* is a central financial exchange where people can trade standardised futures contracts – that is a contract to buy specific quantities of a commodity or financial instrument at a specified price, with delivery set at a specified time in the future.

Gamma
The rate at which an option's delta changes in relation to the underlying futures price.

General average
The apportionment of financial liability for the loss arising from the jettisoning of cargo by dividing the costs among all those whose property (ship or cargo) was preserved by the action.

Handymax
Small cargo ships that carry less than 60,000 tonnes.

Handysize
Ships with a capacity of between 15,000 and 35,000 tonnes.

Hedge

Something that reduces the risk of adverse price movements in an asset: a hedge normally consists of taking an offsetting position in a related security, such as a futures contract. It can, however, consist in taking an offsetting in a different but inversely correlated commodity.

Implied volatility (option)
The value of the volatility of the underlying instrument which, when input into an option pricing model (such as Black–Scholes), will return a theoretical value equal to the current market price of the option.

Import margin
The amount of money per unit that an importer will earn or lose by importing a commodity from the world market to a local market, after having paid all import duties, taxes and logistics costs.

Incoterms
Trading terms published by the International Chamber of Commerce (ICC) that are commonly used in both international and domestic trade contracts.

Index fund
A mutual fund or exchange-traded fund (ETF) that tracks a specified basket of underlying investments: most index funds track prominent commodity indexes like the S&P GSCI, the Bloomberg Commodity Index (BCOM) or the Thomson Reuters/Jefferies CRB Index (TR/J CRB).

Initial margin
A monetary amount that a trader deposits in good faith into an account to enter into a futures contract; sometimes known as **original margin**

Intrinsic value (of an option)
The difference between the market value of the underlying asset and the strike price of the given option.

Inverse
A market structure in which a futures price is lower in the distant delivery months than in the near delivery months; sometimes known as a **backwardation**.

Laytime
The amount of time allowed (in hours or days) in a voyage charter for the loading and unloading of cargo. If the laytime is exceeded, demurrage is incurred. If laytime is not used, despatch may be payable by the ship owner to the charterer.

Laydays

The period of time during which a ship must present itself to the charterer at the load port. If the ship arrives before the laydays specified, the charterer does not have to start loading (depending on the type of charter). If the ship arrives after the laydays, the contract can be cancelled. Laydays are often presented as in a contract as *laydays and cancelling* and can be shortened to *laycan*.

Letter of credit (L/C)
A method of payment whereby a written commitment is issued by a bank after a request by an importer that payment will be made to the beneficiary (exporter), provided that the terms and conditions stated in the L/C have been met, as evidenced by the presentation of specified documents. Also known as a **documentary credit**.

Leverage
The size of the position that can be taken in a futures market relative to the initial margin.

Local trader
A trader on a future exchange who may fill public orders occasionally but will predominantly buy and sell for her own personal accounts.

Long position
An uncovered contractual obligation that will make money if the price of the commodity rises.

Long
An entity or person who has bought a commodity and is holding it in the expectation that price will rise so he can sell it out at a higher price later.

Lot/contract
The standardised minimum quantity of a commodity that you can trade on a futures exchange.

Margin call
A request from a futures broker for variation margins to cover losses on open positions.

Marginal cost
The cost of producing one more unit of a particular product: economics suggests that, in the long term, the price of a commodity is equal to its marginal cost of production.

Marginal price
The price that you'd have to pay to buy or sell one more unit of a particular product; this is, therefore, the price at which you can trade on a market.

Marking to market

A means whereby you record a change in the value of an asset or futures position to reflect its current fair market value; marking to market occurs on the daily close and is used to ensure that a margin account is meeting its minimum maintenance.

Markets in Financial Instruments Directive (MIFID)
A European Union law that provides harmonised regulation for investment services across the member states of the European Economic Area. The directive's main objectives are to increase competition and consumer protection in investment services.

Market makeup
How the open interest on a futures contract is split on the COT report among commercials, non-commercials and non-reportables.

Mass-balance system
A system for sourcing sustainable ingredients whereby a company can sell the same quantity of certified product as they buy, without it having to be the actual product.

Mean reversion
The theory that prices eventually move back toward the mean, or average, price-- the historical average of the price or another relevant average such as the average cost of production.

National Futures Association (NFA)
The self-regulatory organisation for the U.S. derivatives industry.

Negative roll return
The return generated when a long position is rolled from a nearby futures contract into a further forward contract in a contango.

Non-commercial
The CFTC categorisation of a speculator as an entity that is not directly involved in the commercialisation of the commodity on its journey from producer to consumer.

Notice of readiness (NOR)
The NOR informs the charterer that the ship has arrived at the port and is ready in all respects to load or discharge. Presentation of the NOR is the point at which laytime commences.

Notice period
When you buy FOB, you must give your seller notice in advance regarding when your vessel will arrive. The notice period refers to how long in advance you must inform your seller of the vessel's arrival date; it may vary from contract to contract.

Open outcry
A method of communicating and trading on a futures exchange that involves verbal bids, offers and hand signals. Most exchanges have replaced open outcry with electronic trading systems.

Original margin

A monetary amount that a trader deposits in good faith into an account to enter into a futures contract, sometimes known as **initial margin**.

Over the counter (OTC)

A bilateral contract in which two parties agree on how a particular trade or agreement is to be settled in the future; forwards and swaps are examples of OTC contracts.

Panamax

Ships that can transit the Panama Canal; they have an average capacity of 65,000 tonnes.

Paper commodity

A term that describes a commodity traded on the futures market rather than on the physical markets.

Paper trading

Trading on futures and options on an exchange as opposed to trading on the physical commodity.

Physical commodity

One that has a physical form (cf., **paper commodity**). If you load a physical commodity onto a ship, the ship will settle deeper into the water; if you put it into a warehouse, the warehouse will fill up.

Physical premium/discount

The premium/discount to the futures price paid for a particular grade or origin of a particular commodity compared to the futures market. Sometimes referred to a **basis**.

Physical trading

Trading a physical commodity, not trading futures and options on an exchange.

Positive roll return

The return generated if a futures market is in a backwardation when a position is rolled from a nearby futures contract into a further forward contract.

Price maker

An entity whose own transactions will set, or at least influence, the market price.

Price taker

An entity that must accept the prevailing prices in the market for its production or inputs. The entity's own transactions cannot affect the market price.

Price volatility

The rate at which the price of a security increases or decreases for a given set of returns; it's measured by calculating the standard deviation of the annualised returns over a given period of time.

Put option

The right but not the obligation to sell something in the future at a predetermined price.

Quantitative fund
A fund in which investment decisions are determined by numerical methods rather than by human judgment.

Roll
When you liquidate a position in a nearby futures month and reinstate that position in a position further forward (down the board).

Shipment period
On a C&F or CIF contract, the *shipment period* refers to the dates between which it's acceptable for the vessel to have finished loading, not before the first day of the shipment period and not later than the end of the shipment period.

Shipping documents
The documents that must be completed and presented to the buyer before the seller can get paid. These will always include a commercial invoice and a bill of lading but may also include quality and health certificates.

Short position
An uncovered commitment on a market that will make money if prices fall.

Short
Someone who has sold a commodity for forward shipment in the expectation that price will fall and that he can buy it back at a lower price later.

Silo
A storage facility for dry commodities, usually grain.

Speculator
An entity – it could be an individual, a hedge fund, a pension fund or a bank – that is not involved in the physical transformation of the underlying commodity but is taking a position regarding future price movements. A speculator is not directly involved in the commercialisation of the commodity on its journey from producer to consumer.

Spoofing
An example of false messaging when someone places an order with the intention that it will not be executed.

Spot market
Where commodities are traded for immediate delivery, or 'on the spot'.

Spot price
The price of a commodity for prompt or immediate arrival or shipment.

Spot shipment/arrival
> A commodity for prompt or immediate shipment/arrival; **spot** is not a legal term. Exact dates should always be specified.

Spread
> The difference between the price of a specific commodity for one delivery period and another delivery period, sometimes referred to as a **time spread**.

Squeeze
> This usually refers to a situation where someone is short of a physical commodity or a futures contract and is forced to cover his commitment, often at an uncomfortable loss.

Straddle
> An options strategy where you hold a position in both a call and a put with the same strike price and expiration date.

Strangle
> An options strategy involving the purchase or sale of both call and put options of different strike prices that allows the holder to profit based on how much the price of the underlying security moves, with relatively minimal exposure to the direction of the price movement. The purchase of a call and a put is known as a *long strangle*, while the sale of a call and a put is known as a *short strangle*.

Superco
> Supervision or superintendent company hired to survey goods' loading and discharge.

Supply chain
> All the actors and processes involved in bringing a product from the producer to the end consumer.

Surplus market
> When the supply of a particular commodity exceeds the demand for that physical commodity at a particular time.

Swap
> An agreement whereby a floating (or market or spot) price based on an underlying commodity is traded for a fixed price over a specified period.

Terminal (futures)
> A term sometimes used to describe a futures market.

Terminal (port)
> A facility for the loading of bagged or bulk commodities onto a vessel.

Time spread
> See **spread**.

Time value (of an option)
> The portion of an option's worth determined by the length of time before the option is due to expire.

Trading book
    An entity's open (yet to be closed out) futures and physical positions/contracts.

U.S. Department of Agriculture (USDA)
    The U.S. federal executive department responsible for developing and executing federal laws related to farming, agriculture, forestry and food. Also known as the *U.S. Agriculture Department.*

Value-at-risk (VAR)
    A measure of the risk of a position on a market. It estimates how much that position might lose, given normal market conditions, in a set time period such as a day. Firms and regulators in the financial industry typically use VAR to gauge the amount of assets needed to cover possible losses.

Variation margin
    Funds used to bring a commodity-futures account up to a level that covers losses on open positions. This request for funds is referred to as a **margin call**.

Warehouse contract
    A futures market under which the physical commodity is delivered in a warehouse rather than FOB or C&F.

Warehouse receipt
    A document that provides proof of ownership of commodities stored in a warehouse, vault or depository for safekeeping. Warehouse receipts may be negotiable or non-negotiable. Negotiable warehouse receipts allow the transfer of ownership of that commodity without having to deliver the physical commodity.

Wash out
    When a transaction between two parties is cancelled, with or without a penalty.

Wash trade
    When two parties execute prearranged trades to print the market higher or lower or to deny other market participants the opportunity to participate in that trade, effectively bypassing competitive-execution requirements.

References

All links were verified in September 2019

Introduction

1. www.bloomberg.com/news/articles/2019-08-16/top-private-u-s-firms-s-family-owners-get-best-payout-since-2010

Preface

1. solaris-ch.com/ (Solaris started trading in 2012, specialising in the trade of grain from Russia.)
2. www.GAFTA.com (The Grain & Feed Trade Association)
3. www.twitter.com/RussianGrainTra

Chapter One

References
1. *Merchants of Grain: The Power and the Profits of the Five Grain Companies at the Centre of the World's Food Supply* – Dan Morgan – iUniverse (Originally published by Viking Press)
2. *Against the Grain: How Agriculture Has Hijacked Civilisation* – Richard Manning – North Point Press
3. *The King of Oil* – Daniel Ammann – Saint Martin's Press
4. *The Secret Club that Runs the World – Inside the Fraternity of Commodities Traders* – Kate Kelly – Penguin Books
5. *A Culture of Conspiracy: Apocalyptic Visions in Contemporary America* – Michael Barkun – University of California Press

Chapter Two

1. *Command and Control* – Eric Schlosser – Penguin Books 2013
2. *The Wealth of Nations* – Adam Smith – W. Strahan and T. Cadell, London 1778
3. Keynote Address of Commissioner Dan M. Berkovitz at the FIA Commodities Symposium, Houston, Texas, June 2019 www.cftc.gov/PressRoom/SpeechesTestimony/opaberkovitz4
4. www.maynardkeynes.org/keynes-the-speculator.html

5. www.staff.ncl.ac.uk/david.harvey/MKT3008/RussianOct1973.pdf
6. www.bloomberg.com/opinion/articles/2019-09-13/america-s-farmers-need-more-than-a-trade-truce
7. ag.purdue.edu/commercialag/Documents/Resources/Farmland/Land-Prices/2011_09_01_Henderson_Agriculture_Boom_Bust.pdf

Chapter Three

1. As quoted in *Destined for War: Can America and China Escape Thucydides's Trap?* by Graham Allison www.newstatesman.com/politics/international-politics/2012/07/kevin-rudd-west-isnt-ready-rise-china
2. www.forbes.com/sites/timworstall/2012/09/03/it-does-not-take-7-kg-of-grain-to-make-1-kg-of-beef-be-very-careful-with-your-statistics/#4fffb3465f0d
3. Unless otherwise stated, all statistics in this book are from the USDA.
4. www.gingrich360.com/2012/06/ninedaysthatchangedtheworld/
5. www.usda.gov/oce/forum/past_speeches/2017/2017_Speeches/Swithun_Still.pdf
6. thediplomat.com/2019/02/the-dormant-breadbasket-of-the-asia-pacific/
7. *Homo Sapiens,* p. 452
8. digitalcommons.unl.edu/cgi/viewcontent.cgi?referer=&httpsredir=1&article=1006&context=planthealthdoc
9. aae.wisc.edu/aae641/Ref/Duvick_maize_breeding_2005.pdf
10. www.agry.purdue.edu/ext/corn/news/timeless/yieldtrends.html
11. https://ourworldindata.org/employment-in-agriculture

Chapter Four

1. www.macrotrends.net/1369/crude-oil-price-history-chart
2. news.bbc.co.uk/2/hi/americas/6319093.stm
3. www.ft.com/content/a0aa9ef0-d618-11df-81f0-00144feabdc0
4. https://news.un.org/en/story/2007/10/237362-un-independent-rights-expert-calls-five-year-freeze-biofuel-production
5. https://www.npr.org/templates/story/story.php?storyId=89545855
6. https://en.wikipedia.org/wiki/Food_vs._fuel
7. http://www.ethanolhistory.com/
8. https://web.archive.org/web/20120106204543/http://www.detroitnews.com/article/20111224/AUTO01/112240320/1148/auto01/Congress-ends-corn-ethanol-subsidy
9. https://www.usda.gov/oce/climate_change/mitigation_technologies/USDAEthanolReport_20170107.pdf

10. https://www.usda.gov/media/press-releases/2017/01/12/usda-releases-new-report-lifecycle-greenhouse-gas-balance-ethanol
11. https://insideclimatenews.org/news/14062019/trump-ethanol-climate-change-benefit-science-questions-emissions-data-usda
12. https://www.gao.gov/assets/700/698914.pdf
13. https://ethanolrfa.org/wp-content/uploads/2019/02/RFA2019Outlook.pdf
14. https://www.epure.org/about-ethanol/fuel-market/fuel-blends/
15. https://uk.reuters.com/article/brazil-ethanol-corn/brazil-corn-ethanol-industry-booms-as-cereals-output-nears-100-mln-t-idUKL5N22K78C
16. https://www.bloomberg.com/news/articles/2018-03-29/louis-dreyfus-faces-1-05-billion-cash-call-from-brazilian-unit
17. https://www.reuters.com/article/us-bunge-bp/bunge-and-bp-team-up-in-brazil-bioenergy-venture-create-no-3-sugarcane-processor-idUSKCN1UH15O

Chapter Five

1. As quoted in *Commodity Conversations – An Introduction to Trading in Agricultural Commodities*.
2. https://www.trafigura.com/media/1492/2014_trafigura_the_economics_of_commodity_trading_firms_section_i_english.pdf

Chapter Six

1. *Merchants of Grain* p. 326
2. *Merchants of Grain* p. 329
3. *Merchants of Grain* p. 326
4. *Merchants of Grain* p. 331
5. *Merchants of Grain* p. 338
6. https://www.poultryworld.net/Meat/Articles/2018/11/Cargill-expands-its-blockchain-turkey-programme-354938E/
7. https://www.investopedia.com/terms/c/commodity.asp
8. https://www.wsj.com/articles/firms-that-bossed-agriculture-for-a-century-face-new-threat-farmers-1534347514?ns=prod/accounts-wsj
9. National Bureau of Economic Research Working Paper No. 10595, issued in June 2004

10. A *beta fund* tries to outperform the wider market.

Chapter Seven

For further reading please see:

History of Suisse–Atlantique http://www.swiss-ships.ch/reeder/reederei-berichte/suisat/form-suisse-at-story_fr.html
The Multinational Traders – Geoffrey G. Jones 1997
    https://www.amazon.com/Multinational-Traders-Routledge-International-Business-ebook/dp/B000OI103E
Village of Secrets: Defying the Nazis in Vichy, France – Caroline Moorhead Vintage Books
'André & Cie S.A.'s sudden demise'
    https://jacquessimon506.wordpress.com/2017/07/22/andre-cie-sudden-demise/
André & Cie cuts more jobs
    https://www.swissinfo.ch/eng/andr%C3%A9---cie-cuts-more-jobs/1928486
Andre Seeks Bankruptcy Protection, Plans Asset Sales – *Wall Street Journal*
    https://www.wsj.com/articles/SB984346960348092640
André & Cie, 'A Heavyweight by the Shores of Lake Geneva', Swiss Trading & Shipping Association (STSA)
    https://stsa.swiss/knowledge/switzerland/andre-cie
Corporate Trivia
    http://www.corporatetrivia.com/current/2002/switzerland/andre.html
Au bord du gouffre, André cesse ses activités à Lausanne
    https://www.letemps.ch/economie/bord-gouffre-andre-cesse-activites-lausanne
André looks for new strategy
    https://www.lid.ch/medien/mediendienst/detail/info/artikel/getreidehaendler-andre-cie-sucht-neue-strategie/
André ferme la boutique
    https://www.24heures.ch/vaud-regions/2001-Andre-ferme-boutique/story/14789426

Chapter Eight

1. https://www.continentalgrain.com/

2. https://www.nytimes.com/2001/04/12/business/michel-fribourg-87-trader-who-opened-soviet-market.html
3. *Merchants of Grain*, p. 140
4. https://www.forbes.com/2008/09/17/fishman-wamu-subprime-face-markets-cx_es_0917autofacescan02.html#2cf6c895192e
5. https://www.nytimes.com/1998/11/11/business/cargill-set-to-buy-main-unit-of-continental-grain-its-chief-rival.html
6. https://www.foodingredientsonline.com/doc/cargill-to-purchase-continental-grain-0001

Chapter Nine

1. https://www.wsj.com/articles/why-trade-is-so-crucial-for-food-companies-1508119380
2. https://www.adm.com/
3. http://www.soyinfocenter.com/HSS/archer_daniels_midland.php
4. http://www.company-histories.com/ArcherDanielsMidland-Company-Company-History.html
5. https://en.wikipedia.org/wiki/Dwayne_Andreas
6. https://www.nytimes.com/2016/11/17/business/dwayne-o-andreas-former-archer-daniels-midland-chief-dies-at-98.html
7. http://fortune.com/2015/02/03/improving-diapers-and-beers-mouthfeel-8-surprising-facts-about-archer-daniels-midland/
8. https://www.bloomberg.com/news/articles/2015-10-20/archer-daniels-midland-raises-stake-in-palm-oil-giant-wilmar
9. https://www.reuters.com/article/us-wildflavours-archer-daniels/u-s-agribusiness-adm-to-acquire-wild-flavors-for-3-billion-idUSKBN0FC0K320140707
10. https://www.bloomberg.com/news/articles/2018-01-22/adm-bunge-deal-would-create-a-cargill-sized-agribusiness-giant
11. https://www.wsj.com/articles/adm-bunge-takeover-talks-have-stalled-1520611381
12. https://www.reuters.com/article/us-adm-m-a-exclusive/exclusive-adm-ceo-says-wrong-time-for-monster-acquisitions-idUSKCN1PA2H1

Chapter Ten

1. http://www.fundinguniverse.com/company-histories/bunge-ltd-history/
2. https://www.ft.com/content/99242ea0-fd64-11e7-a492-2c9be7f3120a
3. https://www.bloomberg.com/news/articles/2018-10-30/bunge-is-said-near-deal-with-activists-for-board-seats-review

4. https://www.reuters.com/article/us-bunge-bp/bunge-and-bp-team-up-in-brazil-bioenergy-venture-create-no-3-sugarcane-processor-idUSKCN1UH15O
5. https://fox2now.com/2019/08/13/agriculture-tech-giant-bunge-moving-global-headquarters-to-st-louis-county/

Chapter Eleven

1. https://www.bloomberg.com/news/articles/2018-06-07/america-s-largest-private-company-reboots-a-153-year-old-strategy
2. For a full history of Cargill, see Wayne G Broehl's three volumes published by University Press of New England:
    a. *Cargill: Trading the World's Grain.* (1992)
    b. *Cargill: Going Global.* (1998)
    c. *Cargill: From Commodities to Customers.* (2008)
3. *Merchants of Grain* p. 82
4. *Merchants of Grain* p. 132
5. http://www.startribune.com/cargill-executives-moving-out-of-lake-minnetonka-mansion/378543475/

Chapter Twelve

1. https://www.ft.com/content/8e0d7ed2-cf8c-11e7-b781-794ce08b24dc
2. https://www.economist.com/business/2019/02/02/a-chinese-state-backed-giants-rapid-rise-in-global-trading-of-food
3. https://www.bloomberg.com/news/articles/2018-01-29/rags-to-riches-tale-ends-in-disaster-for-noble-group-s-elman
4. See Chapter 13 for a brief history of Phibro.
5. https://www.bloomberg.com/news/articles/2018-12-20/noble-group-says-restructuring-now-effective-as-probe-drags-on
6. https://www.reuters.com/article/cofco-nidera/update-1-chinas-cofco-seeks-over-500-mln-from-former-nidera-owners-newspaper-idUSL8N1QX6VA
7. https://www.reuters.com/article/cofco-nidera/update-1-dutch-court-lifts-asset-freeze-on-ex-nidera-owners-in-blow-to-cofco-idUSL8N1RA5R8
8. https://www.reuters.com/article/brazil-grains/dreyfus-cofco-head-to-head-in-brazil-soybean-export-rankings-data-idUSL1N1ZE162

Chapter Thirteen

1. http://www.fundinguniverse.com/company-histories/groupe-louis-dreyfus-s-a-history/

Source: International Directory of Company Histories, Vol. 60. St. James Press, 2004.
2. *Merchants of Grain*
3. https://www.independent.co.uk/news/obituaries/robert-louis-dreyfus-businessman-who-helped-resurrect-olympique-marseille-football-club-1749706.html
4. *Robert Louis-Dreyfus: The Incredible Odyssey of a Business Rebel* by Jean-Claude Bourbon and Jacques-Olivier Martin (Michel Lafon, 2009).
5. https://www.parismatch.com/Actu/Economie/Robert-Louis-Dreyfus-un-seigneur-qui-voyait-loin-et-visait-haut-140512
6. https://www.reuters.com/article/us-louisdreyfus-results/louis-dreyfus-says-overhaul-steadied-profit-in-tough-grain-market-idUSKBN1GX3BX
7. https://www.bloomberg.com/news/articles/2018-03-29/louis-dreyfus-faces-1-05-billion-cash-call-from-brazilian-unit
8. https://www.reuters.com/article/us-louisdreyfus-metals-sale/louis-dreyfus-completes-466-million-sale-of-metals-unit-to-chinese-fund-idUSKBN1IC1W3
9. https://www.foodbev.com/news/louis-dreyfus-targets-growth-in-china-with-new-oilseed-facility/
10. https://www.reuters.com/article/louisdreyfus-appointment/update-1-louis-dreyfus-appoints-food-innovation-chief-idUSL8N1YM3D6

Chapter Fourteen

1. For a good understanding of Wall Street at that time, read *Liar's Poker* by Michael Lewis, published in 1989 by WW Norton & Co
2. www.phibro.com
3. http://www.kingofoil.com/about/

Chapter Fifteen

1. *Robert Kuok: A Memoir*, with Andrew Tanzer, Landmark Books 2017
2. https://www.bloomberg.com/news/articles/2019-06-12/giant-asian-food-company-eyes-soybean-expansion-in-hard-times
3. https://www.climateadvisers.com/tft-and-climate-advisers-welcome-wilmars-transformative-policies-to-protect-forests-and-people/
4. https://grist.org/food/48-hours-that-changed-the-future-of-rainforests/
5. https://www.theguardian.com/sustainable-business/wilmar-no-deforestation-commitment-food-production
6. https://www.eco-business.com/news/singapore-businesses-mark-10-years-of-csr-push/

Chapter Sixteen

1. https://www.bloomberg.com/news/articles/2019-02-14/commodity-trading-giants-hunting-for-investors-find-few-takers
2. See an interview with Sunny Verghese, Olam's founder and CEO in my earlier book *The Sugar Casino*.
3. https://www.bloomberg.com/news/articles/2019-03-11/commodities-trader-engelhart-plots-revival-after-over-expansion
4. https://www.reuters.com/article/soy-brazil-amaggi/brazils-amaggi-buys-norwegian-non-GMo-grain-firm-idUSN1317759420090713
5. https://www.vicentin.com.ar/historia?lang=en
6. https://www.agd.com.ar/en/our-identity/history
7. http://www.molinos.com.ar/en.aspx
8. https://www.bloomberg.com/news/articles/2018-11-28/former-glencore-executive-vaults-cargill-in-russian-wheat-trade
9. https://www.adm.com/news/news-releases/adm-and-aston-foods-announce-completion-of-sweeteners-and-starches-joint-venture-in-russia
10. https://www.kernel.ua/
11. https://averecommodities.com/
12. http://www.nibulon.com/data/our-company/main-activities/grain-storage-processing-and-transshipment-trade-activity.html
13. https://www.agroprosperis.com/en/apgroup_presentation.html
14. http://www.globalagiting.com/nch-canvespital/
15. https://www.reuters.com/article/us-usa-china-soybeans/u-s-confirms-small-soybean-sale-to-private-chinese-buyer-idUSKCN1UR4TM
16. https://etgworld.com/#/home
17. https://www.enerfogroup.com/
18. https://www.foxbusiness.com/features/glencore-makes-takeover-approach-to-bunge-3rd-update
19. https://blocktribune.com/cofco-international-joins-abcd-initiative-to-bring-blockchain-to-agricultural-sector/

The New Normal – J. F. Lambert

1. https://www.bunge.com/news/bunge-completes-acquisition-ioi-loders-croklaan
2. https://www.bloomberg.com/news/articles/2019-05-07/china-is-said-to-plan-overhaul-of-state-agriculture-giants
3. https://www.reuters.com/article/us-chinatex-m-a-cofco/china-approves-chinatex-merger-with-cofco-idUSKCN0ZV0AS
4. https://www.ft.com/content/f1ba6da0-3346-11e8-ac48-10c6fdc22f03

Made in the USA
Coppell, TX
14 November 2020